Literary Philosophers

Literary Philosophers
Borges, Calvino, Eco

edited by
Jorge J. E. Gracia, Carolyn Korsmeyer,
and Rodolphe Gasché

ROUTLEDGE
New York and London

Published in 2002 by
Routledge
29 West 35th Street
New York, NY 10001

Published in Great Britain by
Routledge
11 New Fetter Lane
London EC4P 4EE

Copyright © 2002 by Routledge
Routledge is an imprint of the Taylor & Francis Group.
Design and typography: Jack Donner

Printed in the United States of America on acid-free paper.

Excerpts from "Peirre Menard, Author of the *Quixote*," "Tlön, Uqbar, Orbis Tertius," "The Circular Ruins," "The Garden of Forking Paths," and "The Library of Babel" are from *Collected Fictions* by Jorge Luis Borges, translated by Andrew Hurley, copyright © 1998 by Maria Kodama; translation copyright © 1998 by Penguin Putnam Inc. Used by permission of Viking Penguin, a division of Penguin Putnam Inc.
    Excerpts from T ZERO by Italo Calvino, copyright © 1967 by Giulio Einaudi Editore, s.p.a., English translation by William Weaver copyright © 1969 by Harcourt, Inc. and Jonathan Cape Limited, reprinted by permission of Harcourt, Inc.

10 9 8 7 6 5 4 3 2 1

Cataloging-in-Publication Data is available from the Library of Congress.

ISBN 0-415-92917-2 (hbk)
ISBN 0-415-92918-0 (pbk)

Contents

Acknowledgments

Several of the essays contained in this collection were read at a conference that took place in Buffalo, October 1 and 2, 1999. The conference was sponsored by the Samuel P. Capen Chair in Philosophy, the Eugenio Donato Chair in Comparative Literature, the Department of Philosophy, the Program in Comparative Literature, and the Department of Modern Languages of the University at Buffalo. We are grateful to them for their support, which made possible both the conference and this volume. We are also particularly indebted to the authors of the essays for their willingness to participate in this project and to adapt to the sometimes unpleasant requirements that go along with the publication of a volume of this kind. A shorter and earlier version of Jorge J. E. Gracia's essay was published in *The Journal of Aesthetics and Art Criticism* and so we must thank the editor, Philip Alperson, for his permission to use parts of it here. Finally, Anthony Mouselong prepared a first draft of the bibliography, which made our task much easier, and Daniel Novotny took care of the index, for which we are most grateful.

CAROLYN KORSMEYER

Literary Philosophers: Introductory Remarks

Though the distinction between "literature" and "philosophy" is often presumed, it can be difficult to pinpoint with any exactness the features that make these enterprises different from each other. Invoking dissimilar purposes of texts—for instance that philosophy aims at the serious discovery of truth and literature at entertainment and diversion—might distinguish Aristotle from Dumas, but it founders on Dante. Although there may be little traditional philosophy that seeks to amuse, there is plenty of poetry and prose that seeks to enlighten. Appeal to genre style also proves of only limited benefit: the presence of plot and character may separate Jane Austen from Kant, but the population of characters in the works of Plato, Berkeley, Kierkegaard, or Boethius defeats the utility of such criteria. One tradition in philosophy maintains that only a level of discussion that is able to make general or universal claims achieves the theoretical system building that marks philosophy, but this is challenged by another school of thought that insists on attention to particulars and to diversity of circumstances in order to arrive at sound conclusions. Even the related appeal to logic and reason over emotion and persuasion has come under scrutiny and argument, most radically with the deconstructionist trend in philosophy that challenges the distinctions among all types of texts.

Despite a recent generation of scholarship that examines anew the practices of philosophy and literary fiction, vexing questions linger about how best to characterize the relationship of these two disciplines. Are they distinct endeavors that happen to deal with some of the same issues, albeit with incompatible approaches? Are they two complementary methods for accomplishing similar ends? Ought they be considered essentially the same, philosophy being—as Richard Rorty has asserted—but a genre of literature? Or are the connections between philosophy and fiction contingent and happenstance, in their variety resisting systematic analysis or generalization?

The works of three particularly clever and cerebral authors epitomize these questions: Jorge Luis Borges, Umberto Eco, and Italo Calvino are as noted for the intriguing philosophical puzzles they present as they are for their inventive literary styles. These three authors are united not only by a taste for philosophy but by their fascination with areas of philosophy not often broached in fiction: epistemology, metaphysics, and logic. Anyone who has reflected on the array of philosophical issues that arise in novels, stories, and poems has probably observed that most of these are chiefly insightful about matters of ethics: morals and manners, social relations, power, politics, insight into character, and self-knowledge. Some, such as the tragedies of classical antiquity or the Zen-inspired novels of Yosunari Kawabata, also presume a metaphysics that informs plot, character, and moral judgment. Only a relatively small portion of philosophical literature, however, is chiefly devoted to the complexities of ontology or logic: Lawrence Sterne and Lewis Carroll come to mind, and also the trio of writers that occupy us in these pages.

In their own quite different styles, these three writers intrigue for their sustained exploration of paradox and puzzle and their sometimes quite deliberate engagement with the perennial questions that define metaphysics. They share mutual interests and influences—both Calvino and Eco acknowledge a debt to Borges—that converge in their engagement with issues such as the problem of the one and the many, of personal identity through time, of induction of purpose from pattern. Their stories, fables, and novels tantalize with sustained confusions of reality and illusion; of identities of self and other; of overlapping fates, inevitable choices, linked stories, and follies. They feature a host of characters engaged in that ultimate epistemic quest, the search for the key to knowledge that will reveal all secrets; invariably their satisfaction is perennially postponed. Perhaps most disturbingly, these authors evoke and tease the compulsion shared by narrators and readers alike to find meaning in an opaque world full of random and ambiguous patterns, in which clues may be false promises and solutions are always yet another page away, even after the story has ended.

Such themes are pursued in ways that are individually distinctive yet similar. There are shared interests in the phenomenon of human consciousness itself and its reflexive twists and turns; in cryptographic systems of metaphysical conceit, such as the Tarot or Cabala; in repetition, imitation, and variation of image, theme, and place. Indeed sometimes the very buildings imagined by our three authors would seem to have been designed by the same architect—one with a taste for labyrinths. None of their works can be read with half a mind; their stories and novels require intense concentration lest the reader become hopelessly lost. Reading is both absorbing and fatiguing, and their works perhaps appeal more to the head than to the heart. But if we are not always deeply moved by the writings of Borges or Eco or Calvino, we cannot fail to be provoked and intrigued, to enter their worlds where inversions of the familiar prompt doubt about previous convictions and plots provoke investigation of the limits of logic and reason. Because of their reflective appropriation of the quests that define metaphysics, logic, and epistemology, the fictions of these authors focus and sharpen the issues regarding the relations between philosophy and literature in general.

In the essays that follow a group of distinguished philosophers, literary scholars, and comparativists explore and debate the philosophical status of the works of Borges, Calvino, and Eco. Needless to say, they do not all agree. Some maintain a fairly traditional distinction between the two disciplines; others are more inclined to follow certain postmodern insights and allow that these texts tread the border where no clear distinction can be discerned. None, however, adopts here outright the radical deconstructionist position that maintains that there is no distinction between logic and rhetoric and therefore none between philosophy and literature either. Indeed, to take this position would eliminate the substance from the issue and make the questions posed more or less moot. Moreover, these essays are not so much directed to the large categories *philosophy* and *literature* and the general features that might define the differences between the two; rather, the questions raised here concern whether, in certain cases, the enterprises are so mixed that texts are *both* philosophy and literature. For some of the contributors, the stories and novels of these three authors are alternative venues for doing philosophy; for others, the literary texts supplant the philosophical in ways that are distinct and incompatible, however intriguing and illuminating they might be about the standard concerns of philosophy. The different perspectives espoused disclose the several issues involved in addressing the question, can philosophy be done in or through or by means of fictional literature? Some of these essays, notably those that open the discussion, explore the general question with the works of Borges or Calvino or Eco in mind as exemplary test cases; others examine particular texts to assess their status in this ambiguous territory. Taken as a group, they provide long, close, and midrange lenses to assess the nature of the philosophical and literary endeavors and the questions that most require address.

One set of such questions clusters around the authors of these texts. Only Eco is formally trained in philosophy, but because not everything that a philosopher writes is thereby philosophy, that fact alone does not distinguish his novels from those of Calvino. The academic standing of these writers is clearly not what is at issue, but we cannot dispense with the matter of authorship quite so simply. A more relevant question is this: do certain of these narratives imply an author with a philosopher's mind? This is something more than the question of whether certain narratives raise philosophical questions, for the latter is easy to answer—yes, they do. Otherwise the question of philosophy in literature would never have arisen. But it is quite possible—indeed, perhaps usual—for philosophical questions to arise more or less secondarily as a consequence of plot and character rather than as the chief and driving point of a narrative. In these cases, the "doing" of philosophy on the basis of literature falls to the reader as much as the writer, for to adapt an idea from Foucault, it may be that the author of a novel is just a writer of philosophical matters. And although the issue is raised less frequently, the reverse is also the case: just because a philosopher employs dialogue and character or has an especially vivid and imagistic style of writing, he or she does not thereby qualify as a crafter of literature.

Unlike the many authors of fiction whose philosophical interests arise as a consequence of conventional literary devices such as plot development, Borges, Calvino, and Eco all write with deliberate philosophic agendas. It is impossible to imagine their narratives could come to be written without significant and intentional pursuit of classic questions of metaphysics or epistemology informing them. Indeed, many of their stories take such questioning as the very point of the narrative, their plots but maps to a philosophical site. Perhaps this is why so many of their characters are almost ciphers, empty of individual personality, for they are in thrall to a metaphysical purpose.

None of the authors in this volume is in doubt that the texts under study grapple intentionally, seriously, and with dedication (however playful) with philosophical matters. Nor do they dispute that the authors are grounded in and deeply engaged with the history and methods of standard philosophy, traditionally conceived. Their differences concern the nature of the texts themselves, the discourses and traditions in which they participate, and the roles of narrative, genre, parody, and style in identifying and classifying bodies of writing.

Granted, texts are not always easy to categorize, and there are plenty of examples of "philosophical" writing that employ the "literary" devices of conversation and character (Plato's dialogues, most famously), or parody and *double entendre* (Plato again, and Machiavelli), or aphorism and provocation (Nietzsche, Adorno). There are philosophers who are praised not only for their original contributions to intellectual culture but for the eloquence of their style (Bertrand Russell, for example, or Schopenhauer), whereas others of equal importance are read for the significance of their ideas despite their numbingly clumsy writing (Kant, most notoriously, despite the accolades he receives for advancing German as a philosophical language). This fact alone suggests a certain detachability of philosophical content from its textual vehicle, for if philosophical writing always required the eloquence of the literary master, there would be less of it on library shelves. Reciprocally, if the thought-provoking novelist needed to develop ideas with the thoroughness of philosophical argumentation, there would be fewer pretenders to our debatable category, "literary philosophers," a term that the attentive reader will have noted is flanked with question marks in the title. But what about the specific authors under study here? For we have already presented Borges, Calvino, and Eco as especially qualified candidates for this classification because of their sustained and central pursuit of philosophy in elegant narrative forms, forms that seem, moreover, honed and streamlined in their hands for the purpose of theoretical exactitude.

This issue invites a number of avenues of address, including reflection on philosophy and literature as practices or traditions, an approach that disposes some of the authors in this volume to retain the division between the disciplines. Deborah Knight, for one, declines to see the works of even these three authors as philosophy dressed in narrative form, more imaginative routes to theoretical truths than one usually finds. As she puts it, "Literature just is not philosophy in a somewhat nattier, more creative, more imaginative form. Literature, like philosophy, is a specific sort of practice, and literature and philosophy are different practices." Thinking of literature and philosophy as disciplinary and writerly practices leads her to consider a third, perhaps bridge practice: interpretation and criticism of literary texts. There are many advocates on behalf of the union of philosophy and literature who cobble the defense of their position onto the interpretation of specific works, seeing in novels of James or Eliot philosophy in imaginative practice. But Knight is suspicious about the ease with which an imaginative reader can discover philosophical significance in just about any kind of text and argues that the deepest and most creative interpretation cannot turn a novel into a work of philosophy. Her review of so-called ethical criticism (which extends philosophy into literature), and rival schools of interpretation that decline to do so, situates the questions raised by Borges, Calvino, and Eco in the larger context of debate that is underway concerning philosophy and literature in general.

What criteria might be used to decide that a text is an example of philosophy and not of literature? These are, as we have already noted, terms that refer to an enormous range of works, and not all of them exhibit the same characteristics. Arguably, both "philosophy" and "literature" are not definable with any exactitude, so how should we address the literary quality of the former and the philosophical status of the latter? Despite the formidable range of works classed in each category, William Irwin proposes that a variation on the concept of family resemblance that he terms "necessary condition family resemblance" can provide a type of criterion. A review of attempts to define both literature and philosophy yields his observation that no essentialist definition can be given for either term that is not merely stipulative. Nonetheless, what we might call an open necessary condition can be articulated: to be a work of literature, a work must have been produced with the intention of fitting the category literature, although the characteristic properties of that category, because they vary with history and tradition, cannot be further determined in advance. "Philosophy" receives a similar treatment: "Among the intentions ... in producing philosophy must be, actually or counterfactually, the intention to produce a text that would fit within the application of the necessary condition family resemblance term 'philosophy.'" (Perhaps this can be seen as a more formal way to state part of what Knight has in mind when she speaks of literary and philosophical "practices.") A consequence of Irwin's survey of definitions and their difficulties is his conclusion that the decision to describe any given work as philosophy or literature—or by the corollary descriptions "philosophical" or "literary"—must proceed on a case by case basis. Therefore rather than issuing a blanket assessment of the entire corpus of even such an author as Borges, he focuses on just one story: that of Pierre Menard, whose production of different but indiscernible objects so intrigues philosophers. That this story is both philosophical and literary is no surprise, but using his necessary condition family resemblance criterion, Irwin concludes that the story is itself not a work of philosophy because it is unlikely it was produced with the intention of fitting into the requisite tradition.

Although the contributors cite a large range of stories and novels in the course of their discussions, Borges's "Pierre Menard" is repeatedly invoked in these essays, more than any other single work. This is understandable, as questions about the ambiguous nature of a piece of writing are intensified by the reflexive trope of Menard's *Quixote*, distilling in one story so many puzzles about the identity of texts. Moreover, this narrative of textual repetition yet new creation deftly focuses one of the major themes that arises over and over in the works of all three authors: mimesis. In their highly self-conscious and reflexive narratives, Borges and Calvino and Eco deploy mimesis and duplication in their plot contents, in the genres they adopt, in their writing style, and sometimes (as in the case of Menard) in their very word order. This renders their texts extremely dense, whether they write with the unique terseness of a Borges or the larger style of the traditional *grand récit* that Eco favors. When imitating the text of another, does the imitator do the same thing as the original author or something different? When a short story writer includes in his or her mimesis the problems and concerns and even argumentative considerations of a philosophy, is the resulting text a story or a treatise?

The guiding question regarding the philosophical or literary status of these authors often meets a teasing resistance from the texts themselves, questioning as they do the exclusiveness of that *"or."* Lois Parkinson Zamora studies the development of Borges's style and his own genre of the short story in terms of "monsters." By monsters, Borges means combinations of things that in reality are discrete but in fiction and myth are combined. Zamora observes that it is by means of unnatural combinations that Borges creates beings that do not just add to our imaginary repertoire but are crafted as exemplars of the problem of universals: single members of their own unique classes (the old *haeccaities* of medieval philosophy). In Borges's hands, the problem of the one and the many is presented by particulars with no kin, a device that not only zeroes in on a standard problem in metaphysics but does so by means of a specifically drawn fictional being. On a more abstract scale, she argues, Borges combines disciplines—including philosophy and literature—creating thereby a "textual monster" with a unique shape of its own. Zamora presents Borges as a "magical idealist," as distinct from the famous magical realism so often associated with Latin American fiction. Borges's signature spare style, his distilled brevity, is the product of careful selection of metaphor and synecdoche that presents in its very form some philosophical issue. Her argument emerges from her compendious presentation of the development of Borges's *oeuvre* and thus also serves as an informative reference point for several of these essays.

It is precisely an admiration of that perfection of form, one that results in inseparability of text from idea, that leads Jorge Gracia to refuse to collapse any literary works into the category of philosophy. He suggests a different sort of criterion by means of which the two sorts of works can be distinguished. He pursues a suspicion implicit in the idea that the essence of philosophy resides in the ideas and arguments presented, and the essence of literary work in the style, imagery, and emotional provocation encountered in fictional narrative: namely, that literature is more embedded in the actual words written by the author, whereas philosophy may be presented without loss in altered language. This idea is familiar among those who see literary works as the imaginative playing out of philosophical ideas, presenting in particular and vivid ways what is usually abstract and general. But Gracia is more precise than this: The criterion he proposes separates the conditions of identity of *text* and *work*: "Text" refers to the actual words written, their precise sequence and form. With works of literature, their conditions of identity include their texts, whereas with philosophy, "work" can be separated from "text" without loss of identity. This is dramatically illustrated with problems of translation from one language to another. Gracia also plays with Borges's story of Pierre Menard, whose rewriting of Cervantes' *Quixote*, although word for word the same as the original, still produces a different work with different aesthetic attributes. How much greater is the difference between texts rendered in different languages from their originals? Strictly speaking, a work of literature cannot be translated without changing its identity, whereas a philosophical text "says" more or less the same thing in whatever language it is presented. That "more or less" qualification does not detract from the power of the ideas of philosophy, but it does impair the literary form, for even a very good translation loses something of the original flavor. This claim suggests that the *aesthetic quality* of literature, embedded in the precise sequence of original words, is indispensable to its identity, whereas with philosophy it is the *intellectual quality* of ideas propounded that is indispensable.

This line of thought raises another point of dispute regarding the cohesion of literature and philosophy: One of the effects of powerful narrative is to engage the reader in a story, arousing emotions and other responses in the process of unfolding a plot. Anyone inclined to see in literature an alternative route to philosophical insight also probably subscribes to the idea that a philosophical argument or thesis is made more powerful, more convincing, and even better philosophy if it has emotive punch. How integral is the emotive response to the philosophy itself? Is it but a device of rhetoric or persuasion, or is it part and parcel of the position, as crucial to convincing reasoning as argumentation and evidence? There are those who regard Sartre's *Nausea* or *No Exit* as the fictional application of the ideas of *Being and Nothingness*; others are more inclined to see them as independent works of philosophy in a more imaginative, indeed perhaps even more persuasive, form. In fact, they might argue, how would *Being and Nothingness* itself read if its many imaginative scenarios were expunged from the text? Arguing that its emotional valence and appeal are integral parts of the writing of theory is an uphill battle, for philosophy has a long-established suspicion of emotion, preferring the cold clarity of reason and assessment of argument to the more underhand persuasions of emotional arousal. Therefore, in considering the status of "literary philosophy" it is necessary also to assess the reader's emotional engagement with narrative fiction: is it diversionary, signaling mere entertainment that sugar-coats the bitter pill of rational argumentation that is more directly presented in treatise and essay? An affirmative answer would separate the literary part of a text from the philosophical part, but those more inclined to see the integration of power of argument with its emotional appeal would maintain that affective response to a text is itself part of what makes the literary works in question philosophical.

Assessing the reader's emotional involvement is somewhat hampered by the intellectual rigor and cerebral tastes of Borges, Calvino, and Eco themselves, for these are not writers noted for their appeal to the heart—unlike, for example, other noteworthy exemplars of philosophical fiction such as Tolstoy or Eliot or Proust. However, our three authors most certainly entertain; if they rarely arouse tears they are intellectual irritants who often provoke laughter, and in this way they beguile as much as they argue. Although as a rule these writers do not arouse strong emotions, they carefully and deliberately situate the reader affectively in relation to the text. This is often accomplished via an intellectual engagement that stimulates curiosity, a mental state Hobbes called an "intellectual appetite." Moreover, it must be granted that the most distanced reader occasionally succumbs to a thrill of fear, an intellectual *frisson*, as plot discloses discovery of an unexpected and dreadful illusion (Borges's "The Circular Ruins"), a foreordained future (Calvino's *Castle of Crossed Destinies*), or a double who threatens the unitary identity of a narrator (Eco's *Island of the Day Before*). Indeed, although Aristotle postulated that philosophy begins in wonder (and ends in amazement, Russell added), Anthony Cascardi observes that according to Borges, it begins in fear and anxiety, seeking amazement as a kind of antidote.

Cascardi pursues the issue of philosophy and literature somewhat differently than our other essayists, for his discussion of Borges folds the latter's famous metaphysical interests into another branch of philosophy: philosophy of art. Borges, the earliest of our three writers, who himself provides much inspiration for the younger two, wrote at a time when theorists of modernism were casting about for a theory of art that could account for a widespread sense that art had no more innovations in its repertoire. With Benjamin's declaration of the recession of the aura of the work of art came a sense that all that lay in store for the artist of the future was repetition of the past. Borges, a short story writer and an artist, as well as an essayist, an omnivorous reader, and a man of his time, was positioned not only to comment upon the state of art of the mid-twentieth century, but to enact its problems and its solutions. Mimesis, the oldest theory of art, was invoked by modernism as having degenerated into mere repetition; but Borges is not merely echoing the plaint of theorists writing in the long wake of Hegel's declaration of the end of art. Mimesis is figured not only as the "abomination of mirrors" proclaimed in "Tlön, Uqbar, Orbis Tertius" but also as magical fabulation—creation ex nihilo, as in "The Circular Ruins." The problem of mimesis, which is a theoretical matter for philosophy and for art, also becomes a personal concern in its metamorphosis into fiction. Cascardi writes, "Borges shares Nietzsche's suspicion that 'philosophy' may have its origins not in wonder but in anxiety, in the desire to quiet the fear that comes from this abandonment of reality's metaphysical grounds." Figured in fiction, in art itself, this anxiety is both theory and plot, abstract idea and affective response. The anxiety is perhaps not allayed, but it is distanced—a variety of therapy for the existential confrontation with doubling and fragmentation of selves by regarding philosophical discourse as a series of engaging puzzles, joining the metaphysicians of Tlön in seeing metaphysics as a branch of fantastic literature. The short stories that play out a metaphysics of repetition and endless mimetic variations can be regarded as both enactments and displays of a kind of metaphilosophy. Because Borges has recast philosophical concerns in terms of his own enigmas of same and different, like and unlike, differentiatable and indiscernible, original and copy—it is almost churlish to drag in traditional standards to argue that the works are mere stories. The inseparability of expressive mode and philosophical problem arguably renders these texts indissolubly both philosophy and fiction.

The anxiety at the root of philosophy is not always so apparent in these writers, for the characters that populate the works of Borges or Calvino or Eco often lack familiar traits with which the reader may sympathize. For this reason, some of their works are readily seen in terms of comedy, and as Elizabeth Millán-Zaibert notes, Calvino himself considered both philosophy and literature to have roots in comedy—a dramatic form that plays with wonder and amazement in order to subdue fear with laughter. She proposes that to consider Calvino philosophical is to open oneself to another view of the philosophical method—an "aesthetic method." Initiated by early German romantic writers such as Schlegel, the aesthetic method construes philosophy not as an ally of science that pursues deductive or conclusive arguments, but as the expression of a "longing for the infinite" that in principle is unreachable. Therefore it can be approached only indirectly by means of allusion and irony. Irony in particular is a method for reflecting on the gap between representation and reality, but one that does not expect definitive answers to ensue. Millán-Zaibert, perhaps more than any of these contributors, is sympathetic to the position espoused by Derrida and Rorty that shrinks or even erases the line between a philosophical and a literary text, and she maintains that the situation of the philosophically self-conscious and ironic Calvino bears this out.

Much of the work of this trio involves not only irony but parody, which is not only a comic genre but also one that, as Zamora observes, mirrors another, absent text. How many of those absent texts contain philosophical systems is brought into prominence in Henry Sussman's discussion of the asystematic writings of Borges and Calvino. Sussman outlines twelve ways of looking at a system, ways that resonate not only with the nineteenth-century system-builders Kant, Hegel, and Schopenhauer but with their fun-house counterparts in Borges, Calvino, Kafka, Blanchot, and other writers who relentlessly invert logic and progression into the building of their own repetitious universes whose nonsystems assert yet violate predictability. Sussman terms his tribute to Borges and Calvino "the writing of the system," and indeed it is the possibilities and limits of language itself that these authors advance, sometimes by means of covert and indirect parody. As Sussman remarks of one of Borges's stories, "Fiction bears the trace of system to the same extent that system is already discombobulated by the inherent play and radicality of the medium—language—making it up." For Calvino, who grounds his fiction not in grand possibilities but in the phenomenology of the everyday world, systems here are less mock-philosophies than familiar annoyances writ large. Such is the case with the traffic patterns of clogged cities that are mapped in labyrinthine form in "The Chase." By contrast, the counteruniverses Borges writes into being reach toward a kind of sublime—that Kantian point at which the human mind reflexively recognizes both its own limits and the existence of possibilities beyond it, an intuition of which reveals the capacity of the mind to extend itself beyond the limits of nature. For both authors, the "writing of systems" at once refers to philosophical systems, parodies those systems, deconstructs systematic thinking, and simultaneously discloses "the systematic parameters imprinted upon theoretically aware writing itself." Sussman's approach casts Calvino and Borges as metaphilosophers whose inversions illuminate the nature of philosophical endeavor.

It is notable how often not just philosophy but *meta*philosophy arises in these discussions. Metaphilosophy—reflection, diagnosis, second-order reflection on the character of philosophy—is an undertaking that is ordinarily classified as one of the purviews of philosophy proper. However, unlike the standard areas of the discipline that concern themselves with first principles or the foundations of knowledge or right conduct and (some would argue) require rigid discipline to come to fruition, metaphilosophy would seem to have no such limits. Indeed, assessing a discipline or a practice often positively demands a stance from outside the familiar boundaries of the field. Borges, Calvino, and Eco, as we have seen, straddle those boundaries; and insofar as their works constitute metaphilosophy they demonstrate how that endeavor in fiction achieves the salutary distance and perspective required for rumination on the conduct and writing of philosophy.

Like Sussman, Rocco Capozzi, Wladimir Krysinski, and Ermanno Bencivenga stress the extent to which writing about writing itself occupies these three authors. Capozzi explores the intertextuality of Eco's novels, which borrow, parody, quote, allude to, and play within familiar literary forms. Eco's version of playful mimesis, a deliberately nonoriginal deployment of genres, marks a creativity of Eco's own postmodern sort. Eco's texts are hybrids of others (rather like Borges's "monstrous texts") and their combinatory possibilities awaken related philosophical and linguistic issues. Eco grounds the production of meaning not just in the texts of literature and philosophy, but also in technology and the phenomena of the internet. The World Wide Web, Capozzi points out, represents for Eco the ultimate intertextuality, with its hyperlinks that take one click by click deeper and deeper into a net of references and associations. Eco's novels do not just display but enact intertextuality, inviting readers to participate in the construction of the labyrinths in which they then wander. More than Borges or Calvino, Eco powers his intricate plots with the use of references to actual philosophers and recognizable theoretical problems; he depicts in the complexity of his mammoth novels a virtual line-up of philosophical possibilities. Capozzi refers to these novels as "cognitive tools with a great potential for stimulating literary and philosophical discussions through a myriad of analogies and intertextual echoes."

Krysinski analyzes all three of our authors as writers of "metafictions," by which he means fiction that reflects upon itself and upon the production of meaning. Because metafiction in its many forms queries the nature of texts, meanings, and the multiplicity of interpretation, it may be viewed in terms of philosophy, that is, as an interrogation about truth and the limitless attempts to locate order and comprehensibility in a universe devoid of fixed center or evident purpose. The fluidity and self-reflection of metafiction dissolve the boundaries between philosophical and literary texts partly because the identity of narrative is constantly questioned. Borges, for example, "tactically telescopes philosophical, interpretive, and argumentative discourse and can at any moment effectuate a detour through philosophy." Calvino, he argues, synthesizes reason and art, turning his literature into a mode of reflection on the conditions of knowledge and meaning. Metafiction sometimes takes the form of a new, perhaps parodic, use of genre, as Eco does with the Gothic novel or the mystery (as Capozzi also noted). Deploying familiar genres to strange ends is a means of using peculiarly literary devices as philosophical means, enticing the reader into mazes of interpretive possibilities that force meaning and writing into a mode of analysis as we read—even for fun. Krysinski insists that labyrinths in these writers are more than colorful and mystifying plot devices but narrative components that drive philosophical self-consciousness. In the hands of Borges, Calvino, and Eco, the trade between fictional narrative and metafictional philosophy is so entwined that the two become one: narrative is philosophy and philosophy is narrative.

Bencivenga also stresses the self-conscious writing about writing that Calvino performed, his stories demonstrating the nature of words themselves and their referential and creative limits. Calvino, he argues, was increasingly interested in philosophy, and as his work developed he folded philosophy into his stories and novels until it became their sole purpose. Bencivenga sees philosophy and literature as enterprises that share the same quest, one that seeks the truth. (Both Knight and Bencivenga—as well as Calvino—attach themselves to this stern, old-fashioned value.) The combination can liberate the reader from habitual attachments both to familiar assumptions and the solid resistance of the one possible world in which we all must live. Because of this real liberatory potential, he notes, it is important for the reader that Calvino's worlds focus on transformation of ordinary lived realities, a process that requires narrow selection of familiar events or objects at the expense of everything else—creating a void within which stories emerge. He makes the everyday strange and isolates its inherent puzzles. As Bencivenga says, "Both philosophy and literature aim at disconnecting us from our ordinary context; the end of both is liberation, and the agility of mind that goes with it, and the more extensive knowledge and greater adaptiveness that issue from that agility. Within this general liberating task, they play distinct but comple-mentary roles." As he traces these roles in Calvino's work, moreover, it becomes clear that there is a closer tie between the two types of writing than just shared purposes. The drive to understand and to pursue the truth is not only a "rational" stimulus to do philosophy because it is a drive from the imagination as well as from the intellect—and one with emotive power as its engine. As Bencivenga concludes: "The demand for truth, therefore, is not *external* to imagination; it structures it from the inside. . . . I like to think of the invention component of this operation as belonging to the literature side of it, and of the demand for truth that structures that invention as belonging to the philosophy side; and I like to think that, when both work together well, liberation does ensue—one does indeed find oneself floating through space, free for once of some of one's chains." Philosophy and literature may be distinguishable, but the texts in which they appear are not always distinctly one or the other. And indeed, in this closing contribution to the volume, Bencivenga slyly enacts his own merger of philosophy and literature. He more than just quotes from the works of his subject; he incorporates segments of Calvino's tales into his reflections on philosophy, literature, and the pursuit of meaning and truth. Bencivenga's appreciation of writing that provides wisdom, where "philosophers could not avoid being poets," resonates with Krysinski's comparison of philosophers and narrative artists as guests at a "Spanish tavern," "where philosophers and writers convivially lodge together though each of them brings heterogeneous subjects to the tavern."

Dining companions, genial monsters, builders of labyrinths, metaphilosophers and metafictionalists, artists whose imaginations reach toward the truth—these and other descriptions are proffered here to explore the cooperative tension between philosophy and literature. In the order in which this volume has been arranged, there is some measure of progression from essays that discuss the more general issues of philosophy and literature to those that focus quite specifically on the works of Borges or Calvino or Eco and the status of their fictions. This has yielded as well a certain progression from authors who are inclined to be skeptical about assigning the classification "philosophy" to literary works to those who are more willing to endorse the collapse of the two disciplines and genres of writing, especially in the cases of the three writers under study here. In the fictional worlds of Borges, Calvino, and Eco, where sequences of causality are reversed, individuals switch identities, and stories of one person mirror those of others, why should we be surprised if literature becomes philosophy and philosophy is stood on its head—along with the rest of the world? Perhaps that inverted position permits both artists and philosophers to recognize the possibilities and limits of their endeavors and to entertain a playful dose of mutual revelation.

2

DEBORAH KNIGHT

Intersections: Philosophy and Literature, or Why Ethical Criticism Prefers Realism

The relationships between literature and philosophy are many, and they are complex, and people, as you might expect, hold different views. One view insists that philosophy is just a type of literary discourse—a species of the genus, as it were. Richard Rorty thinks so. Another states that literature and philosophy are antithetical to each other. Plato thought so. Both these positions seem deeply unsatisfactory. If our job here is partly defined by the question of whether Borges, Calvino, and Eco are literary philosophers, then we have to think a bit about literature and philosophy.

Of our three authors, Borges exerts a special fascination for philosophers, both Continental and Anglo-North American ones. Recall what Michel Foucault wrote in the Preface to *The Order of Things*: "This book first arose out of a passage in Borges, out of the laughter that shattered, as I read the passage, all the familiar landmarks of my thought—*our* thought."[1] The passage is not philosophical, but as Foucault indicates, by means of it we can see questions of major philosophical importance.

The Borges work most beloved by philosophers is "Pierre Menard, Author of the *Quixote*." "Menard" exemplifies what many take to be the foundational philosophical question: how can we tell the difference between two things that seem to be identical? We must be able to answer this question if we are to get anywhere in metaphysics or epistemology or moral philosophy. Without an answer we cannot tell reality from appearance, truth from lie, moral from immoral actions. The problem of indiscernibles goes back to the very beginnings of Western philosophy. More recently, Arthur C. Danto has ornamented his philosophical career with the invention of numerous fanciful and exotic examples of indiscernibles. One example is the Exhibit of Red Squares, with which his book, *The Transfiguration of the Commonplace*, begins. In this imaginary exhibit, we find side by side perceptually indistinguishable square canvases, each painted a uniform red. Are these works all the same? They certainly all look alike. But they are not. The first is a painting of the Israelites crossing the Red Sea (of which its artist said, "The Israelites had already crossed over, and the Egyptians were drowned"). Commenting on that work, the Danish wit Sören Kierkegaard said that it seemed to express his mood, and indeed the next painting in the exhibit, influenced by that remark, is entitled "Kierkegaard's Mood." Then there is the "clever bit of Moscow landscape" ("Red Square") and the "minimalist exemplar of geometrical art" ("Red Square"), and the other paintings Danto describes. Danto's indiscernibles are every bit as dazzling as Borges's encyclopedia entry. And just as we laugh when we read about the Chinese encyclopedia, we laugh when we read Danto, whose own fictions about indiscernibles are far more fun than the actual artworks that inspired them—much wittier, for instance, than Warhol's *Brillo Box* or Duchamp's *Fountain*.[2]

Danto takes Borges to have been inspired by the same thought, the thought of indiscernibles. It "must follow" from a Leibnizian argument that if Cervantes' and Menard's word-for-word identical *Quixotes* have all the same properties, they must be identical. But as Danto tells us, Borges's point is that they do not have all the same properties, and so cannot be identical after all: "They have only in common those properties that the eye as such might identify. So much the worse for the properties that meet the eye, then, in individuating works of art. Borges's example has the philosophical effect of forcing us to avert our eye from the surfaces of things, and to ask in what if not surfaces the differences between distinct works must consist."[3]

But the essence of Borges's greatest insight may be more dizzying even than Danto suggests, as Michael Wood points out in the *London Review of Books*.[4] The moment of real conceptual vertigo surely occurs when we see on the page the two quotes, one from Cervantes, the other from Menard—each obviously word-for-word identical, but the second quote, Menard's, introduced by the delicious line, "Menard, *on the other hand*, writes. . . ." Both Wood and Danto delight in this phrase. What Borges does, and does repeatedly, is not merely confront us with two perceptually indiscriminable things. Rather, he gives us individual things without fixed identity, which are and are not the same, or which somehow split into two, as Borges does himself: "It's the other one, Borges, that things happen to," he writes. These are not simply variations of the foundational philosophical question, how to distinguish appearance from reality. The "Menard" is refracted through this persistent theme of non-self-identity, a theme that, taken seriously, would be the undoing of Western philosophy, and is captured by the thought: "I am not what I am."

Borges confronts us with the challenge to "apprehend in one great leap." But as Foucault saw, sometimes what we apprehend is only our inability to think *that*, to think, for instance, what it would mean to assert, "I am not what I am." This dazzling effect of apprehending in one great leap is sometimes achieved by philosophy. Sometimes it isn't achieved. I doubt anyone has ever experienced it reading, say, Grice or Kripke, though I can't be sure. I know

I've experienced it often reading Wittgenstein. But although the effect can be produced by both literary and philosophical means, it does not follow that literary works that produce this effect are therefore philosophical—except, possibly, in the honorific sense.

Philosophy is not philosophy just because it adopts a recognizable style—and that despite the fact that even today the tendency Danto noted in "Philosophy as/and/of Literature" is perfectly evident in the English-language professional journals, where the professional article still inclines toward the ideal of being "a unit of pure philosophy, to the presentation of which the author will have sacrificed all identity."[5] Of course, this ideal style of philosophy is much narrower than the actual range of philosophical styles, which as Danto reminds us runs from dialogue through meditation and unscientific postscript to lecture notes and grammatologies. Nor are all contemporary Anglo-North American philosophers as anonymous as the professional model suggests: Jerry Fodor, Daniel C. Dennett, not to mention Danto himself are all immediately recognizable as the authors of their works. But they are interested in what the other, less identifiable philosophers are interested in, which is saying something true about a philosophical issue of some importance. As Danto says, "No one could conceivably be interested in the form of life defined by the literary form in issue [that is, the ideal form of the philosophical paper as an anonymous unit of pure philosophy], were it not believed that this is the avenue to philosophical truth.[6]" Which raises the question of whether literature can be an alternative avenue to philosophical truth.

The answer here must be yes and no. Yes, clearly, as the Borges examples show, literature can be an avenue to philosophical truth, at least when it is the avenue for someone interested in philosophical truth to apprehend something in one great leap. But science and history and personal experience are also avenues to philosophical truth, and apprehension in any of these cases can also happen in one great leap. Literature does not get to sneak in as philosophy merely on the grounds that it sometimes allows us to recognize philosophical matters more clearly than philosophical discourse. So no, literature by itself is not an alternative avenue to philosophical truth unless someone comes along who wants to interpret literature philosophically. Even Sartre, whose novels illustrated his philosophy more vividly than his philosophy alone (compare *Being and Nothingness* with *La nausée*), did not write philosophy when he wrote literature. Literature just is not philosophy in a somewhat nattier, more creative, more imaginative form. Literature, like philosophy, is a specific sort of practice, and literature and philosophy are different practices.

Nevertheless, the two become intertwined. Indeed, they become most entangled when philosophers trawl great literary works looking for philosophical insight. Consider an example that has been largely bypassed, and undeservedly so, in the philosophy of literature: Peter Jones' *Philosophy and the Novel*.[7] It is a slim volume with five chapters: the first four deal in turn with *Middlemarch*, *Anna Karenina*, *The Brothers Karamazov*, and *A la recherche du temps perdu*, and the final chapter offers a philosophically oriented theory of the interpretation of literary fiction. The theory of interpretation is philosophically oriented because the book as a whole is written to reveal what Jones takes to be significant *philosophical aspects* of these four novels. The chapter titles give you a good sense of what counts as a "philosophical aspect": "Imagination and Egoism in *Middlemarch*," "Action and Passion in *Anna Karenina*," "The Self and Others in *The Brothers Karamazov*," and "Knowledge and Illusion in *A la recherche du temps perdu*." The question has to be: is Jones, a philosopher, still doing philosophy when he writes about these canonical novels? He would say yes. That is because his theory of interpretation, the "creative interpretation" theory, holds that "one way in which a novel may be described, justifiably, as philosophical is if it displays philosophicalness without philosophy."[8] He would say that the philosophicalness of the text can be perceived just because what he is doing is philosophical, rather than say literary, analysis.

It would follow for Jones that Borges's, Eco's, and Calvino's works are philosophical if they "display philosophicalness without philosophy." And it would not be hard to show that many of them do. What might be interesting would be to get a sense of which novels *do not* display philosophicalness, viewed by a philosopher who was interested in discovering it. Could Jones be thinking of novels by, say, John le Carré or Jackie Collins? But even works of popular literature, indeed of mass literature, can and do display philosophicalness. So it is not obvious what would be excluded as meriting being described as philosophical, if not on Jones' own terms, at least on ones very like his.

Jones' "creative interpretation" theory notes very sensibly that "writers create texts; readers interpret texts."[9] This distinction between texts and interpretations means that literary texts are "cut off" from their authors. Interpretations are therefore multiple and nonconverging, and the author exerts no authority over the validity of any interpretation. So Jones does not claim that George Eliot or Tolstoy or Dostoevsky or Proust is a philosopher (although Tolstoy's *What Is Art?* is still part of the canon in the philosophy of art). It is Jones as creative interpreter who discerns the philosophicalness of these texts. By extension, even if we find philosophicalness in the novels and stories of Borges, Calvino, and Eco, it would not be correct to infer that the authors are to be thought of as philosophers, even honorifically. In the meantime, the approach Jones recommends for the interpretation of literature would certainly not be applied by him to, say, Descartes or even to Danto.

The question is: does Jones' method really cash out as philosophy? Arguably not. What he seems to do is produce literary criticism from a philosophical perspective. Indeed, Jones exemplifies a tendency apparent in Anglo-North American philosophers of literature from Monroe Beardsley to the present. This tendency links philosophers writing about literature with what I would call traditional humanistic literary criticism—I'm thinking of F. R. Leavis as the paradigm here. Certainly these philosophers of literature have more in common with that sort of literary criticism than they have with either philosophical writing or with literary scholarship inspired by the sorts of theoretical problems that arose with poststructuralism and its many thematic offspring and variations, for instance, postmodernism, gender theory, and postcolonialism.

Contemporary Anglo-North American philosophers of literature are often humanists. Humanism is the cornerstone of, for instance, Peter Lamarque and Stein Haugom Olsen's impressive *Truth, Fiction, and Literature*,[10] published in 1994, and for that matter of Susan Feagin's *Reading with Feeling*,[11] published in 1996. In Peter Lamarque's introduction to his *Fictional Points of View*[12] (also 1996), he emphasizes a "binding theme [which] informs the whole and provides a general motivation" for his work, and calls this "a 'humanistic' approach to literature and to fiction." He explicates his version of humanism this way: "The core idea is that works of literature, through the medium of fiction, can serve the end of advancing, helping to develop and understand, exhibiting through their themes and vision, matters of general, perhaps universal, human interest." Literary fiction is "an important, even indispensable, vehicle for exploring human concerns." Furthermore, it allows us to "engage seriously with issues that matter in the real world, and, in stirring the imagination, can clarify thought and enliven perception." Lamarque himself admits that all this might seem "old-fashioned" and that, at least in some quarters, it is taken for granted that such values "have been discredited finally and irrefutably."[13] But humanism is what we find, and it then becomes tricky to know whether philosophers of literature are still doing philosophy when they offer extended analyses of literary texts.

Having looked at the relationships between philosophy and literature, we find ourselves in the center of an important distinction: between philosophy *of* literature and philosophy *and* literature. What, you might ask, could the difference possibly be? These areas represent two-thirds of the field surveyed in Danto's "Philosophy as/and/of Literature." For our purposes, we are not likely to be concerned with that paper's third area, the idea of philosophy *as* literature. This is a good thing. As Danto argues, to view philosophy *as* literature is in a fundamental way to mistake what philosophy is aiming at. Many texts fall to the status of "literature" precisely because they can so easily be read without a sense of what we might call their historical intentionality— a point Danto makes when he says that "to rotate [philosophical] texts in such a way that the secondary facets [i.e., style, form, etc.] catch the light of intellectual concern puts what we regard as the primary facets in shadow."[14]

To accept the notion that philosophy *just is* literature, as Rorty does, risks making the point of philosophy disappear in the same way that treating the Bible *as* literature makes the point of the Bible as divine revelation disappear. But this is not our worry here. By contrast, we do seem to be very much interested in the question of literature *as* philosophy.

The difference between "philosophy and literature" and "philosophy of literature" can be set out, roughly, as follows. Philosophy *of* literature is a metadiscourse that attempts to determine what literature is, and along the way tries to identify what characterizes literary (as opposed to nonliterary) discourse as well as what makes literature valuable. Philosophers of literature inquire into topics such as truth and reference, as well as the dubious onto-logical status of fictional entities, including fictional characters and the worlds they "inhabit." Lamarque and Olsen have flatly decided to defend a "no-truth" theory of literature, thus confounding all philosophers keen to put a good spin on the oxymoron "fictional truth." As for reference, over a decade ago Danto remarked with a certain mordant glee that "this is scarcely the place to tell the chilling tale of fictional reference."[15] Nor is this the place to tell the tale, which remains chilling. Philosophy *and* literature is a rather warmer area, and fuzzier. Philosophy *and* literature creates a space to examine philosophical themes—for instance, metaphysical, epistemological, or ethical themes—as they appear in literary texts. These themes will typi-cally be humanist ones, and the texts cited will typically be canonical.

I want to turn now to the topic of ethical criticism. At first glance, ethical criticism looks like a very good wedding of philosophy *and* literature and phi-losophy *of* literature. It is interdisciplinary, allowing philosophers, literary scholars, and others to work on a common set of issues. It is concerned with just the sorts of philosophical themes and questions exemplified in Peter Jones' *Philosophy and the Novel*. Additionally, and especially under the influ-ence of Martha Nussbaum, ethical criticism has made close reading and tex-tual analysis a central part of its methodology—something that has not been typical in philosophy of literature. Moreover, ethical criticism wants to reunite our experiences as readers of literature with our "real life" experi-ences because reading can have consequences for us as moral agents. Ethical critics claim that the appreciative reading of at least some exemplary works of literary fiction can help us live better lives.

The two primary figures in ethical criticism are Martha Nussbaum and Wayne Booth. Alexander Nehamas notes that Richard Rorty occasionally espouses a position very like that of ethical criticism.[16] However, Rorty's basic take on ethics diverges significantly (one might almost say wildly) from that of Nussbaum and Booth. To treat ethical criticism as just another oppor-tunity for "keeping the conversation going" distorts its purpose, so Rorty cannot be considered an ethical critic *bona fides*. Slightly further back in the genealogy, at least on the philosophical side, we find figures such as Hilary

Putnam and Alasdair MacIntyre. There are also persuasive opponents of ethical criticism—including Nehamas, Lamarque and Olsen, and Richard A. Posner.

What, then, is ethical criticism? Booth has devoted an entire book, *The Company We Keep: An Ethics of Fiction*, to the topic.[17] Nussbaum has written numerous essays, many gathered together in book form, including *Love's Knowledge* and *Poetic Justice*.[18] In 1998, their APA debate with Posner on the topic of ethical critism was published in *Philosophy and Literature*.[19] For both Booth and Nussbaum, the ethical is basically the realm located by answers to the question, "How should we live?" This question is clearly Aristotelian. Nussbaum (like MacIntyre) breaks with Kantian and utilitarian ethics to link the governing issues of ethics to Aristotle's notion of *phronesis*, practical action, and to his diagnosis of the *phronemos*, the person engaged in practical action. Nussbaum argues that moral philosophy properly construed requires supplementation from a small number of literary works that, as Posner tartly observes, are "chosen to illustrate, rather than to shape, her moral stance."[20] Additionally, she focuses on specific groups of people faced with pressing practical issues to decide, and recommends to them—again—a small, preselected group of fictions that should improve their ability to make practical judgments. Her target group lately has been lawyers. She advises that lawyers (and others) will be better positioned to make the sorts of decisions they have to make if they become good, committed readers of specific novels that she recommends as beneficial for "citizenship."[21]

Booth, by contrast, takes ethical criticism to be a very widespread, and very varied, practice.[22] Indeed, for Booth, ethical criticism describes any interpretation of literature that has "ethical appraisal" as a central feature.[23] Notice that on this construal Rorty is brought back in as an ethical critic, but if these are the conditions of membership, it is not clear who besides ultraformalists would be excluded. Although Booth grants that *overt* ethical criticism is frequently not a recognized critical position—and indeed is a position that, when identified, is generally denounced or derided—nevertheless he argues that even dogmatic theorists wind up practicing ethical criticism much of the time.

One reason why ethical criticism is such a commonplace of literary criticism is that, as Booth argues, "all narratives are in a sense didactic."[24] Now, any claim concerning a narrative's didacticism normally suggests a moral lesson that is conveyed at the level of paraphrasable content. This is not primarily what Booth is talking about. Rather, the sort of didacticism he is interested in results from the fusion in address of narrative content and form. That is, it is an element of narrative *rhetoric*. So Booth wants to turn our attention away from "paraphrasable content"—which tends to reduce the moral dimension of narratives to something like "the moral of the story"—and toward a focus on the transformation of the reader when that reader "genuinely 'listens to the story.'"[25] And the sort of conversation—and thus the sort of "listening" relationship—is one of *friendship*, at least potentially. The metaphor Booth explicitly employs is one of "people meeting as they share stories."[26] Such friendship is strictly indexed in terms of the individual reader, the story's implied author, the story, and the time of reading. And the friendship in question is of course importantly virtual, for the conversation we are having is not with the story's actual, historical author, but rather with its *implied* author—and the implied author is to a significant degree something we construct or project. For instance, if we fail to recognize a work as ironic, we will be mistaken about the intentions of its implied author. In the meantime, our status as readers is also a virtual one, disconnecting us from many of our everyday connections to the world and focusing us on our engagement with the text at hand. Despite this virtuality, Booth claims that all narratives propose the real offer of friendship. Nor is the offer keyed to a particular narrative mode—realism, say. Rather, Booth claims that "for our purposes, all stories, even those modern novels that use elaborate distancing tricks to subvert realism and prevent identification, can be viewed not as puzzles or even as games but as companions, friends—or [at least] as *gifts* from would-be friends."[27]

We can see now, I think, why both Booth and Nussbaum gravitate toward the notion of "ethical criticism." For both of them, reading trains us in perhaps the most fundamental sort of attentive and caring interpersonal relationship, one that is the basis for personal and social interaction as well as political community. For both of them, what matters is not simply the story but the story as told by a teller. The normativity of this position should be obvious. The ethically best works will also be the ones we should read; everything else being equal, the ethically worst are probably best left unread. This reaffirms a view of the literary canon as one based primarily on moral rather than aesthetic critieria. It will also, in all likelihood, direct us to read so-called High Literature rather than Low, Popular, or Mass Literature. Nussbaum clearly does not concern herself with popular fictions. Booth, ever open to the rich diversity of literary narratives, would I think be quite happy to promote ethically praiseworthy popular fictions. But this would just be a case of fine-tuning the long-standing division between high and low fictions. Where they differ is with regard to the scope of ethical criticism and the literary works that support it. As Posner so nicely puts it: "Booth's essential claim is that ethical criticism of literature is inescapable, and Nussbaum concedes that it is not."[28] Indeed, Nussbaum concedes that even interpretations of her preferred canon of ethical texts need not be ethically motivated.[29]

Several aspects of Nussbaum's thought merit critical attention, but for our purposes the most important is its *particularism*. Here we face the predicament Stuart Hampshire drew attention to in 1952: "When in Aesthetics one moves from the particular to the general, one is travelling in the wrong direction."[30] Nussbaum also believes that in the ethical criticism of literature, moving from the particular to the general is a movement in the wrong direction. The literary texts she is concerned with, says Nussbaum, are so finely rendered, so precise in their description of character and situation, so exact, that critical paraphrase is, strictly, both impossible and unjustifiable. But if we accept the literary work's absolute particularity, then there is no way to tell how we might derive any principles for human action, or even principles for our own action, from literary texts. As readers, we are concerned with the actions of Maggie and the prince in *The Golden Bowl*, not with ourselves. If we are "loving and attentive" readers, as Nussbaum wishes us to be,[31] perhaps we might be able to fathom how *they* should act, or we might come to moral judgments about *them*. How we might imagine these decisions to ramify for our own conduct, or the conduct of those around us, remains quite obstinately opaque.

The same problem haunts discussions of literature that are broader than Nussbaum's. As Posner remarks, "the moral content of a work of literature is likely to be obsolete whether or not it conforms to our current moral views."[32] Consider *Othello*. It is not obvious that there *is* a fixed moral sentiment that can be read off the play. But even if there were, and accepting Nussbaum's particularism, how do we imagine it to be applied in our own lives? Why would we imagine it *should* be applied in our own lives? Or consider *Casablanca*, which has long been interpreted as an allegory about the need for Americans to finally commit themselves to action on behalf of the Allies fighting Hitler. Whatever effect this moral bromide might have had on Americans in the early 1940s, two things are clear. It was hardly the only expression of this sort of political sentiment. And its applicability to contemporary viewers—especially those younger viewers for whom World War II is nearly as vague and mythic as the fall of Rome—is surely negligible. Like the golden bowl itself, Nussbaum's philosophical project is flawed. Ethical criticism construed as exemplifying that project is probably just ideologically driven literary criticism by another, and somewhat grander, name.

It should be obvious why ethical criticism, especially as practiced by Nussbaum, prefers realism. In fact, it should be obvious why such criticism tends to prefer canonical texts with basically Aristotelian plots and richly developed psychological characters engaged in courses of action that are serious and demand second-order reflection from the characters as well as from readers. Such texts can easily be drafted into service as possible answers to the question, "How should we live?" They tend to promote reader identification, encourage responses such as sympathy and empathy for characters, and might be considered valuable for our moral education because the issues facing characters are at root moral ones. We should ask: what is this humanistic ethical criticism to do when faced with the sorts of self-conscious and self-reflexive metafictions written by Borges, Calvino, and Eco? What sense will it be able to make out of the mock-essay, that fabulous Borgesian genre, that completely subverts both the expectations of realist literary fiction and any straightforward application of the idea that as readers we are in communion with an author (however implied) who is merely communicating things to us as known fact? What is ethical criticism to make of *Mr. Palomar* as he tries to imagine what it is like to be a gecko? It does not seem obvious. Which suggests one major limit of philosophy of literature, one that the essays in this volume will do much to redress.

The problem of literature as philosophy seems to have the form of Danto's favorite philosophical problem, the identity of indiscernibles. What would it take for two physically indiscernible texts to be categorized: this one literature, that one philosophy? But that is an unusual case. What we usually have to decide is the category to which a particular text properly belongs. Who among philosophers could serve as a precedent of the *literary* philosopher? Let's take Nietzsche. Is Nietzsche's work philosophy, or some bizarre new literary genre that invokes a lot of the history of philosophy as parody or pastiche or outright invention? Was Nietzsche a literary postmodern *avant la lettre*? You may know that Arthur Danto wrote a highly regarded and eloquent book about Nietzsche,[33] and in its aftermath one wag remarked, speaking in the voice of Nietzsche's mother: "Little Friedrich used to say the darndest things until he visited the arthurdantist." It seems that if Danto, especially Danto, recognizes in Nietzsche's work a genuine philosopher, then the matter is pretty much at an end, and those philosophers who scorn Nietzsche reveal only their prejudice against him. And surely Nietzsche, despite his many eccentricities of style and argument, is a philosopher, concerned as he is with the basic metaphysical and epistemological questions, such as the nature of truth.

To return to our question, are Borges, Calvino, or Eco literary *philosophers*? Would a trip to the arthurdantist reveal to us that they have been philosophers all along? No. Nietzsche could go and come out recognizably as a philosopher because he was one already. All the arthurdantist did was make this apparent for those with a taste for philosophy construed as "a unit of pure philosophy, to the presentation of which the author will have sacrificed all identity."

The more interesting question, it seems to me, is this: Is our philosophical analysis of these authors, or indeed of any literary authors, itself philosophy? Can those of us who are philosophers make literary authors into philosophers through our creative interpretation of their work, through our intentional reading of their work along philosophical lines? Martha Nussbaum says yes. Peter Jones sensibly says that we can reveal the philosophicalness of the literary text, but this does not impact the status of the authors. Peter Lamarque and Stein Olsen and I, siding with Jones, say no. Philosophers do not get to translate literary authors into philosophers any more than Humpty

Dumpty gets to mean anything he likes by what he says. We cannot do it by decree any more than Nussbaum herself can make Henry James into a moral philosopher. And quite frankly we cannot make certain literary texts proper supplements to philosophy any more than Nussbaum can turn certain James' novels into necessary supplements to moral philosophy.

It seems to me plain that when philosophers turn to authors such as Calvino and Eco and the incomparable Borges, what we do when we talk about them constitutes literary analysis, possibly even literary criticism. Are we any good at literary criticism? Some of us are, some of us are not. Can we use literature to exemplify central philosophical issues? Of course, at least if we have interpretive skill and critical acumen. Can we learn from literature? Certainly. Can we learn from literary criticism? Yes, we can learn much, and indeed we can learn from literary criticism to appreciate literature for its contributions to metaphysics, and even to moral philosophy. What this means is that we are all in the same boat when we read Borges or Calvino or Eco. Philosophers do not get any special privileges as readers of literary texts. If interpretation is as Jones thinks to a large extent creative interpretation, then all of our best interpretations, whether we start out as philosophers or not, will add to a greater understanding of these texts and their main themes and concerns. Arguably what we need for Borges, Calvino, and Eco is not a philosophy of literature, but as Professor Krysinski's essay recognizes, a philosophy of metafiction.

Notes

1. Michel Foucault, *The Order of Things: An Archaeology of the Human Sciences* (London: Tavistock, 1970), p. xv. As Foucault reminds us, "The passage quotes a 'certain Chinese encyclopedia' in which it is written that 'animals are divided into: (a) belonging to the Emperor, (b) embalmed, (c) tame, (d) sucking pigs, (e) sirens, (f) fabulous, (g) stray dogs, (h) included in the present classification, (i) frenzied, (j) innumerable, (k) drawn with a very fine camelhair brush, (l) *et cetera*, (m) having just broken the water pitcher, (n) that from a long way off look like flies."
2. Arthur C. Danto, *The Transfiguration of the Commonplace: A Philosophy of Art* (Cambridge, MA: Harvard University Press, 1981), p. 1.
3. Danto, *The Transfiguration of the Commonplace*, p. 35.
4. Michael Wood, "Productive Mischief," *London Review of Books* 21, no. 3 (4 February 1999): pp. 7–9.
5. Arthur C. Danto, "Philosophy as/and/of Literature," in *Literature and the Question of Philosophy*, ed. Anthony J. Cascardi (Baltimore: Johns Hopkins University Press, 1987), p. 6.
6. Danto, "Philosophy as/and/of Literature," p. 6.
7. Peter Jones, *Philosophical Aspects of the Novel* (Oxford: Clarendon Press, 1975). See also C. G. Prado, *Making Believe: Philosophical Reflections on Fiction* (Westport: Greenwood Press, 1984) for a development of Jones' "creative interpretation" theory.
8. Jones, *Philosophical Aspects of the Novel*, p. 181.
9. Jones, *Philosophical Aspects of the Novel*, p. 182.

10. Peter Lamarque and Stein Haugom Olsen, *Truth, Fiction, and Literature: A Philosophical Perspective* (Oxford: Clarendon Press, 1994).
11. Susan L. Feagin, *Reading With Feeling: An Aesthetics of Appreciation* (Ithaca, NY: Cornell University Press, 1996).
12. Peter Lamarque, *Fictional Points of View* (Ithaca, NY.: Cornell University Press, 1996).
13. Lamarque, *Fictional Points of View*, p. 3.
14. Danto, "Philosophy as/and/of Literature," p. 4.
15. Danto, "Philosophy as/and/of Literature," p. 8.
16. Alexander Nehamas, "What Should We Expect from Reading (There Are Only Aesthetic Values)," *Salmagundi* 111 (Summer 1996), pp. 27–58.
17. Wayne Booth, *The Company We Keep: An Ethics of Fiction* (Berkeley: University of California Press, 1988).
18. Martha Nussbaum, *Love's Knowledge: Essays on Philosophy and Literature* (New York: Oxford University Press, 1990); *Poetic Justice: The Literary Imagination and Public Life* (Boston: Beacon Press, 1995).
19. Martha C. Nussbaum, "Exactly and Responsibly: A Defence of Ethical Criticism," *Philosophy and Literature* 22, no. 2 (October 1998), pp. 343–365; Wayne C. Booth, "Why Banning Ethical Criticism Is a Serious Mistake," *Philosophy and Literature* 22, no. 2 (October 1998), pp. 366–393; Richard A. Posner, "Against Ethical Criticism: Part Two," *Philosophy and Literature* 22, no. 2 (October 1998), pp. 394–412. This debate was in part inspired by Richard A. Posner, "Against Ethical Criticism," *Philosophy and Literature* 21, no. 1 (April 1997), pp. 1–27.
20. Posner, "Against Ethical Criticism," p. 18.
21. Nussbaum, "Exactly and Responsibly: A Defence of Ethical Criticism," p. 350.
22. Booth, *The Company We Keep*, p. 25.
23. Booth, *The Company We Keep*, p. 4.
24. Booth, *The Company We Keep*, p. 201.
25. Booth, *The Company We Keep*, p. 201.
26. Booth, *The Company We Keep*, p. 170.
27. Booth, *The Company We Keep*, p. 175.
28. Posner, "Against Ethical Criticism: Part Two," p. 395.
29. Nussbaum, "Exactly and Responsibly: A Defence of Ethical Criticism," p. 347.
30. Stuart Hampshire, "Logic and Appreciation," in *Aesthetics and Language*, ed. William Elton (Oxford: Basil Blackwell, 1959), p. 169.
31. Nussbaum, *Love's Knowledge*, p. 27.
32. Posner, "Against Ethical Criticism," p. 7.
33. Arthur C. Danto, *Nietzsche as Philosopher* (New York: Columbia University Press, 1980).

3

WILLIAM IRWIN

Philosophy and the Philosophical, Literature and the Literary, Borges and the Labyrinthine

In reading the short stories of Jorge Luis Borges one is struck, prompted, and awakened by his exploration of philosophical themes. This lover of labyrinths calls our view of reality into question as he throws us into fictional worlds of illusion and allusion, halls of mirrors, and roads less traveled. He forces us to consider the ontology and epistemology of texts in "Pierre Menard, Author of the *Quixote*," the nature of time and parallel universes in "The Garden of Forking Paths," the unexpected origin of fate and chance in "The Lottery in Babylon," and the importance of forgetting and the horrors of memory in *Funes, His Memory* (to name just a few of his better known short stories).

Beyond simply challenging our unreflective beliefs about the nature of reality, the short stories of Borges call into question the nature of literature and philosophy. Are these *ficciones* literature? Are they philosophy? If there is one lesson to draw from Borges, it is that we cannot and should not necessarily trust our usual take on things. We must first ask ourselves, What is literature? What is philosophy?

As we shall see, the many attempts at defining literature and philosophy provide much insight but ultimately fail. Why? Not for lack of diligence or ingenuity, but because we cannot define "literature" and "philosophy" in terms of necessary and sufficient conditions, that is, give essential definitions of them. Rather, I shall argue that they are terms akin to, though not the same as, Wittgensteinian family resemblance terms. Having argued this, what can we say about the short stories of Borges? Are they literature? Are they philosophy?

Family Resemblance?

As is well known, Wittgenstein articulated the notion of family resemblance in the *Blue Book*[1] and the *Philosophical Investigations*,[2] giving the classic example of games. What makes something a game is difficult or perhaps impossible to specify, but any competent speaker of English knows how to properly use and apply the term "game." Wittgenstein's ingenious, yet straightforward, explanation is that games share a family resemblance; each of them bears some resemblance to, that is, shares something significant in common with, at least one other, but not all other, games.

In the *Blue Book* Wittgenstein tells us, "games form a family, the members of which have family likenesses. Some of them have the same nose, others have the same eyebrows, and others again the same way of walking; and these likenesses overlap."[3] I would argue that we can give a better account of things such as games if we coopt and make use of family resemblance by looking to this passage from the *Blue Book*. What we will offer then is not what Wittgenstein and his followers mean by family resemblance but something significantly different. We will coopt and transform Wittgenstein's antimetaphysical notion for our own metaphysical purposes.

When we consider what it means for two people to share an actual family resemblance, we must note that there are right and wrong attributions of it. Two close friends may be mistaken for brothers; a stranger may even say that they look alike and so share a family resemblance. The stranger is right to notice the similarities but wrong to attribute them to a family resemblance. So, noticing similarities and thinking there is a family resemblance are not always sufficient for there actually being one. In the case of actual family resemblance, there must ultimately be an appeal to shared genetics.[4] Shared genetics is a necessary, although not a sufficient, condition for being a person of whom it is correct to say he or she bears the family resemblance.[5]

If actual family resemblance works this way, then perhaps there is a necessary, but not sufficient, condition for the correct application of family resemblance terms. The condition would, of course, depend on the case at hand. To be clear, Wittgenstein would not agree. Rather, he would maintain that there is neither a necessary nor a sufficient condition for the correct application of family resemblance terms. What we are offering then is inspired by, developed out of, and transforms Wittgenstein's notion; it is not identical to it. To distinguish our conception let us call it "necessary-condition-family-resemblance."

Let us see how this conception of necessary-condition-family-resemblance works in the case of a game. For something to qualify as a game, it must be intended, actually or counterfactually, as a game by at least some of the people playing it at the moment, or, if not being played at the moment, must have been intended, actually or counterfactually, as a game by the players.[6] This clearly applies to all cases of actual games from paradigms, such as basketball, to odd cases, such as *Dungeons and Dragons*. Still, intending[7] something to be a game is not a sufficient condition for it being a game. Arsonists may (in their own demented minds) intend the burning of orphanages to be a game, but that does not make it a game. Burning orphanages does not fit the necessary-condition-family-resemblance. How do we know and correctly object that something does not fit the resemblance? It is in fact absurd in many cases to ask someone to justify the claim that a necessary-condition-family-resemblance term does not apply to a certain entity. As Michael A. Simon aptly says, "We are no more called to account for why we do not call fishing a game than we are for why we do not call reading or washing a game. Reasons can ordinarily be given for declining to apply a predicate to a particular case, to be sure, but they are always of a negative sort and do not differ in principle from why a cat is not called a primate or why a blackboard-eraser is not called an automobile."[8] We can know that a necessary-condition-family-resemblance term applies even when we cannot clearly say why we know it or what our evidence is.[9]

As we observed, a person may look like he shares the family resemblance even if he does not. It is the same with necessary-condition-family-resemblance terms. Something may not be a game although it is game-like. For example, literary allusions with their sense of play are ludic, game-like, but are not games. We should also note that actual family resemblance is open ended and subject to change, with intermarriage and the addition of new members. In the same way then, the proper application of a necessary-condition-family-resemblance term is subject to change and development. What we call a game today may bear only the faint resemblance of a distant ancestor to what we call a game a thousand years from now.

What Is Literature?

In asking the question, what is literature?, we are not speaking of literature in the sense of the secondary meaning of the word,[10] in which it means anything written down—the sense in which we speak about the literature on cloning or Columbus, for example. Rather, we mean literature in the primary, although broad, sense of the word. The range of texts that historically has been classified as literature is indeed broad, and some would like it to be even broader. The poet Shelley wanted to include some legislative statutes as literature,[11] and E. D. Hirsch, Jr., argues that some of the writings of Niels Bohr should be classified as literature, given the way they engage the heart and mind.[12]

How are we to define literature? Hirsch observes that all attempts at a definition of literature end up being stipulative definitions about how the term *ought to be used* rather than describing how the term actually *is used*.[13] Of course a stipulative definition may be fine for certain purposes, but it will not do for our purpose of articulating an objective account of what literature is. I shall argue that Hirsch[14] is on the right track; to use our terminology, literature is a necessary-condition-family-resemblance term.[15]

Although we cannot even begin to examine every definition of literature proffered by scholars through the ages, we can inspect some of the more promising definitions.[16] Monroe C. Beardsley argues, "it is on my view, not the presence of aesthetic merits per se but the aesthetic intention they evince that distinguishes literary works of art from other discourses."[17] This talk of intention at first seems strange coming from the co-author of "The Intentional Fallacy,"[18] but his definition sheds some light on the matter: "'aesthetic intention'—that is, the intention to make something capable of affording aesthetic satisfaction to one who properly approaches it."[19] Beardsley's emphasis on aesthetic intention, rather than simply aesthetic merit, is sensible. Aesthetic merit alone is neither necessary nor sufficient for a text's being literature. To see why it is not sufficient consider the following possibility. If a text has aesthetic merit but we have good reason to believe there was no intention, counterfactual or otherwise, to produce literature, then individuals may choose to read the text *as* literature but it would be odd and potentially offensive to say it *is* literature.[20] So we may read the Bible or the Koran *as* literature, but this does not necessarily imply that these texts *are* literature. It appears that Beardsley can avoid the problem of imposing normative standards of aesthetic merit and so avoid giving a stipulative definition.

Beardsley has not given us a satisfactory essential definition of literature, however. It is not a necessary condition that an instance of literature manifest an aesthetic intention. It could be that a text has no aesthetic intention behind it, or that it is not clear and manifest that there was such an intention, yet, for other reasons we shall discuss subsequently, we might be correct in classifying the text as literature. It is not a sufficient condition for a text to manifest an aesthetic intention to be an instance of literature; it is possible to construct a text that has and manifests an aesthetic intention and yet is not literature. Consider, for example, a towering marble sculpture of the text "SAY YES TO LIFE." Certainly this would be art but it would not be literature. Beardsley's definition at first does not appear to be stipulative, but indeed it is—as was shown in establishing that aesthetic intention is not a necessary condition. Aesthetic intention may be a primary characteristic of paradigm cases of literature, but it is not a necessary condition of literature. A text can be an instance of literature, although likely a fringe example, with no aesthetic intention. Thus to assert that a piece of literature must manifest an aesthetic intention is tantamount to stipulating it. Although it was not Beardsley's intention to give a stipulative definition he has done so nonetheless. And beyond that, this stipulation is not innocuous. As Hirsch argues, literature is not essentially aesthetic,[21] and "the narrowness of a predominantly aesthetic definition can lead, and sometimes has led, to a narrowness of educational goals."[22] Other criteria, such as capacity to move the heart and elevate the spirit, may, despite the lack of aesthetic intention or even aesthetic merit, in some cases be enough to classify a text as literature. For this reason it can at least be argued that even Aristotle's *Poetics* or Darwin's *Origin of the Species* is an instance of literature. To restrict literature in terms of the aesthetic is to narrow the class too far, although admittedly not by much.

In his article "What Is Literature?" Robert Stecker concludes with the following definition:

> A work w is a work of literature if and only if w is produced in a linguistic medium and
> 1. w is a novel, short story, tale, drama, or poem, and the writer of w intended that it possess aesthetic, cognitive, or interpretation-centered value, and the work is written with sufficient technical skill for it to be possible to take that intention seriously, or
> 2. w possesses aesthetic, cognitive or interpretation-centered value to a significant degree, or
> 3. w falls under a predecessor concept of literature and was written while the predecessor concept held sway, or
> 4. w belongs to the work of a great writer.[23]

To be clear, each of the four conditions is intended as sufficient, although none is intended as necessary. In condition 1 Stecker avoids the problem Beardsley faced in restricting literature in terms of aesthetic intention, allowing that other values may suffice in lieu of the aesthetic. A text may have cognitive value, presenting stimulating ideas, or may have interpretation-centered value, being the kind of text open to numerous and varied interpretations. There are other values Stecker should have included, for example, the emotive, the ability to stir the emotions in a sense that is not necessarily aesthetic. There are also other genres that should be included, such as the memoir.

In condition 2, Stecker misses the distinction between an entity being literature and being taken or used *as* literature. A linguistic entity may manifest aesthetic, cognitive, and/or interpretation-centered value to a significant degree, and yet, if there was no intention to manifest these (or this) values (value), the entity may be taken or read *as* literature although it would be mistaken to say it *is* literature. (We made this point above in the context of aesthetic merit.) In condition 3, the predecessor concept is given too much power. Simply because a text was at one time regarded as an instance of *belles lettres*, for example, does not necessarily imply that we should now regard it as literature. Condition 3 may commonly be the case, but there is no reason to accept that it is always the case. In condition 4, what "belongs to the work of a great writer" is terribly vague, a point that Stecker concedes somewhat.[24] Certainly we do not necessarily want to consider everything an author ever wrote as included in his or her "work." Laundry lists, for example, would not ordinarily count, but what about personal letters? Is the music criticism of Shaw, for example, part of his "work" and thus literature? Is T. S. Eliot's doctoral dissertation in philosophy part of his work and thus literature?

Stecker gives us a thorough and insightful definition but one that is nonetheless inadequate. In the end what he has given us is, as we shall see, a list of some of the things that go into the necessary-condition-family-resemblance indicated by the term "literature." Before proceeding to our account of literature as a necessary-condition-family-resemblance term, however, we must consider one last definition.

In *Truth, Fiction, and Literature* Peter Lamarque and S. H. Olsen give the following account: "A text is identified as a literary work by recognizing the author's intention that the text is produced and meant to be read within a framework of conventions defining the practice of ... literature."[25] Lamarque and Olsen point toward a necessary, although not sufficient, condition for literature. The condition is necessary because, as I have argued, unless the text is intended, actually or counterfactually, as literature then it *is not* literature, although it may be read *as* literature.[26] The condition is not sufficient, however, because unless the text can actually be identified as intended to fit the framework they mention and actually does fit that framework, it is not literature. For example, the writing of a child may be sincerely intended as literature, although no one can recognize that intention, or, even if that intention is recognized, the writing may not actually fit the framework of literature.

On the other hand, a text produced at a time or in a culture with no conception of literature could still be literature, despite the lack of an actual intention to fit the framework. A counterfactual intention would suffice. That is to say, if (hypothetically and counterfactually) the author of the text were presented with the notion of literature, would the author agree that the intention was to produce a text that fits the necessary-condition-family-resemblance of literature? If the answer is yes, then we have a counterfactual intention to fit the resemblance. This is very much like asking whether the author of a living will or advance directive would have intended artificial nutrition and hydration to be prohibited by the declaration of "no extraordinary care." If the patient had actually considered the issue of nutrition and hydration we are ferreting out an actual intention; if the patient had not actually considered nutrition and hydration, then we are ferreting out a counterfactual intention. In either case our search for the intention is legitimate. The epistemological difficulty of discovering counterfactual intentions does not disqualify them, no more so than does the epistemological difficulty sometimes involved in discovering actual intentions. In fact, some counterfactual intentions are abundantly clear. For example, although the framers of the Constitution did not actually intend the free speech guaranteed by the First Amendment to cover cyberspace communications, it is clear that they counterfactually intended it. That is to say, they obviously did not actually consider cyberspace communications, but if presented with the possibility of such communications they would have intended for them to be covered by the First Amendment.[27]

Lamarque and Olsen's definition places only one very broad requirement on a text being literature, that it be intended and recognized as intended to fit the framework of conventions defining literature. I would suggest that the framework of conventions that "define" literature does not truly define it, but simply enables us to give a rough account of literature.[28] That is, we cannot give a nonstipulative definition of literature in terms of necessary and sufficient conditions. Rather, like other necessary-condition-family-resemblance terms, literature has a necessary, although not sufficient, condition. Among the intentions (which may be many and varied) of the author in producing literature must be, actually or counterfactually, the intention to produce a text that would fit within the application of the necessary-condition-family-resemblance term "literature." This is a necessary but not a sufficient condition, for if the text does not fit the resemblance despite the intention, it is not literature. Because the proper application of a necessary-condition-family-resemblance term, in this case "literature," can never be conclusively settled, there is no hope of combining the caveat that the text must fit the resemblance with the necessary condition that it be intended to fit the resemblance. In combining these two demands we would simply be left with an account that is correct but that does not settle the matter in terms of an essential definition. The chief specification of the definition would rest on something that could not be conclusively settled, that is, how we know if something appears to fit the resemblance.

This is not to suggest that we are in the dark when it comes to knowing what kind of things we look for in judging whether a text fits the necessary-condition-family-resemblance of literature. In judging whether an entity is a game we may consider things such as whether it involves skill or luck, has a winner and loser, provides entertainment and diversion, etc. In a similar way there are characteristics to look for in judging whether a text is an instance of literature. Our preceding discussion and criticism of proposed definitions of literature make a number of those characteristics clear: belonging to a genre such as poetry or the novel normally considered part of literature, having aesthetic intention and merit, being fictional discourse, making extraordinary use of language, being diversionary or nonpragmatic discourse, having cognitive, interpretation-centered, or emotive value, having been accepted by a predecessor concept such as *belles lettres*, belonging to the work of a great writer, etc. As is the case with "game," though, neither any single characteristic of literature nor any combination of characteristics yields a nonstipulative definition in terms of necessary and sufficient conditions.

"Literature," as a necessary-condition-family-resemblance term, potentially has a rather broad application; it is not restricted normatively. Still, there are two considerations to keep in mind with regard to the application of the term "literature" that keep it from becoming a vacuously broad notion. First, although the use of the term "literature" is not stipulatively restricted by normative standards, this does not preclude us from talking of good and bad literature. We simply do not decide in advance that all literature must be "good" in accord with certain set standards. We are free to employ our own aesthetic standards, however, we may have determined them, in judging the merit of an instance of literature. For example, because they clearly are intended to and actually do fit the resemblance, I take John Milton's *Paradise Lost* and John Grisham's *The Firm* to be literature. I judge the former to be great literature and I judge the latter to be poor literature. Others may disagree with my judgments, and that is fine. Judgments of aesthetic merit are not purely subjective, but they do allow room for disagreement. Further, these judgments involve a normative element, which is not our interest here.

The second consideration is that there can be (and are) texts that approach, but fall short of, or to the side of, being literature (texts that are "literature-like") and other texts that can be read *as* literature although they *are not* literature. I would suggest that texts that fit either of these descriptions can aptly be called *literary*. For example, the philosophical writings of William James are literary, even if they are not literature. The literary, then, is a broad category including texts that are "literature-like," texts not intended to *be* literature that may still be fruitfully read *as* literature, and literature itself (it would be odd and mistaken to deny that an example of literature is literary). So, if we were to agree that the latest physics textbook is not literature we could still describe it as literary if there were sufficient reason to do so—a judgment of some "literary flair" might do. Also, if we were to agree that the Koran was not intended to fit the resemblance of literature (whether or not this is actually the case) and so is not literature, we could still judge it to be literary. This, I believe, allows for an important compromise with those who seemingly want to take a very broad range of texts (including their own works of criticism) as literature. Our response to them is that we can agree with them that such texts are literary and can be read *as* literature, although we would not say they *are* literature.

To return to our motivating interest, let us ask: Are the short stories of Borges literary? Are they literature? They certainly share much in common with paradigmatic works of literature, being of aesthetic, cognitive, and inter-pretation-centered value. The short story is also normally recognized as a subgenre of literature. Borges's *ficciones* are indeed imaginative fictions; they can be diversionary and nonpragmatic; and Borges is commonly regarded as a great writer. Certainly this is more than enough to say that the *ficciones* are literary. In fact, given that these texts of Borges evince the intention to have all of these qualities and there is no external evidence to suggest the qualities were not intended, it is clear that the texts were intended to, and actually do, fit the necessary-condition-family-resemblance of literature. The short stories of Borges are literature. There is no surprise in this conclusion, but it does lead us to the next question, one with a potential for surprise in its answer. Are the short stories of Borges philosophy?

What Is Philosophy?

As is well known, the English word "philosophy" comes from the Greek word φιλοσοφια (*philosophia*), love of wisdom. It is, then, in its etymology and original use an extremely broad term. As Pythagoras conceived of it, philosophy is living the life of the mind as opposed to living the life characterized by love of bodily pleasure.[29] Its objects of study have been many and various, and thus it is in some sense a truism that philosophy is "a more or less general theory of everything." The serious problem faced in answering the question, What is philosophy?, is that there may be no good definition to be had, that is, no essential definition in terms of necessary and sufficient conditions. It may also be that most, or all, definitions, including those that do succeed in giving necessary and sufficient conditions, will be stipulative. Giving a definition of philosophy based on necessary and sufficient conditions is inevitably restrictive. For, if it is not to be vacuous, it will exclude certain candidates, and that exclusion is inevitably, it seems, a normative matter. In the end, then, we may not be able to *answer* the question, What is philosophy?, but only *respond* to it. Perhaps "philosophy," like "literature," is a necessary-condition-family-resemblance term. Before jumping to this conclusion, however, let us consider some of the more promising definitions of philosophy.[30]

Howard Kainz defines philosophy as, "what Socrates said and did ... systematic re-examination of accepted meanings and values in his culture, for the explicit purpose of increasing self-consciousness of oneself and society."[31] This is a fine definition in certain respects. Historically, much philosophy has been systematic (and perhaps still can be, at least to an extent). The examination of meanings and values is a prime activity of philosophy, and raising the self-consciousness of both or either oneself and society is a primary goal of philosophy. And finally, there could not be a better model of philosophy than Socrates. Kainz, by articulating the Socratic paradigm of philosophy, has offered a definition that will fit most, if not all, paradigms of philosophy. At first it seems difficult to deny that this definition offers a sufficient condition for philosophy, but given the division of labor in the modern academy the difficulty disappears. A number of other disciplines could rightfully claim to offer "systematic re-examination of accepted meanings and values in culture, for the explicit purpose of increasing self-consciousness of oneself and society." Sociology and political science come immediately to mind, but history and literature[32] might also take this as part of their task. It cannot be objected that this is *only* part of the task of these other disciplines, since in fact it is *only* part of the task of philosophy too. That is, there are things with which philosophy is concerned, for example, concepts and the nature of ultimate reality, that are not explicitly part of this definition. And also, not all of what the definition offers is necessary to philosophy. For example, some philosophy, such as Nietzsche's, eschews not only systems but the systematic.

Husserl and other phenomenologists are not concerned with meanings and values but with descriptions and eidetic essences.[33]

In his article, "The Conditions of the Question: What Is Philosophy?," Gilles Deleuze tells us that "philosophy is the art of forming, inventing and fabricating concepts." [34] Moving further in the direction of Nietzsche, Deleuze says "philosophy more rigorously understood is the discipline that consists of *creating* concepts."[35] "[T]o create ever new concepts—this is the object of philosophy."[36] This is an important contribution to the conversation, and philosophers from various camps would nod approvingly at the inclusion of concepts in an account of philosophy. Still, rather than discovering, investigating, and interrogating concepts, Deleuze would have the philosopher fabricate and create them. Although no doubt it is true that much great and original philosophy has done just what Deleuze describes, it is hard to see how it is necessary. Much that has traditionally been considered philosophy would be excluded. As Deleuze says, "[philosophy] is neither contemplation, nor reflection, nor communication, even if it can sometimes believe itself to be one or the other of these because of the capacity of every discipline to engender its own illusions."[37] Although it would be fine to define philosophy stipulatively in these terms, and perhaps that is all Deleuze seeks to do, this will not work as the kind of definition we seek. Deleuze's account stipulates that only what creates new concepts counts as philosophy, a normative condition that simply is not a necessary condition outside of this stipulative context. The creation of concepts will also not work as a sufficient condition for philosophy. Disciplines other than philosophy create concepts, psychology, and literature, for example.

Rather than stipulating the importance of concepts for philosophy, we could focus on some other concern instead. Russell and many Anglo-American partisans might insist that there is no philosophy without analysis (not necessarily analytic philosophy per se but analysis in a sense that would include Plato, Aristotle, et al.).[38] Like Deleuze's glorification of concepts, this worship of analysis can serve only to stipulate normatively the definition of philosophy, and this will not do for our purposes.

My position is that we cannot give a nonstipulative definition of philosophy in terms of necessary and sufficient conditions. Like other necessary-condition-family-resemblance terms, philosophy has a necessary, although not sufficient, condition. Among the intentions (which may be many and varied) of the author in producing philosophy must be, actually or counter-factually, the intention to produce a text[39] that would fit within the application of the necessary-condition-family-resemblance term "philosophy." This holds for the same reason that the counterpart intention to fit the resemblance holds in the case of literature. This is a necessary but not a sufficient condition, for if the text does not fit the resemblance despite the intention, it is not philosophy. Because the proper application of a necessary-condition-family-resemblance term, in this case "philosophy," can never be conclusively settled, there is no hope of combining the caveat that the text must fit the resemblance with the necessary condition that it be intended to fit the resemblance. In combining these two demands we would simply be left with an account that is correct but that does not settle the matter in terms of a proper definition. The chief specification of the definition would rest on something that could not be conclusively settled: how we know if something appears to fit the resemblance.

This is not to suggest that we are in the dark when it comes to knowing what kind of things to look for in judging whether something fits the neces-sary-condition-family-resemblance of philosophy. There are characteristics to look for in judging whether something fits the resemblance of philosophy, but neither any single characteristic of philosophy nor any combination of characteristics yields a nonstipulative essential definition.

"Philosophy" as a necessary-condition-family-resemblance term poten-tially gives it a rather broad application; it is not restricted normatively like a stipulative definition. Still, there are two considerations to keep in mind with regard to the application of the term "philosophy" that keep it from becoming a vacuous notion. First, although philosophy is not stipulatively restricted by normative standards, this does not preclude us from talking of good and bad philosophy. Our necessary-condition-family-resemblance account does not specify in advance that all philosophy must be "good" in terms of standards all must adopt. The necessary-condition-family-resem-blance of philosophy can be, and is, shared by even its black sheep and embarrassing uncles. We are free as individuals or as followers of a particular school to employ our own standards of what good philosophy is. For example, because they clearly are intended to, and actually do, fit the resem-blance, the writings of Derrida and Searle are both correctly considered philosophy. We may differ in our evaluations of their writings, but that is another matter altogether.

The second consideration is that there can be (and are) texts that approach, but fall short of, or to the side of, being philosophy (texts that are "philosophy-like") and other texts that can be read *as* philosophy although they *are not* philosophy. I would suggest that texts that fit either of these descriptions can aptly be called *philosophical*. The philosophical, then, is a broad category including texts that are "philosophy-like," texts not intended to *be* philosophy that may still be fruitfully read *as* philosophy, and philos-ophy itself (it would be odd and mistaken to deny that an instance of philos-ophy is philosophical). So, if we were to agree that the latest physics textbook is not philosophy, we could still describe it as philosophical if there were sufficient reason to do so—for example, if it clearly gestured toward meta-physics. Also, if we were to agree that the Koran was not intended, even counterfactually, to fit the family resemblance of philosophy (whether or not this is indeed the case) and so is not philosophy, we could still judge it to be philosophical. Similarly, even if Henry James did not intend his novels to be philosophy they are philosophical.[40] This, I believe, allows for an important compromise with those who seemingly want to take a very broad range of texts as philosophy. Our response is that we can agree with them that such texts are philosophical and can be read *as* philosophy, although we would not say they *are* philosophy.

So, what is and what is not philosophy? This is the kind of question that needs to be answered on a case-by-case basis, and so I will do my best to avoid broad generalizations.[41] Our method for arriving at an answer has been articulated, and that is all we need for the moment.[42] Is literature philosophy? Certainly it can be, in a given case, if it is intended to fit the necessary-condition-family-resemblance and does indeed fit. That philosophers can produce literature that is also philosophy seems uncontroversial; indeed many of the existentialists seem to have considered it necessary for their projects. But is all literature philosophy? Clearly the answer is no, inasmuch as a great deal of literature is not intended to fit the resemblance of philosophy. More difficult cases are those in which the instance of literature is undeniably *philosophical*. Some instances of literature, such as Homer's *Odyssey*, Dante's *Divine Comedy*, Cervantes' *Don Quixote*, Shakespeare's *Hamlet*, Tolstoy's *The Death of Ivan Illyich*, and Kafka's *Metamorphosis*, are undeniably *philosophical*. Many would argue that they are indeed philosophy, and many more would not hesitate to teach them in their philosophy courses. As I have suggested, we need to examine such texts on a case-by-case basis, and we must remember that the *philosophical* is not necessarily *philosophy*.[43]

Borges?

Are the short stories of Borges philosophy? We cannot hope to answer that question for all of his *ficciones* here, given that we must answer on a case-by-case basis. And so we shall restrict our primary focus to one of his short stories, and then speculate on how our findings may or may not generalize to the others. The short story we shall discuss, "Pierre Menard, Author of the *Quixote*," is one that has become a popular object of discussion by philosophers, particularly with the increased interest in textuality and hermeneutics in recent years.[44]

In this story, Borges's narrator tells of the life and work of his recently deceased friend, Menard. He begins with a catalogue of Menard's "visible" work, which includes sonnets, literary criticism, and monographs on the history of philosophy, among other items. All of this, however, is said to pale in comparison to "the other, the subterranean, the interminably heroic production, the *oeuvre nonpareil*, the *oeuvre* that must remain—for such are our human limitations!—unfinished. This work, perhaps the most significant of our time, consists of the ninth and thirty-eighth chapters of the Part I of *Don Quixote* and a fragment of Chapter XXII."[45] Borges's story immediately raises the issue of the ontology of authorship. How can one be the author of a text that has already been written? It would be possible, although unlikely, for two authors to independently produce texts that appear identical. (Consider that Leibniz and Newton are said to have independently arrived at the calculus.) Still, this cannot be the case for Menard, who is not ignorant of Cervantes' *Don Quixote*; Menard has indeed read it, some parts more than once. Simply copying the text would not do either, and that was not Menard's plan. Rather, "His admirable ambition was to produce a number of pages which coincided—word for word and line for line—with those of Miguel de Cervantes" (p. 91). Menard's plan raises yet another question: Is it possible for two authors to independently produce such a long and complex text? It is a difficult, some would say impossible,[46] task simply to understand the author as he intended to be understood. Still others, including Schleiermacher,[47] would say we in fact must attempt to understand the author better than he understood himself. Menard, we are to take it, was an extraordinary man and would have had no trouble in assuming the mindset of Cervantes in producing his *Don Quixote*. In fact this was his first approach at the task. "Initially, Menard's method was to be relatively simple: Learn Spanish, return to Catholicism, fight against the Moor or Turk, forget the history of Europe from 1602 to 1918—*be* Miguel de Cervantes" (p. 91). The whole method sounds not only impossible but absurd, yet the narrator tells us that Menard was quite capable of it. "Pierre Menard weighed that course (I know he pretty thoroughly mastered seventeenth-century Castilian) but he discarded it as too easy" (p. 91). Not only was it too easy but it was not interesting enough. "Being, somehow, Cervantes, and arriving thereby at the Quixote— that looked to Menard less challenging (and therefore less interesting) than continuing to be Pierre Menard and coming to the Quixote *through the experiences of Pierre Menard*" (p. 91). Is this possible? In theory, we must suppose it is; different causes can have the same effect, after all.[48] Despite the limitations of ordinary human beings, the narrator tells us that this exceptional Menard succeeded in independently writing the *Quixote*, although he did not finish the task before his untimely passing.

Menard's success raises another question regarding the ontology of texts: Are two texts that are indiscernible the same text? The answer is, not necessarily. Clearly, this happens all the time with simple texts. The text of an advertisement, "big furniture sale!" could mean that the store is offering terrific savings in one context and that it is selling huge chairs and couches in another context. So, logically speaking this could occur for longer and more complex texts as well. Menard's success at arriving at the *Quixote* would result in a text different from Cervantes' yet identical in appearance. The two texts would embody different intentions and their differing historical contexts would result in differences in style. As the narrator tells us, "The contrast in styles is equally striking. The archaic style of Menard—who is, in addition, not a native speaker of the language in which he writes—is somewhat affected. Not so the style of his precursor, who employs the Spanish of his time with complete naturalness" (p. 94). The narrator also tells us that despite the affectation of Menard's archaic language, his *Quixote* is actually superior to that of Cervantes. "Menard's fragmentary Quixote is more subtle than Cervantes'. Cervantes crudely juxtaposes the humble provincial reality of his country against the fantasies of the romance, while Menard chooses as his 'reality' the land of Carmen during the century that saw the Battle of Lepanto and the plays of Lope de Vega" (p. 93).

Menard's *Quixote*, in its writing, points toward new ways of reading, given that his text is far less clear in its intention. As the narrator tells us, "The Cervantes text and the Menard text are verbally identical, but the second is almost infinitely richer. (More *ambiguous*, his detractors will say—but ambiguity is richness)" (p. 94). Ambiguity, this celebrated virtue on which the poets thrive, is there in spades for the reader of Menard's text. But why go through the trouble of the Menardian project? Who among us could hope to achieve it anyway? Why not simply read texts *as if* they were written by someone else? Haven't Foucault and Barthes buried the author anyway? Aren't readers free to read any text as if they were the author, or, if they prefer, as if someone else were the author? As the narrator tells us, "Menard has (perhaps unwittingly) enriched the slow and rudimentary art of reading by means of a new technique—the technique of deliberate anachronism and fallacious attribution" (p. 95). Noticing the narrator's parenthetical statement, we cannot be sure that Menard himself would approve of this new technique of reading, but it is already too late. Menard has opened Pandora's box. Now a feminist need not rewrite *Hamlet*; she can simply read the text as if it were written by Judith Butler or Toni Morrison. A homosexual need not rewrite *Zarathustra*; he can simply read it as if its author were gay—and as if Zarathustra were seeking an erotic tryst with the Übermensch. As the narrator tells us, "That technique, requiring infinite patience and concentration, encourages us to read the *Odyssey* as though it came after the *Aeneid*, to read Mme. Henri Bachelier's *Le jardin du Centaure* as though it were written by Mme. Henri Bachelier. This technique fills the calmest books with adventure. Attributing the *Imitatio Christi* to Louis Ferdinand Céline or to James Joyce—is that not sufficient renovation of those faint spiritual admonitions?"(p. 95).

I would not claim that Borges intended us to agree with the conclusions the narrator draws or those that the story points to, nor am I agreeing with them. Given his playful nature, I suspect Borges himself believed quite the opposite and would have had a hearty laugh at those who took his narrator seriously. Even the character Menard, we are told, often said the opposite of what he meant and believed. With regard to Menard's invective against Valéry, the narrator tells us, "which diatribe, I might add parenthetically, states the exact reverse of Menard's true opinion of Valéry; Valéry understood this, and the two men's friendship was never imperiled" (p. 89–90).

Clearly, "Pierre Menard, Author of the *Quixote*" is philosophical in that it raises issues and asks questions that are of concern to philosophers. Any one of the issues would be a worthy subject for a journal article in the *Philosophical Review*. Still there is little more surprise in saying that one of Borges's short stories is philosophical than there is in saying it is literary. The more pressing question is: Is "Pierre Menard" an instance of philosophy? To ask this question is, first, to ask whether it was intended to fit the necessary-condition-family-resemblance of philosophy, and although I cannot say for certain, I suspect with good reason that it was not. Borges certainly read philosophy and had a love for and affinity with certain philosophers, but there is no indication that he regarded himself as a philosopher and, more importantly, there is no indication that he intended his "Pierre Menard" or other short stories to be philosophy. A writer of short stories would need to make clear that the stories were intended to be philosophy for them to be taken as philosophy. Otherwise the natural presumption of the reader is that they are literature, albeit philosophical literature, and so the author's goal and intention would be thwarted.

As I admitted, it could be that I am wrong and that Borges did in fact intend his "Pierre Menard" to be philosophy. In that case "Pierre Menard" would fulfill the necessary condition of being philosophy; it would be a text intended by its author to fit the necessary-condition-family-resemblance. This, however, would not be sufficient because the text would also have to actually fit the resemblance, which it does not. The short story is not ordinarily accepted as fitting the resemblance of philosophy; in fact, I know of no short story offered by its author and generally accepted as fitting the resemblance. "Pierre Menard" in particular does nothing to change that. It raises interesting and important philosophical issues, but it neither argues for, nor provides answers. I suspect, although I will not assert here, that we could say the same of Borges's other *ficciones*. I could go on in saying why "Pierre Menard" does not fit the resemblance, but that would be to verge on the absurd. Simply recall what Simon argued, "Reasons can ordinarily be given for declining to apply a predicate to a particular case, to be sure, but they are always of a negative sort and do not differ in principle from why a cat is not called a primate or why a blackboard-eraser is not called an automobile."[49]

Let us not leave the labyrinth on a negative note, however. Although "Pierre Menard" is not philosophy, it is certainly philosophical. Given that Borges likely did not intend this short story to be philosophy, it is no criticism of it or him to say that it is not—no more than to say that it is not science. Nonetheless, Borges can, and perhaps should, be read by philosophers, and particularly students of philosophy—as he has the ability to awaken and excite an interest in the philosophical that may spur on philosophy.[50]

Notes

1. Ludwig Wittgenstein, *The Blue and Brown Books* (Oxford: Basil Blackwell, 1958), p. 17.
2. Ludwig Wittgenstein, *Philosophical Investigations* (New York: Macmillan, 1953), 65ff.
3. *Blue Book*, p. 17. Cf. L. Pompa, "Family Resemblance," *Philosophical Quarterly* 17 (1967), p. 65.
4. Cf. Erich Kahler, "What Is Art?" in *Problems in Aesthetics*, ed. Morris Weitz (New York: The Macmillan Company, 1959), p. 160; and Maurice Mandelbaum, "Family Resemblances and Generalizations Concerning Arts," *American Philosophical Quarterly* 2 (1965), pp. 220–221.
5. Mother and father can partake in the family resemblance through sharing genes in common with their offspring.
6. Or counterfactually would be if they stopped to consider it.
7. In his discussion of family resemblance and the arts Mandelbaum draws attention to the importance of intention in a similar way but does not fully endorse the importance of intention. Cf. pp. 220, 222, 223 n16, and 225.
8. Michael A. Simon, "When Is a Resemblance a Family Resemblance?" *Mind* 78 (1969), p. 415.
9. Even reflecting upon our knowledge may not yield a good answer. It is sometimes a matter of intuition, not in the mystical sense of the word but simply in the sense of not fully knowing how we arrive at the conclusion. For example, a husband may have an intuition that his wife is being unfaithful. We need not attribute this to some mysterious power but simply to reasons he cannot clearly identify. In the same way I may recognize that a word is of Greek origin, intuitively, without being able to clearly identify my reasons for being able to identify its etymology.
10. That is, we do not mean to be faithful to the etymology of the word. Etymologically, literature means anything in print. Cf. René Wellek, "What Is Literature?" in *What Is Literature?*, ed. Paul Hernadi (Bloomington: Indiana University Press, 1978), p. 16.
11. Cf. E. D. Hirsch, Jr., "What Isn't Literature?" in *What Is Literature?*, ed. Paul Hernadi (Bloomington: Indiana University Press, 1978), p. 30.
12. Cf. Hirsch, p. 32.
13. Ibid.
14. Hirsch gives his own admittedly stipulative definition. "Literature includes any text worthy to be taught to students by teachers of literature, when these texts are not being taught to students in other departments of a school or university" (p. 34).
15. For a related view on using family resemblance to account for art see Morris Weitz, "The Role of Theory in Aesthetics," *The Journal of Aesthetics and Art Criticism* 15 (1956), pp. 27–35. For arguments against the possibility of family resemblance, particularly as applied to the arts, see Kahler, pp. 157–171; Haig Khatchadourian, "Common Names and Family Resemblances," *Philosophy and Phenomenological Research* 18 (1957–58), pp. 341–358; and A. R. Manser, "Games and Family Resemblances," *Philosophy* 42 (1967), pp. 210–225.
16. Some examples of faulty definitions and accounts of "literature" include literature as imaginative writing, literature as a matter of form, and literature as nonpragmatic discourse. Cf. Terry Eagleton, *Literary Theory: An Introduction*, 2nd edition (Minneapolis: University of Minnesota Press, 1996), pp. 1–7. Richard Ohmann in "Speech Acts and the Definition of Literature," *Philosophy and Rhetoric*, 4 (1971) offers an innovative approach to this elusive definition. "A literary work is a discourse whose sentences lack the illocutionary forces that would normally attach to them. Its illocutionary force is mimetic" (p. 14). This definition seems promising at first glance, but it turns out to be only a sophisticated version of the

claim that literature is imaginative writing. Monroe C. Beardsley's first definition of literature as presented in his *Aesthetics* (New York: Harcourt, Brace & World, 1958) is as follows: "A literary work is a discourse in which an important part of the meaning is implicit" (p. 126). Colin Lyas in "The Semantic Definition of Literature," *The Journal of Philosophy* 66 (1969) exposes the inadequacy of Beardsley's so-called semantic definition. We can have instances of literature that leave nothing to the imagination, much nonfiction for example (cf. p. 84). Jean-Paul Sartre's account contends that literature utilizes words in engaged social and political commitment. Both the writer and reader are free but situated. Notably, Sartre does not include poetry in this utilitarian account. See Bernard Frechtman, trans., *What Is Literature?* (New York: Philosophical Library, 1949), pp. 19, 45, and 51.

17. Monroe C. Beardsley, "Aesthetic Intentions and Fictive Illocutions," in *What Is Literature?*, ed. Paul Hernadi (Bloomington: Indiana University Press, 1978), p. 166.
18. W. K. Wimsatt and Monroe C. Beardsley, "The Intentional Fallacy," in *The Verbal Icon: Studies in the Meaning of Poetry* (Lexington: University of Kentucky Press, 1954), pp. 3–18.
19. Beardsley (1978), p. 165. Even in "The Intentional Fallacy" Wimsatt and Beardsley did not deny the role of authorial intention altogether; they simply denied the validity of appealing to intentions not manifested in the text, for example, consulting the author about his intentions.
20. It is potentially unethical as well. See my *Intentionalist Interpretation: A Philosophical Explanation and Defense* (Westport, CT: Greenwood Press, 1999), pp. 50–54.
21. Hirsch, p. 29.
22. Ibid., p. 34.
23. Robert Stecker, "What Is Literature?" *Revue Internationale de Philosophie* 4 (1996), p. 694.
24. Stecker, p. 694.
25. Peter Lamarque and S. H. Olsen, *Truth, Fiction, and Literature* (Oxford: Oxford University Press, 1994), pp. 255–256. They go on to specify the conventions of literature in mimetic and aesthetic terms. Cf. Stecker, p. 685.
26. For a different view on causal conditions and conditions of identity see Jorge J. E. Gracia, "Borges's 'Pierre Menard': Philosophy or Literature?," this volume, pp. 85–107.
27. For further discussion of counterfactual intention see E. D. Hirsch, Jr., "Counter-factuals in Interpretation," in *Interpreting Law and Literature: A Hermeneutic Reader*, ed. Sanford Levinson and Steven Mailoux (Evanston, IL: Northwestern University Press, 1988), pp. 55–68.
28. Cf. Deborah Knight on the "practice" of literature in "Intersections: Philosophy and Literature, or Why Ethical Criticism Prefers Realism," this volume pp. 15–26.
29. For Pythagoras' definition, see Howard Kainz, "The Definition of Philosophy," *Epistemologia* 17 (1994), p. 201.
30. These will be, for the most part, definitions offered in print by people addressing the question, what is philosophy? To be clear, the definitions we shall consider have been removed from the contexts in which they were originally offered. We do not mean to attack a straw man, but only to point out that typical definitions of philosophy do not provide necessary and sufficient conditions while remaining nonstipulative. Indeed, many or most do not even make this their goal.
31. Kainz, p. 202.
32. In his contribution to this volume Gracia argues that philosophy can be distinguished from literature in that a work of philosophy can be translated whereas a work of literature cannot. This is debatable, given that arguably some works of philosophy, such as Heidegger's *Sein und Zeit* or *The Analects* of Confucius, cannot

be translated without producing a different work. In any event, Gracia's account does not aim to provide essential definitions of "literature" and "philosophy."

33. Other definitions of philosophy include F. E. Sparshott in "On Saying What Philosophy Is," *Philosophy in Context* 4 (1975), "Philosophy is what philosophers do. But who is a philosopher? Someone who understands someone who tells him what philosophy is" (p. 27). Edward O. Sisson, in "What Is Philosophy: A Proposed Definition," *Philosophical Review* 57 (1948), offers a definition of philosophy in terms of its function. "The function of philosophy is to observe and systematize the maximal characters of the Universe" (p. 169). Chris Dicarlo, in "What Is Philosophy?: A Causal Explanation," *Eidos* 6 (1987), offers a definition of philosophy in terms of its cause, "our inability to know what is real" (p. 130). As he says, "philosophy is the attempt to construct an understanding of one's experiences in the face of philosophy's very cause for being—namely, ignorance" (p. 131). Cf. Anthony J. Cascardi on Borges's take on philosophy, "Mimesis and Modernism: The Case of Jorge Luis Borges, this volume pp. 109–127. Martin Wolfson, in "What Is Philosophy?" *The Journal of Philosophy* 55 (1958), defines "original philosophy" as follows: "Every original philosophy is an autobiography. Thus to philosophize is to express one's discontent with what is; to show that what was, or what is, was and is in error" (p. 323). Joseph Flay, in "What Is Philosophy?" *Personalist* 47 (1966), answers the question by citing "the following characteristics of philosophy: (1) Its objects are the activities of men and the conditions under which they take place; (2) the cultural matrix partially defines the orientation of the philosopher involved; (3) there is a continuity or historical nexus which links the philosophical systems of the various epochs in some way" (p. 212). To be fair, Flay seems to intend to give a description or explanation, not a definition in terms of necessary and sufficient conditions. Archie Bahm, in "What Is Philosophy?" *The Scientific Monthly* 52 (1941), responds to the question by saying, "Philosophy is a kind of attitude, a kind of method, a group of problems, and a group of theories" (p. 553). He then proceeds to describe each of these elements of philosophy in loose and open-ended terms. Another possible way of defining philosophy is to distinguish it from literature by asserting that what is essential to philosophy is only ideas, not the texts that express those ideas. Whereas literature is essentially about texts, philosophy is essentially about ideas; cf. Gracia in this volume. In "Philosophy and Literature in Calvino's Tales" Ermanno Bencivenga tells us that philosophy aims at disconnecting us from our ordinary contexts, demands truth, and leads to liberation, this volume.

34. Gilles Deleuze, "The Conditions of the Question: What Is Philosophy?" (trans. Daniel W. Smith and Arnold I. Davidson), *Critical Inquiry* 17 (1981), p. 471.

35. Deleuze, p. 473. Cf. Friedrich Nietzsche, *The Will to Power*, trans. Walter Kaufmann and R. J. Hollingdale (New York: Vintage, 1967), pp. 220–221.

36. Deleuze, pp. 473–474.

37. Ibid., p. 474.

38. Gerald F. Kreyche, "What Is Philosophy?" *Listening* 21 (1986), pp. 56–65.

39. Using the term "text" rather loosely and including mental and spoken texts.

40. Cf. Knight, this volume p. 25.

41. Is work in the history of philosophy, philosophy? We cannot answer in the affirmative or negative in advance of considering the case in question. We must ask of the case at hand, was it intended to fit the resemblance of philosophy and does it fit the resemblance? Some cases are easy to answer in the affirmative; for example, whatever one's judgment of Heidegger, it is clear that his *Kant and the Problem of Metaphysics* was intended to, and does, fit the resemblance. Other cases are easy to answer in the negative; for example, Jostein Gaarder's *Sophie's World: A Novel about the History of Philosophy* was neither intended to, nor does it, fit the resemblance.

What about accounts of the history of philosophy, such as those offered by Guthrie, Copleston, and Jones? These cases are not immediately clear. What were their intentions? To produce philosophy, or simply to present the facts and interpret them in the manner of the historian? I do not claim to know, nor is this the appropriate place to launch such an investigation. Does what they offer fit the resemblance of philosophy? If it does not, then their intentions will be moot. I will not, in the short space allotted me, be so arrogant as to answer here, in what I suspect is a close case.

42. According to our account, Eastern thought and Western precursors to philosophy, in the contemporary sense of the term, are instances of philosophy if they meet the necessary condition account established.

43. We can find strong examples of the *philosophical* outside of literature as well. The list of texts and figures I would assert (but cannot here argue) are *philosophical* but not philosophy or philosophers includes some of the writings of Benjamin Franklin, the American Declaration of Independence, Hume's history of England, Skinner, Freud, Jung, Lacan, Einstein, Hawking, and Dawkins.

44. For examples of philosophers who discusses this story, see Arthur C. Danto, *The Transfiguration of the Commonplace: A Philosophy of Art* (Cambridge, MA: Harvard University Press, 1981), pp. 33–38; Jorge J. E. Gracia, *A Theory of Textuality: The Logic and Epistemology* (Albany: SUNY Press, 1995), pp. 117, 242, 254, and 263; Robert Stecker, "Apparent, Implied, and Postulated Authors," *Philosophy and Literature* 11 (1987), pp. 261–262; in this volume see the essays by Knight, Gracia, Cascardi, and Krysinski.

45. Jorge Luis Borges, "Pierre Menard, Author of the *Quixote*," in *Collected Fictions*, trans. Andrew Hurley (New York: Penguin Books, 1998), p. 90. Further page references to this story are given parenthetically in the text.

46. Hans-Georg Gadamer, *Truth and Method*, 2nd revised edition (New York: The Continuum Publishing Company, 1989), cf. p. 296.

47. See E. D. Hirsch, Jr., *Validity in Interpretation* (New Haven, CT: Yale University Press, 1967); and my *Intentionalist Interpretation*.

48. Cf. Gracia (1995), pp. 104–105.

49. Simon, p. 415.

50. I wish to thank Jorge J. E. Gracia, Carolyn Korsmeyer, Gregory Bassham, and Megan Lloyd for helpful criticisms of an earlier version of this essay. I also wish to thank my audiences at the Eastern Division Meeting of the American Society for Aesthetics, The Mid-South Philosophy Conference, and the Philosophy Club at the United States Military Academy at West Point.

4.

LOIS PARKINSON ZAMORA

Borges's Monsters: Unnatural Wholes and the Transformation of Genre

> The probing of the philosopher is deliberate, as the role of logic in philosophy demonstrates. . . . On the other hand, the probing of the poet is fortuitous.
>
> —Wallace Stevens, *Opus posthumous*

> Every object whose end is unknown to us is provisorily monstrous.
>
> —Jorge Luis Borges, "A Vindication of the Cabala"

Jorge Luis Borges would be pleased with the fervor surrounding the centenary of his birth, and also a little perplexed. Pleased to wander into the bookstores of Mexico City or Buenos Aires and encounter great quantities of new and reprinted editions of his work, stacked on tables devoted solely to him. Perplexed, though, to find that these stacks do not routinely include the work that has made him, for many early twenty-first-century readers, *the* indispensable writer of our time. There are new collections of juvenalia, journalism, and miscellany,[1] new editions of Borges's lectures and literary conversations,[2] and an illustrated collection of his *milongas*.[3] There are also recent critical studies of Borges's work from a variety of disciplinary perspectives: psychoanalysis,[4] cultural history,[5] and philosophy.[6] Yet despite this array of critical commentaries and new anthologies of his occasional writings, fully two-thirds of Borges's work remains uncollected, and thus inaccessible to all but the most diligent, Spanish-speaking researchers. Borges's *Obras completas* are, alas, far from complete.[7]

Everywhere present and yet two-thirds absent, Borges's work is apparently also endlessly polysemic. He has become *the* man for all seasons and disciplines, a multipurpose postmodernist, a marvelously mobile source of authority for every point of view. His work is routinely invoked to illustrate a vast array of theories and critical positions—some held by such diametrically different critics as, say, Michel Foucault and Harold Bloom, each of whom cites Borges at the outset of his most influential book, Foucault in *Les mots et les choses* and Bloom in *The Anxiety of Influence*. Not to mention Umberto Eco, who casts Borges as both medieval monk and paradigmatic postmodernist. Of Borges's amazing versatility, the Argentine critic Beatriz Sarlo writes that he

> obliquely discusses in his texts the major topics of contemporary literary theory. This has turned him into a cult writer for literary critics who discover in him the Platonic forms of their concerns: the theory of intertextuality, the limits of the referential illusion, the relationship between knowledge and language, the dilemmas of representation and of narration.[8]

Furthermore, Borges's narrative strategies are designed to suspend authorial adjudication in favor of interpretative possibility: ideas are presented for their narrative and symbolic potential, not for their superior truth claims. Borges recognizes this fact in his epilogue to his 1952 collection, *Other Inquisitions*. He writes that these "miscellaneous essays" revealed to him his own tendency "to evaluate religious or philosophical ideas on the basis of their aesthetic worth and even for what is singular and marvelous about them."[9] It is as much the shape of an idea as its substance that draws Borges to it.

The present collection of essays recognizes this fact, for we, too, have cast Borges as Everyman, and his writings as Everything. We cross not only disciplinary boundaries but also geographical, cultural, and historical ones. The Argentine Borges is housed here with two writers who are both of a subsequent generation and both Italian. Eco and Calvino inevitably occupy a common position with respect to European and Latin American traditions that Borges did not—not the least difference being the presence of Borges in those traditions.[10] So, then, our interdisciplinary undertaking necessarily implies this question: what is it about Borges's expressive forms that makes them move so fluently across disciplines and cultures, even though his subject matter is often dense and difficult? What is it about his miniature narratives that makes them seem to expand to contain the universe?

I will approach these questions by invoking the animal oddities that Borges loved to catalogue and describe, and then move to speculate about Borges's *narrative* oddities, his idiosyncratic combinations of disciplines and genres. Indeed, as we will see, these oddities are related: monsters are associated with, or inhabit, Borges's most characteristic metaphoric structures—the labyrinth, the mirror, the dream, the circular ruin—and become themselves metaphors of being. His monsters are part of their creator's lifelong exploration of the status of the real, and more particularly, his exploration of the relations of philosophical idealism and literary form.

First, though, we must consider the intellectual culture of Argentina in the 1920s and 1930s. Disciplines are not immune from their changing cultural and historical contexts, so we will want to inquire about the cultural priorities and textual traditions that Borges inherited as he developed his own idiosyncratic art. How did the fervor of Buenos Aires, as he titled his first volume of poems, compel (and empower) him to redraw the boundaries between disciplines and genres, to universalize the particular, and to make myths and monsters of all kinds?

Borges's Argentina

Among the stacks of Borges's newly reprinted work in the bookstores of Mexico City and Buenos Aires are his first three books of prose from the 1920s: *Inquisiciones* (*Inquisitions*, 1925), *El tamaño de mi esperanza* (*The Measure of My Hope*, 1926), and *El idioma de los argentinos* (*The Language of Argentines*, 1928).[11] These volumes are filled with the elaborations of a young writer who had not yet established his style. Borges opposed their republication for fully sixty years, but before his death he did give permission to the editors of La Pléiade edition of his complete works to add a selection from these early repudiated books.[12] Then in 1994, eight years after his death and despite his stated wishes, Seix Barral reprinted all three volumes. The contrast of his early work to the spare Borgesian style we have long taken for granted suggests how self-consciously during the late 1920s and 1930s Borges worked to free himself from prevailing Argentine aesthetic norms. These reprinted collections from the 1920s have focused my attention on the collections of the 1930s to see how, in them, the great work of the 1940s, collected in *Ficciones* (1944) and *El aleph* (1949), became possible. I will attend in particular to the work in Borges's collections from the 1930s: *Discusión* (1932), *Historia universal de la infamia* (*A Universal History of Infamy*, 1935), and *Historia de la eternidad* (*A History of Eternity*, 1936).

Beret Strong's study *The Poetic Avant-Garde: The Groups of Borges, Auden, and Breton* compares Borges's avant garde movement, *ultraísmo*, in Buenos Aires in the 1920s, to the somewhat later avant garde groups of Auden in England and Breton in France. She reminds us that these were years of cultural crisis and artistic response, and also years of personal exploration for the young cosmopolite polyglot Borges, struggling with his identity as an Argentine writer. Despite his residence in Europe during World War I and following, and also because of it, Borges returned to Argentina in 1921 with the sense that it was his duty and his calling to write like an Argentine.[13] His three essay collections of the mid-1920s reflect that sense of duty. Underlying mere duty, though, is the larger question of cultural nationalism facing virtually all American writers at the time, both in the United States and in Latin America: how to establish a literary culture distinct from that of the colonizing elite, how to separate authentic cultural identity from imposed identities, how to validate local traditions and at the same time face their limitations. In fiction, *costumbrismo* (social realism in a regionalist mode) reigned not only in Argentina but throughout Latin America. Beatriz Sarlo affirms that Borges sought to "avoid the pitfalls of local colour, which can only produce a regionalist and narrowly localist literature, without relinquishing that density of culture which comes from the past and is part of our own history."[14] Of course Borges eventually *does* embody universal categories in regional Argentine figures—gauchos and *compadritos*: as we will see, the stories in which he does so ten years later are breakthrough stories for him, surely in part because he had discovered the means to instantiate the ideal in the most particular of Argentine popular types. For now, however, his challenge was to create a usable past larger than the local and situate himself in relation to it as a citizen of the New World.[15] His later insistence that there is no original idea or text, only commentaries on previous texts, surely derives in part from this historicizing process.

This dual imperative of recuperation and renovation is clear in the poetics of *ultraísmo*, the avant garde movement that Borges single-handedly transplanted from Spain to Argentina upon his return in 1921. "Make it new" was hardly the battle cry of the *ultraístas*, despite their rejection of certain Argentine precursors. Their stated purposes were to create a "new" poetics that would avoid worn-out metaphors but nonetheless foreground metaphor as such, eliminate rhyme in favor of free verse, and, in Beatriz Sarlo's terms, "construct a literary language for Buenos Aires and also give to the city a mythic dimension."[16] In their call for cultural recovery and reconstruction, the *ultraístas* proposed an essentially conservative project that more resembles their contemporaries in England, Ezra Pound and T. S. Eliot, than it does expressionism or surrealism or any other European avant garde movement of the time. Pound's imagism, with its focus on metaphor, and Eliot's preference for the seventeenth-century "metaphysical" conceits of John Donne and George Herbert parallel Borges's emphasis on the renovation of figurative language in poetry. Furthermore, Eliot's antiromantic conception of the impersonality of poetry, the poet's embeddedness in all literature (as opposed to the poet's singularity or originality), and the transindividual nature of tradition per se parallel Borges's universalizing aesthetic, which was taking shape at the time. In Eliot's poetics, as in Borges's, the priority of the individual poet's feelings was replaced by the priority of poetic structure, and by the relations among the parts that make up that structure. Wimsatt and Brooks say of Eliot that he "transposed poetic theory from the axis of pleasure versus pain to that of unity versus multiplicity"[17]—a statement that might be equally applied to Borges. As early as 1920, Borges wrote that "ultraism is perhaps nothing other than the splendid synthesis of ancient literature,"[18] thus foretelling his own aspiration to enter and extend the Western literary tradition by creating synthesizing narrative strategies and structures of his own.

I have already suggested that *Inquisiciones, El tamaño de mi esperanza*, and *El idioma de los argentinos*—1925, 1926, and 1928—adopt the ornate style current in Argentine letters at the time and focus on Argentine literary topics and attitudes. Immediately after the publication of the third of these volumes, however, Borges began to work on quite another project, which he called an "invisible" style—the style that we now take for granted as Borgesian. This must also have seemed to Borges an "international style," and thus a help in laying aside the idea current at the time that an Argentine must write *about* Argentina. During the 1920s, the nation was struggling to establish its identity amidst a flood of European immigration and internal relocation. Fully one-third of the population of Buenos Aires at this time was foreign born. As Beret E. Strong notes:

> Because foreign influences were so strong, the nation had to make a special effort to remain aware of its colonial roots. *Hispanismo*, or Spanish heritage, became a positive value in the quest for Argentine identity.... For writers who came of age when Argentina was torn between the pressures of international cultural exchange and an urgent need to assert national identity, the conflict between the domestic and the foreign was divisive and confusing.... Borges had contradictory loyalties to both sides of the decade's binary division between European cosmopolitanism, characterized by Domingo Sarmiento's "civilization," and the innate "barbarism" of *argentinidad* based on violent folk heroes and the sprawling pampas. (pp. 43–44)

Beatriz Sarlo puts it more succinctly: "The tension created by this double origin is at the heart of Argentine literature" (p. 47). What we know is that Borges used Argentine types and locales in several of his best *ficciones*, but we also know that during the late 1920s and early 1930s, he was able to liberate himself from the culturally imposed obligation to do so.

He also liberated himself from the generic conventions of literary realism. During this period, Borges was consciously engaged in dismantling the barriers separating genres and disciplines, particularly those between literature and philosophy. I have said that he had inherited Argentine *costumbrismo*—precisely the "local color" fictions of "violent folk heroes and sprawling pampas"—and also the ornate Argentine literary language of the time. Both of these legacies would seem to separate what was considered "literary" expression from the more abstract discourse of European philosophy. But genres and disciplines have never been as cleanly separated in Spain as elsewhere in Europe. There are no specialized words for either "nonfiction" or "short story" in Spanish, only recent coinages of convenience, and the word *historia* means both history and story. Romanticism, which still conditions literary representation in the rest of Europe and the United States, did not flourished in Spain or in Latin America. And the baroque, never an important demarcation in English literary history, marks the apogee of Spanish letters and still operates importantly in Latin American literature, including (as I will argue) in the work of Borges. Nor were the Spanish philosophical traditions that Borges inherited the same traditions inherited by writers in much of Europe or the United States. Put another way, he inherited what they did, and more.

Argentina and Spain

Borges's own dual heritage of English and Spanish is well known, and is epitomized in the detail that he himself liked to recount: as a child, he first read *Don Quixote* in his father's library in English, and when he later read it in its original Spanish, "it sounded like a bad translation."[19] In the cultural context of Buenos Aires of the 1920s, Argentine intellectuals felt compelled to position themselves with respect to Spain and Spanish, and Borges was no exception. His ambivalence in this regard—his *"querella hispánica"* (quarrel with Spain)—has been widely discussed by Latin American critics, as has his countervailing passion for certain Spanish writers of the sixteenth and seventeenth centuries (Quevedo, Gracián, Cervantes, Góngora) and his affinity with certain contemporary Spanish intellectuals and writers (Américo Castro, Ortega y Gasset, Gerardo Diego, Unamuno, García Lorca, Rafael Cansinos-Assens). Although not wishing to limit Borges's enormous range of reference to his Spanish precursors and contemporaries, I do want to suggest that these passions and affinities form an enduring substratum that will affect both his philosophical *and* his literary modes of expression.

Borges goes back to medieval Spain, to the three-part flowering of Judaism, Islam, and Christianity that lasted for 700 years, until Muslims and Jews were expelled from Spain by the Catholic Kings in the late fifteenth and early sixteenth centuries. The Mexican writer Carlos Fuentes celebrates this historical recuperation as Borges's "supreme narrative synthesis" of the cultural heritage of Spanish America: "I certainly would not have had this early, fraternal revelation of my own Arab and Jewish heritage without such stories as 'Averroes' Search,' 'The Zahir' and 'The Approach to al-Mu'tasim.'"[20] Because these traditions are theological as well as philosophical, they depend upon story to a far greater extent than most European philosophical discourse. In the Jewish and Arabic traditions of medieval Spain, Borges found confirmation of his intuition (cited below in the section "The Monstrous Trinity") that theology is a branch of fantastical literature. The Kabbalah and the tales of Scheherazade are prime examples of sources from these alternative traditions, and certainly not the only ones. In many of his stories, Borges's cryptic reference to Hebrew and Arabic texts and contexts heightens their mysterious ambiance and mythic resonances.

During the 1920s, Borges internalized the work of the Spanish Basque philosopher Miguel de Unamuno. Borges had returned to Europe in 1923, where he established himself for the better part of a year in Madrid. There he read Unamuno exhaustively, corresponded with him, and later sent him his books as they appeared.[21] This is significant for our purposes because Unamuno himself crossed the boundaries between fiction and philosophy in generic experiments he called *nívolas* or *ficciones*. Unamuno's promotion of Spanish mysticism over European science, his theme of life as a dream, his commentary on the Quixote as a philosophical text, and his expressive strategies are reflected in the *ficciones* that Borges would himself eventually write.

At this same time, Borges met another forbiddingly versatile Spanish intellectual, José Ortega y Gasset, a philosopher and great cultural conduit: Ortega was *the* disseminator of European philosophy and literature to Latin America at this time, through his *Revista de occidente* and also through the press he helped to found, Espasa-Calpe. And yet another polymath would cross Borges's path two years later, in Buenos Aires: the Mexican writer, Alfonso Reyes, who was posted as Mexico's ambassador to Argentina in 1926. Essayist, poet, fiction writer, and philosopher in the same intellectual tradition as Unamuno and Ortega, Reyes was deeply aware of his own American need for a usable past: he mastered the Western tradition and placed himself, as a Mexican, within it. Borges's association with these nonsystematizing philosophers surely inspired and nurtured his creation of his own inclusive, hybrid *ficciones*.

José Ortega y Gasset's Phenomenology of Form

Unamuno and Reyes became mentors to Borges, but it is Ortega's phenomenological speculations that matter most during this period, as Borges searched for adequate expressive forms. If the relations of Unamuno and Reyes with the young writer were cordial and supportive, that between Ortega and Borges was otherwise. Borges explicitly dismissed Ortega's influence in an essay published at the time of Ortega's death in 1955.[22] But the break would have come long before—after Borges's return from Spain to Argentina in 1924, probably around 1930, when Ortega began to make offensive pronouncements about the Argentine national character.[23] Critics have tended to accept Borges's repudiation of Ortega at face value. This is too bad, for it is impossible that the young Borges, writing for the new magazine *Revista de occidente* while in Madrid and then actively organizing avant garde movements and magazines in Buenos Aires, would not have been aware of Ortega's cultural production.

Clearly Borges's quarrel with Ortega was political and social. Ortega's condescension to Latin America is well known, even as he published widely in Argentina and resided there for nine months in 1916, five months in 1928, and again for three years from 1939 to 1942. Cultural historians affirm

Ortega's immense influence on Argentine intellectual life beginning with his first appointment to the Chair of Spanish Culture at the University of Buenos Aires in 1916.[24] His analysis of Argentina's traditions of positivism and idealism (and his forceful critique of the former), his seminar on Kant, and his introduction of Husserlian phenomenology began a process of reassessment and renovation that the Argentine cultural historian José Luis Romero refers to as a "revolución filosófica." Ortega was an intellectual catalyst in Argentina, but more to the point here is the fact that his aesthetic concerns coincided with those of the young Borges, especially in his exploration of the expressive potential of literary genres, and in his phenomenological engagement of the competing claims of idealism and realism. Although I recognize that to focus on any one of Borges's precursors is to risk a reductive argument, I would nonetheless assert that Borges's transition from ultraist poet to *ficcionista* reflects the literary and philosophical explorations of Ortega during the same period. Without depriving Borges of his explicit disavowal and clear dislike of Ortega, but also feeling that he protests too much, I want to outline briefly their shared conceptual territory.

Two of Ortega's early works, *Meditaciones del Quijote* (*Meditations on Quixote*, 1914) and *La deshumanización del arte e ideas sobre la novela* (*The Dehumanization of Art and Ideas on the Novel*, 1925), are crucial. Borges would have read *Meditations on Quixote* and taken Ortega's discussion of literary genres into serious account. Borges, in the process of recognizing the need to create his own narrative genres, would have understood perfectly Ortega's assertion that the writer's choice of genre reflects "at one and the same time a certain thing to be said and the only way to say it fully."[25] Ortega insisted: "Literary genres are . . . the poetic functions, the directions, in which aesthetic creation moves" (p. 112). Borges would, of course, move beyond Ortega's notion of the strict separation of genres according to particular historical epochs and cultural needs, but Borges's attentiveness to the expressive potential of literary form is surely informed by Ortega's. Beyond Ortega's detailed discussion of genre and his implied comparison of literary and philosophical discursive modes, his use of the melancholy idealist Don Quixote would have compelled Borges's attention. Ortega engages Cervantes' fiction in order to negotiate the extremes of idealism and realism and to adjudicate his own dual attraction to German formalism and phenomenologically based existentialism. For Ortega, it is the psychology of character, not the structure of plot, that is memorable in literature. In a later text, he writes: "We are fascinated by Don Quixote and Sancho [as characters], not by what is happening to them. In principle, a *Don Quixote* as great as the original is conceivable in which the knight and his servant go through entirely different experiences."[26] Borges, who disagreed about the centrality of psychology, would nonetheless prove him right.

Borges would also have shared Ortega's understanding of Cervantes' historical circumstances. Ortega locates Cervantes on the cusp of modernity, with its foreclosure of myth and magic in favor of psychological and material causation. Ortega applauds this modern turn as Borges does not, but the question of the relation between myth and mind is nonetheless urgent for him.[27] Ortega's short chapters on the mythic potential of realistic narration are relevant. In chapters entitled "Myth, Leaven of History" and "Reality, Leaven of Myth,"[28] Ortega laments the limitations of modern scientific rationalism with a reference, as it happens, to monsters. In a footnote in the latter, he writes: "For Aristotle the centaur is possible; for us it is not, because biology, natural science, does not tolerate it" (p. 138).

Ortega's discussion of modern art was certainly also well known to Borges. *The Dehumanization of Art and Ideas about the Novel* was published in 1925, the year after Borges's stay in Madrid, and its argument corresponds in certain ways to Borges's ultraist poetic practice. As I have said, *ultraísmo* departed from contemporary European avant garde movements in its aim to recover a more traditional metaphoric poetics. Ortega celebrates metaphor as "one of man's most fruitful potentialities. Its efficacy verges on magic. . . . The metaphor alone furnishes an escape; between the real things, it lets emerge imaginary reefs, a crop of floating islands."[29] Himself using a metaphor that again resonates with Borges's attention to monsters, Ortega returns to his emphasis on expressive form: "Just as every animal belongs to a species, every literature belongs to a genre. . . . A literary genre, the same as a zoological species, means a certain stock of possibilities."[30] Given Borges's interest in *zoología fantástica* and its connection to generic hybridity, Ortega's metaphor evokes uncannily Borges's eventual morphology of genres.

Ortega's apology for modern art and its counterrealisms would not have escaped Borges's notice as the young writer challenging the conventions of Argentine local color realism, nor Ortega's idea that each generation has new circumstances to address, and must create new modes of being. Furthermore, Ortega's consideration of the status of the real no doubt nourished what was to become Borges's central philosophical concern: the relation of real instances to ideal categories. Ortega's defense of counterrealism was at once a critique of idealism in art and a confirmation of its necessity. If, as Rockwell Gray paraphrases Ortega, "all we can ever really have of the world is the ideas we form of it, it [is] idle to cling to overt representations of man and nature." For Ortega, "painting solved the problem by eschewing representational images; the experimental novel did so by reducing the narrative element to an absolute minimum."[31] Borges's own defense of narrative minimalism—his preference for the short story over the novel, for metaphorical suggestion over detailed physical description—echoes Ortega's position. In the following passage from the final paragraph of *The Dehumanization of Art*, another "imaginary centaur" resonates powerfully with Borges's literary practice. Ortega, echoing Husserl, writes:

There may be no corresponding reality to what our ideas project and what our thoughts think; but this does not make them purely subjective. A world of hallucination would not be real, but neither would it fail to be a world, an objective universe, full of sense and perfection. Although the imaginary centaur does not really gallop, tail and mane in the wind, across real prairies, he has a peculiar independence with regard to the subject that imagines him. He is a virtual object, or, as the most recent philosophy expresses it, an ideal object. This is the type of phenomena which the thinker of our times considers most adequate as a basis for his universal system.[32] (pp. 129–30)

Surely Borges is such a thinker. His "ideal objects"—the aleph, the library of Babel, the labyrinth, the garden of forking paths, the circular ruins—are universalizing, as are the creatures of his "intellectual teratology"—his centaurs, minotaurs, the Trinity, and all the other composite wholes in his fantastic zoology.

In sum, to reread Ortega is to find Borges everywhere—a classic case of a writer influencing his precursor. Borges's keen awareness of the logic of literary form and his phenomenological understanding of universals as showing themselves in particular instantiations were, I propose, nurtured by Ortega's work, as were his lifelong negotiations between conceptual and perceptual realms—between philosophical abstraction on the one hand and narrative realism on the other. Borges extends and enriches these Ortegan concerns in many ways, including those that I will explore below. Whether this relation amounts to direct influence (including resistance and misreading) or to a coincidence of concerns in a shared cultural context is less important to my project than to suggest the ways in which the philosophical and literary ideas of Ortega and Borges overlap. More generally, their shared concerns call attention to the unusually close conjoinings of philosophical and literary discourse at this moment in Spain and Latin America.

The Argentine Writer and Tradition

Borges, having considered the nature of literary realism for fully a decade, declared his independence from prevailing literary constraints and cultural myopias in his essay "The Argentine Writer and Tradition," published in *Discusión* (1932). A religious text provides the metaphor for Borges's developing conception of narrative realism. He famously (if incorrectly[33]) points out that there are no camels in the Koran. Declaring this circumstance analogous to that of Argentine literature, he argues that Argentine writers need not depict local Argentine realities.

> [W]e should feel that our patrimony is the universe; we should essay all themes, and we cannot limit ourselves to purely Argentine subjects in order

to be Argentine; for either being Argentine is an inescapable act of fate—and in that case we shall be so in all events—or being Argentine is a mere affectation, a mask.

I believe that if we surrender ourselves to that voluntary dream which is artistic creation, we shall be Argentine and we shall also be good or tolerable writers.[34]

One can be an Argentine writer and also be universal: with this essay, Borges grants himself permission to begin his move from Buenos Aires to Tlön, Uqbar, Orbis Tertius. That is, he identifies the process of generic transformation, impelled by a powerful dynamic between realism and idealism, whereby his *ficciones* will become a vehicle for philosophical speculation.

Achieving the balance between camel and Koran had become, by 1932, Borges's central aesthetic and philosophical concern. And it clearly continued to be so until the mid-1940s, as witness Borges's anachronistic reference in this 1932 essay to his 1941 story "La muerte y la brújula" ("Death and the Compass"). *Discusión* was reprinted in 1942, and Borges obviously took the opportunity to revise the essay by adding a reference to the story he had just written. (He also added book reviews, to which I shall refer shortly.) Borges names "Death and the Compass," notes that it was written "about a year ago," and asserts that he has at last managed to negotiate the competing claims of realistic description and his universalizing intention. He writes that he inadvertently captured "the flavor of the outskirts of Buenos Aires. . . . Precisely because I had not set out to find that flavor, because I had abandoned myself to a dream, I was able to accomplish, after so many years, what I had previously sought in vain" (pp. 181–182).

In this same essay, Borges considers the Argentine tradition of gaucho poetry. He notes that *Martín Fierro* is for Argentines "our Bible, our canonical book" (p. 177). Tracing its generic lineage and language, he locates the moment in which it, too, manages to transcend the local and universalize:

> *Martín Fierro* is cast in a Spanish of gauchesque intonation, and for a long while never lets us forget that it is a gaucho who is singing; it abounds in comparisons taken from country life; however, there is a famous passage in which the author forgets this preoccupation with local color and writes in a general Spanish, and does not speak of vernacular themes, but of great abstract themes, of time, of space, of the sea, of the night. (p. 179)

Borges does not mention the other "Bible" of Argentine literature, but he might as well have. *Facundo, o la civilización y la barbarie (Facundo, or Civilization and Barbarism* (1845), by Domingo Faustino Sarmiento, is in prose what *Martín Fierro* is in poetry: an idiosyncratic mixture of genres and styles that is firmly located in Argentine culture while at the same time aspiring to universality (as Sarmiento's subtitle makes clear). Argentine literature offered Borges a rich heritage of hybrid genres and narrative styles.

My point is this. Both the philosophical and the literary climate of Buenos Aires in the 1920s and 1930s would have lent themselves to a young writer with a metaphysical bent looking for appropriate narrative forms. For despite Borges's claim to have abandoned himself to dream, he had set out to develop a realistic style that could encompass reality's mythic dimensions—a project quite compatible with the literary and philosophical currents that I have mentioned here. Borges recognized early that to engage narrative realism in the service of his more abstract intentions, he must devise forms that could turn something commonplace into something mythic without distorting its status *as real*. How can the single self, realistically represented in narrative, transcend its singularity? How does the writer turn one man into all men and still work in a realistic medium? How does the writer represent the physical reality of ideas, the flesh and blood of forms, while at the same time conveying their status *as ideas*, as archetypes? Devoted to philosophical spec-ulation as he was, these questions place Borges firmly in the realm of litera-ture, not philosophy. His concerns involve realism and representation, the multiple relations of signifier to signified, the narrative forms and uses of metaphor, archetype, myth—in short, the concerns of a writer. Borges was devising a logic of possibility through a logic of literary form, and he used monsters to assist him in doing so.

Borges's Monsters: Natural Parts, Unnatural Wholes

Borges was fascinated by imaginary beings of all sorts. Beyond his taste for monsters and the literature that contains them—Germanic saga, Greek myth, fantastic tales from Homer and Scheherazade to Poe—he was inter-ested in monstrosity as such. Monstrosity is a state of being that he defines as the unnatural combination of natural parts, the possible permutations of which, he tells us, "border on the infinite." This definition, from Borges's preface to his *Manual de zoología fantástica* (*The Book of Imaginary Beings*, 1957), is buttressed by examples: the centaur combines horse and man; the minotaur, bull and man, and so on, his list implying an interminable prolif-eration of possible combinations: "it seems we could evolve an endless variety of monsters—combinations of fishes, birds, and reptiles, limited only by our own boredom or disgust."[35] Borges's monsters are not, then, necessarily grotesque or terrifying or even marvelous, but they are *always* dangerous because they challenge the Western binarism between nature and culture. Monsters inhabit at once the realms of nature *and* artifice—they are man-made species, so to speak. Because monsters slip suggestively between nature and culture, between real and imagined, they often open the way to chaos, deformity, and dream. Their combinatory capacity, their "infinite" possibility, makes them volatile, unpredictable, and fortuitous. Perhaps it is this kind of creative possibility that Wallace Stevens has in mind when he asserts that writers probe fortuitously.

Borges's interest in *ars combinatoria*—its disjunctions and permutations—might have led him to ally himself with the European surrealists, but it did not. At precisely this time, the surrealists were surrendering themselves to related principles of juxtaposition—recall the famous example of the umbrella and the sewing machine. However, to assume that Borges's combinatory monsters were a predictable outcome of avant garde poetics of juxtaposition is to impose European ideologies upon Argentine practice. Borges's *ultraísmo* did not engage combinatory tactics as a creative principle, nor did any other Latin American avant garde movement, for that matter. There was no call to create metaphors out of disparate elements, as in European surrealism, nor any investment in psychic automism, as there would have been if metaphors were to be created out of sheer unlikeness. Borges would have viewed such arbitrary juxtapositions as invention without discovery and, indeed, in a list of the century's ills, he includes "traffickers in *surréalisme*."[36] Borges was not seeking to *transcend* the real by means of disjunctive combinations, as were the surrealists, but rather to use disjunction to *amplify* the real, and to discover and develop expressive capacities commensurate to the task. The result is not surrealism but magical realism, or what I will eventually call Borges's magical idealism.

The *ars combinatoria* or, rather, *ars disjunctoria* of Borges's monsters has more to do with T. S. Eliot than the surrealists. I have already mentioned Eliot's recovery of certain seventeenth-century poets on the basis of their poetics of disjunction. Recall the eighteenth-century English critic Samuel Johnson's depreciation of Donne and Herbert as "metaphysicals": Johnson charged that their metaphors "yoked by violence together" the "most heterogeneous ideas."[37] To which Eliot, almost two centuries later, responds that heterogeneity and incongruity are necessary to poetry: "a degree of heterogeneity of material compelled into unity by the operation of the poet's mind is omnipresent in poetry."[38] The poet's task is to synthesize in his literary structure what resists synthesis in the world. This is not juxtaposition for its own sake but rather a movement from separation to integration. Borges's monsters may well be considered in Dr. Johnson's terms as "metaphysicals" "yoked by violence together," and also in Eliot's terms, as "amalgamating disparate experience" in the whole of the literary structure.

Indeed, Borges stresses the yoked nature of his heterogeneous monsters. As early as 1926, in an essay entitled "A History of Angels," published in the second of his three self-banished collections, Borges writes about the proliferating meanings of monsters, among which he included angels. Angels are, after all, an unnatural combination of human and bird: they are, according to a certain German theologian whom Borges cites, immaterial yet capable of materializing, aspatial ("neither taking up any space nor being enclosed by it") and everlasting ("with a beginning but without end"). Furthermore, he reports, the Hebrews had no trouble in merging angels with the stars. Borges asserts that of all the monsters created by the human imagination, only angels survive.

> The human imagination has pictured a horde of monsters (tritons, hippogrifs, chimeras, sea serpents, unicorns, devils, dragons, werewolves, cyclopes, fauns, basilisks, demigods, leviathans, and a legion of others) and all have disappeared, except angels. Today, what line of poetry would dare allude to the phoenix or make itself the promenade of a centaur?[39]

Yours, we want to answer, for hindsight allows us to glimpse in this very early essay Borges's as-yet-unformulated intention to rescue these extraordinary beings from oblivion. Why else his delicious catalogue of extinct monsters, why his delicate approach to "this world of wings and mirages"?

Borges's monsters evolve during the 1920s and 1930s in ways that are carefully designed to unsettle our usual sense of the relations of parts and wholes. They are at once unique *and* universal—universal *because* they are unique. They violate the law of compossibility, of simultaneous mutual coexistence, for each species is its own genus, each individual a type, their identity not a matter of communal likeness but of unlikeness to all but themselves. Consider Borges's most psychologized monster, in "La casa de Asterion" ("The House of Asterion"). We discover only at the end of the story that Asterion is the minotaur and his house is the labyrinth. He is alone and knows that there is no other like him. At first he proclaims his uniqueness and equates it to "all that is vast and grand," but soon enough he invents a game with an imaginary other—"the other Asterion." As if to justify his desire for an alter ego, he lists the things in his house that are repeated—the mangers, drinking troughs, courtyards, pools. Then he realizes that seas and temples are also many. "Everything exists many times, fourteen times, but there are two things in the world that apparently exist but once—on high, the intricate sun, and below, Asterion."[40] The pathos of this monster is unusual among Borges's imaginary beings, and it emphasizes Asterion's status as one of a kind. His monologue ends wistfully with his speculation about who will liberate him: "Will he be bull or man? Could he possibly be a bull with the face of a man? Or will he be like me?" (*CF* p. 222). The narrator concludes by reiterating Asterion's desire for a duplicate, and dramatizing the futility of his hope.

Borges's monsters, like the stories that contain them, oscillate between the poles of phenomenological particularity and philosophical abstraction, between realistic parts and ideal wholes. Their hybridity includes the human longing for its opposite: for unity, uniformity, identity both in its literal sense of likeness and in its figurative sense of self-knowledge based on shared characteristics, whether biological, tribal, familial, national. Borges's monsters, again like the *ficciones* that contain them, address this human instinct for wholeness. Consider Borges's homage to the dragon in his preface to *Manual de zoología fantástica*:

> We are as ignorant of the meaning of the dragon as we are of the meaning of the universe, but there is something in the dragon's image that appeals to our human imagination, and so we find the dragon in quite distinct places and times. It is, so to speak, a necessary monster, not an ephemeral or accidental one.[41]

A necessary monster: not "ephemeral or accidental," but rather archetypal, essential, a synecdoche of being. Borges's monsters combine Aristotle and Plato, substantial nature and ideal form. They are baroque in their asymmetrical inclusiveness: as such, they become for Borges realistic devices by means of which the universal may be embodied and materialized.

This ontological complexity is underscored by Borges in this same preface to the *Manual de zoología fantástica*, where he distinguishes between the "zoo of reality" and the "zoo of mythologies." Envisioning the visit of a child to the "zoo of reality," Borges invokes Plato:

> A small child is taken to the zoo for the first time. This child may be any one of us or, to put it another way, we have been this child and have forgotten about it. . . . Plato (if he were invited to join in this discussion) would tell us that the child had already seen the tiger in a primal world of archetypes, and that now on seeing the tiger he recognizes it. (p. 13)

Then Borges shifts his view to the "zoo of mythologies," and although he does not mention Aristotle here, his reference to the endless possible permutations of monsters recalls his discussion of Aristotle and metaphor in an essay entitled "La metáfora," published in *Historia de la eternidad* in 1936. He writes:

> In the third book of his *Rhetoric*, Aristotle observed that all metaphors arise from the intuition of an analogy between dissimilar things. . . . Aristotle, as we see, bases the metaphor on things and not on language. . . . [my translation][42]

Aristotle's metaphors and Borges's monsters are closely related: they reorder reality by joining dissimilar things. Physical dislocation reveals metaphysical possibility, and allows the archetypal to enter.

The relations of the part to the whole are also unsettled by the smallness of Borges's *ficciones*. In Spanish, *monstruoso* can mean "prodigious," "capacious," "enormous." If monsters are often considered to be gigantic and rarely, if ever, minuscule, it is nonetheless true that miniatures are also unnatural wholes. There are small creatures in nature, but no miniatures, for the miniature as such results from the manipulation of perspective. Susan Stewart, in her book *On Longing: Narratives of the Miniature, the Gigantic, the Souvenir, the Collection*, argues that the miniature "offers a world clearly limited in space but frozen and thereby *both particularized and generalized* in time—particularized in that the miniature concentrates upon the single instance and not upon the abstract rule, but generalized in that the instance comes to transcend, to stand for, a spectrum of other instances."[43] Although Stewart is writing about painting, I would propose that her reference to the synecdochal function of the miniature, in which the instance comes to stand for a "spectrum of other instances," is applicable to Borges's *ficciones* as well. I will return to Borges's synecdochal strategies, but here it is enough to say that compression of form tends to enhance the archetypal potential of any narrative, a point that Borges recognizes in his frequent praise of the short story over the novel. So monsters prowl Borges' miniature narratives, an irony of disproportion compounded by the vastness of their universalizing function.

It is obvious by now that Borges's metaphysical engagement of monsters departs radically from their traditional literary uses. Monsters have long terrorized and fascinated fictive enclaves of civilization with their inordinate size, their deformity, and their multiple assaults upon the social and psychic order. Their hybridity is taboo in a very literal sense, for one of the primary functions of taboo is to prevent the confusion of kinds. Anthropologists agree that societies, both traditional and modern, have regularly created mechanisms to discourage (and punish) the crossings of bloodlines, races, religions, gender, and other culturally determined boundaries. In these cases, the survival of the group is deemed by the collective to depend upon the perpetuation of existing structures of exclusion—hence the prohibition of mixture, which is equated with debasement, disaster, and dissolution. In related fashion, both Freudian and Jungian psychology uses monstrosity as a cipher of otherness, and the irruption of monsters in hallucination or dream may be a sign of the return of the repressed. If Borges's monsters seem mild-mannered talismans (his necessary dragon, his angels, Asterion), their hybridity is nonetheless offered as an affront to logic and order. Recall the opposition between civilization and barbarism that had, since at least the middle of the nineteenth century, been a trope in Argentinian literature. Borges's monsters ironize this opposition. Their hybridity transgresses the traditional boundaries between culture and nature, order and dissolution, modernity and its atavistic sources. If modernist writers (Woolf, Forster, Faulkner, Fuentes) have often held their art up against an unruly reality, Borges does something very nearly its opposite. He deploys his monsters to disrupt the realistic surface of his narratives, to move his stories from their terse rationality to the vast and volatile realms of myth, ritual, and archetype—to a world in which signification always exceeds the capacity of signifiers to express it.

The Monstrous Trinity

In his 1932 collection *Discusión*, Borges refers three times to a very particular monster, the Christian Trinity. By including the Trinity among his imaginary beings, he confirms his commitment to their ontological complexity, and emphatically calls attention to the point. At the time, Argentina was thoroughly conservative and Catholic; Borges, a self-declared "amateur Protestant,"[44] knew exactly the consternation that his inclusion of the Trinity would provoke. For Borges, the Trinity epitomizes an unnatural whole: it is the quintessential instance of a creature's symbolic slippage from real to ideal. Doctrinally, the three distinct parts of the Trinity are one seamless, universal whole—flesh and spirit, temporal and eternal, finite and infinite, magic and real. In "Una vindicación de la Cábala" ("A Vindication of the Cabala"), dated 1931 and collected in *Discusión*, Borges examines this doctrine at some length, citing the "necessity" of its fundamental mystery and also its "arbitrary" nature. He writes:

> It is impossible to name the Holy Spirit and silence the horrendous three-fold society of which it is a part. Lay Catholics see it as a united body—infinitely correct yet also infinitely boring; the liberals, as a useless theological Cerberus. . . . The Trinity of course surpasses these formulas. Imagined all at once, its concept of a father, a son, and a ghost, joined in a single organism, seems like a case from intellectual teratology, a deformation which only the horror of a nightmare could spawn. This I believe, but I try to reflect that every object whose end is unknown to us is provisorily monstrous.[45]

Here, Borges amplifies his definition of monstrosity significantly: the monstrous is not only a hybrid combination of disparate parts but also a state whose end is unknown to us. This amplification coincides with the etymology of monster, a word based in the Latin root *monere*, to warn, hence a portent of the unknown, a figure of mystery. Borges continues with images of the Trinity:

> Dante tried to depict them as the reverberating of diaphanous circles of diverse colors; Donne, as entangled serpents, rich and inseparable. *Toto coruscat trinitas mysterio*, wrote Saint Paul; the Trinity shines in full mystery. (p. 23)

Again, Borges invokes monstrosity and ends with mystery.

Two short reviews written in 1942 refer to the Trinity as a hybrid and hydra. Establishing a practice that would become habitual—that of including new works in later editions of a given collection—Borges included these reviews in a second edition of *Discusión*. Their posterior inclusion reinforces my thesis that Borges was consciously using monstrosity as a metaphor and motor for his own generic transformations, and the Trinity as an extreme example. One of these anachronistic additions to *Discusión* is "Sobre el doblaje" ("On Dubbing") and the other is "After Death."

"On Dubbing" is a review not of a single film but of what was then the relatively recent phenomenon of dubbing, which Borges treats as a monster, the combinion of one person's voice and another person's body. The review begins: "The possibilities of combining are not infinite but they are often terrifying. Thus the Greeks engendered the chimera, a monster with the head of a lion, the head of a dragon, the head of a goat."[46] We may object that the chimera is not ordinarily depicted with three heads but is, rather, a being comprised of three parts—the head of a lion, the body of a goat, and the tail of a serpent or dragon. Nonetheless, it is a three-*headed* chimera that Borges envisions, so we are not surprised by his next example, also three-headed: "theologians of the second century [engendered] the Trinity, in which Father, Son and Holy Ghost are inextricably joined." (p. 283, my translation). The paragraph continues with examples of a Chinese bird, a cube that encloses an infinite number of cubes, and the monsters that dubbing creates. How, Borges concludes ironically, is it possible not to admire this "phonetic-visual anomaly"?

The second review added to *Discusión* is of a book by one Leslie D. Weatherhead entitled "After Death." Here, Borges makes his famous argument that theology is a branch of fantastic literature:

> I have recently compiled an anthology of fantastic literature. While I admit that such a work is among the few that a second Noah should rescue from a second deluge, I must confess my guilty omission of the unsuspected major masters of the genre: Parmenides, Plato, John Scotus Erigena, Albertus Magnus, Spinoza, Leibniz, Kant, Francis Bradley. What, in fact, are the wonders of Wells or Edgar Allan Poe—a flower that visits us from the future, a dead man under hypnosis—in comparison to the invention of God, the labored theory of a being who is in some way three and who endures alone *outside of time*?[47]

The paragraph continues with further rhetorical questions, including the following: "what are all the nights of Scheherazade compared to an argument of Berkeley's?" and "who is the unicorn compared to the Trinity?"[48]

Borges's repeated reference to the monstrous Trinity in *Discusión* might seem surprising, given his utter lack of interest in critiquing specific aspects of Christian doctrine or practice. Although Borges certainly expressed his dislike of the authoritarianism of Argentine Catholicism, his monstrous Trinity is obviously not about the church or dogma or theological debate. Rather, it epitomizes for Borges the idealizing potential of the unnatural whole, and foresees a theme that will run throughout his work: the nature of infinity and eternity. Indeed, the relations of parts and wholes will become for Borges a means of symbolizing infinity and eternity—these most unnatural wholes, these otherwise unimaginable states of being. In an essay written at this time, "A Doctrine of Cycles" in *A History of Eternity* (1936), Borges refers to a work entitled *Mathematics and Imagination*, by the mathematician Georg Cantor, and he dwells on Cantor's conception of infinity. Borges paraphrases Cantor's discussion of parts and wholes: "an infinite whole is a whole that can be the equivalent of one of its subsets. The part, in these elevated numerical latitudes, is no less copious than the whole."[49] Paradoxically, the part is equal to the whole and is also infinite. And again in "Personality and the Buddha," written in 1950, Borges addresses the paradoxical relation between parts and wholes in a second-century Buddhist text: "[Man] is not matter, form, impressions, ideas, instincts, or consciousness. He is not the combination of these parts, nor does he exist outside of them."[50] And in "Pascal's Sphere," referring to the medieval conception of God's presence in his creation, Borges writes: "God is in each one of his creatures, but is not limited by any one of them. 'Behold, the heaven and heaven of heavens cannot contain thee,' said Solomon (I Kings 8:27)."[51] Seeing the whole in the part, or the whole as the parts, allows Borges to test the limits of ideal wholes—infinity, eternity, being—and then devise strategies for making realistic narratives into universal structures of meaning.

Borges's Morphology of Genres

In a lecture on the detective story, Borges raises the question of whether literary genres exist. Responding to his own musing, he says: "A fitting reply to this would be that although all individuals are real, to specify them is to generalize them. . . . To think is to generalize, and we need these useful Platonic archetypes in order to say anything."[52] For Borges, literary genres are like his monsters: "useful Platonic archetypes." Like the child who has "already seen the tiger in a primal world of archetypes" and thus recognizes a tiger in the zoo, so too the reader recognizes literary works in relation to their generic type. Both imaginary beings and works of literature involve the relation of particular instances to overarching categories, the relation of singularity to universality. If, as I have argued, Borges's monsters unsettle these relations by means of combinatory devices, so, too, his generic experiments during the 1920s and 1930s reflect Borges's *ars combinatoria*. His literary forms are metaphorical monsters by his own definition: they are unexpected combinations of disparate parts from fiction, myth, philosophy, theology, bestiaries, travel narrative, folktale, epic, allegory, and from a vast array of historical periods and world cultures, combined to create narrative structures whose "ends are unknown to us." In Borges's generic transformations, we come close to the Greek sense of the word "dynamism"—power realized in form—but it is "morphology" that I will engage to describe his project.

Morphology is a branch of both biology and grammar, and in both disciplines, it situates and studies individuals within a generalizing schema. In biology, morphology is the study of the form and structure of plants and animals; in grammar, it is the study of patterns of word formation according to inflection, derivation, composition, and so on. By means of a self-consciously devised morphology of genres, Borges deploys instances to create fictional worlds that are eclectic and inclusive, and narrative structures that, for all their tense compression, remain expansive and open. We might approach Borges's morphology in Derridean terms by saying that Borges has abandoned the book for the text,[53] or in Hayden White's historiographic terms by saying that he prefers chronicle to history,[54] or in Eco's semiotic terms by contrasting the structures of dictionary and encyclopedia.[55] It hardly matters, for as I have said, Borges lends himself to others' theories.

Synecdochal Strategies

Borges's *ficciones* are often presented as single instances of a universal phenomenon, or as parts of a larger whole—a summary, a review, an annotation, a footnote, an epigrammatic event or personage or passage, a suspended series, an erudite commentary on ideas and texts from other cultures and traditions. These partial structures necessarily point to a larger entity beyond the realistic details of the narrative itself, a strategy that depends upon the rhetorical figure of synecdoche. Synecdoche, in which the part stands for the whole, facilitates the transformation of the local into the universal, and narrative realism into idealizing Borgesian *ficciones*. Everywhere in Borges's mature fiction we find narrative structures that move from particular instances to universal propositions, whether the universal is conceived as infinite and eternal (encompassing all spaces and times), archetypal (encompassing all types), or baroque (encompassing all ideas, places, and persons). Borges's metaphors also operate synecdochally. The garden of forking paths points to all gardens—all narrative possibilities—even as we read only one. The library of Babel contains all possible books—a complete description of everything under the sun. Pierre Menard writes the entire *Quixote*, of which a small fragment suggests the whole text and an entire literary tradition.

The evolution of Borges's universalizing strategies can be traced in the collections of the 1930s. In his "Autobiographical Essay," the author states that the "sketches" in *A Universal History of Infamy* (1935) are "the real beginning of my career as a story writer."[56] He writes that at this early point, he considered the short story to lie "beyond my powers, and it was only after a long and roundabout series of timid experiments in narration that I sat down to write real stories" (p. 238). The "timid experiments" are those that comprise *A Universal History of Infamy*, and they are, according to Borges, less stories than "hoaxes and pseudo-essays" (p. 239). "The Approach to al-Mu'tasim," written in 1935 and published in the subsequent volume *A History of Eternity* (1936), was also a "hoax and a pseudo-essay" that "now seems to me to foreshadow and even to set the pattern for those tales that were somehow awaiting me, and upon which my reputation as a storyteller was to be based" (pp. 239–240).

Borges explicitly relates his narrative dependence upon synecdoche to the universalizing intention announced in his title: *A Universal History of Infamy*. He writes in his preface that "these exercises in prose narration . . . overly exploit certain tricks: random enumerations, sudden shifts of continuity, and the paring down of a man's whole life to two or three scenes."[57] It is especially his "trick" of "random enumerations" that allows him to pretend to the encyclopedic coverage promised by his title. A handful of instances stands for all instances. The irony of proposing these seemingly random examples of infamy as a universal history is clear enough when reading the short accounts: a small time hoodlum, a stupid con-man, a Chinese woman pirate, Billy the Kid, and a few others ending with "Streetcorner Man." These figures are hardly worthy ground upon which to build a universal history of anything, but this is just Borges's point: "there is nothing, however humble, that does not imply the history of the world and its infinite concatenation of causes and effects."[58] His oft-repeated insight that one man is all men, that the individual is a microcosm, "a symbolic mirror of the universe,"[59] is an aspect of the same principle, as is his speculation that "universal history is the history of the various intonations of a few metaphors."[60]

Borges's *ficciones* frequently dramatize the "involvement" of insignificant facts or single selves with universal history. The author does so, as I have already suggested, by installing in his realist description synecdochal devices that oblige the reader to move beyond the specificity of the singular and turn that very specificity to the service of an idealizing whole. These devices are quintessentially Borgesian and immediately recognizable to his readers: the list-of-unlike-parts—the "random enumerations" we have just seen—are made to stand for all things; so, too, Borges's handful of metaphors—labyrinth, mirror, dream, monsters, metaphor itself—which stand for all space, all time, all forms, all men, all meanings; and his unnamed characters, who are constructed in order to project the condition of being as such. Take the *compadritos* and small-time hoodlums in *A Universal History of Infamy*, or the Argentine antagonists in "The Challenge," a reprise of "Streetcorner

Man," of whom Borges writes that they "and many others whom myth has forgotten or has absorbed in these two, doubtless held this manly faith [in their own strength], and in all likelihood it was no mere form of vanity but rather an awareness that God may be found in any man."[61] Borges asks his readers to accept that the instance, however arbitrary it may seem, *is* the whole, that it does not just stand for, but contains the universe.

If, in *A Universal History of Infamy*, Borges is not always successful in maintaining a simultaneous level of realistic particularity and idealizing universality, a decade later, in his stories in *Ficciones* (1944) and *El aleph* (1949), he does so with consummate skill, and synecdoche becomes *the* central device for doing so. One thinks immediately of "The Aleph," where a partial list stands for all things. It is a list whose possible permutations not only border on the infinite but are proposed as infinity itself. "How," the narrator asks, "can I translate into words the limitless Aleph, which my floundering mind can scarcely encompass? Mystics, faced with the same problem, fall back on symbols."[62] Symbols, it seems, and lists: Borges's narrator, faced with the problem, enumerates. His list *is* a symbol: together its unlike parts symbolize "the unimaginable universe." In his commentary on this synecdochal strategy, Borges describes its challenge: "The task, as is evident, is impossible, for such chaotic enumeration can only be simulated, and every apparently haphazard element has to be linked to its neighbor either by secret association or by contrast."[63] Borges's randomness is carefully constructed. His list points not to a disembodied ideal world but rather to the sum total of everything, everywhere.

"The Circular Ruins" uses a similar strategy to describe an infinite god. The god is the sum of unlike parts, and he is also a monster. A man, who finds himself in the circular enclosure, dreams of a statue that becomes a god: "In the dream it was alive, and trembling—yet it was not the dread-inspiring hybrid form of horse and tiger it had been. It was, instead, those two vehement creatures plus bull, and rose, and tempest, too."[64] This "multiple god" is described by means of a short list (bull, rose, tempest) that is clearly meant to symbolize all things. So, too, in "Funes the Memorious," the improbable list of remembered items is offered as proof of Funes' total recall. And in "The Library of Babel," the combinatory potential of language *is* the library of Babel, where again, a short list confirms that "everything" is contained therein. Borges's narrative idealism expresses itself in contingent, contradictory, "random" accumulations of all possible phenomena: bull, rose, tempest. The parts of his unlikely lists are unrelated yet compossible; they suggest the plenitude of being, the baroque.

The disorderly orderliness of Borges's lists, and their synecdochal status, is flaunted in Borges's 1941 story "The Analytical Language of John Wilkins." This story is cited by Michel Foucault as the very inspiration for *Les mots et les choses*, his study of the organization of knowledge in the West. The list that Foucault cites is one that Borges's narrator says he recalls because of its "ambiguities, redundancies, and deficiencies." It catalogues all possible categories to which animals can belong in a certain Chinese system. The narrator attributes the list to a certain Dr. Franz Kuhn, who in turn cites an "unknown (or apocryphal) Chinese encyclopedist." The list is itself monstrous in its disjunctions:

> (a) those that belong to the Emperor, (b) embalmed ones, (c) those that are trained, (d) suckling pigs, (e) mermaids, (f) fabulous ones, (g) stray dogs, (h) those that are included in this classification, (i) those that tremble as if they were mad, (j) innumerable ones, (k) those drawn with a very fine camel's hair brush, (l) others, (m) those that have just broken a flower vase, (n) those that resemble flies from a distance.[65]

Foucault states that "and" has been rendered impossible by Borges's taxonomy: that the "fragments of a large number of possible orders glitter separately"; that no universal order is implied, nor any possible.[66]

Perhaps. But Foucault fails, in my opinion, to read the rest of the story. After enumerating this list, the narrator muses that "there is no classification of the universe that is not arbitrary and conjectural. . . . But the impossibility of penetrating the divine scheme of the universe cannot dissuade us from outlining human schemes, even though we are aware that they are provisional" (p. 104). For Borges, the list-of-unlike-parts leads to the contemplation of universal mystery; for Foucault, it leads to the impossibility of meaning. That Foucault reads this story to suit his own position reinforces what we already know: Borges's *ficciones* are endlessly open to philosophical and literary speculation.

Whitman's Limited Catalogue of Endless Things

In a lecture given in 1964, Borges elevates the list to the status of a poetic figure, saying that "in order to be beautiful, [a list] must consist of heterogeneous elements."[67] He is speaking of Taliesin, a Welsh poet of the sixth century, but he had already written repeatedly of his preferred maker of beautiful lists, Walt Whitman. Borges first read Whitman in German as a youth in Geneva in 1917; he sent for *Leaves of Grass* in English and "for a time, I thought of Whitman not only as a great poet but as the *only* poet. In fact, I thought that all poets the world over had been merely leading up to Whitman until 1855, and that not to imitate him was a proof of ignorance."[68] It is Whitman's capacity to create "limited catalogues of endless things," and his related capacity to universalize the individual, including his own poetic

persona, that Borges consistently celebrates.[69] As early as 1922, Borges refers
to Whitman in an essay entitled "The Nothingness of Personality," which
explores Berkeleyan idealism and the psychology of the individual.[70] In 1932,
he publishes two essays on Whitman in *Discusión*, "El otro Whitman" and
"Nota sobre Whitman"; the latter he publishes a second time, slightly
revised, in *Otras inquisiciones* (1952), although it is the first version that is
included in the *Obras completas*. Beyond these essays, his poem on Whitman
in 1964 concludes, "Yo fuí Walt Whitman" (I was Walt Whitman);[71] and in
1969, his translation of parts of *Leaves of Grass* carries a prologue celebrating
the archetypal persona of the poems.[72] Indeed, Borges refers constantly to
Whitman throughout his essays over the course of six decades and more.

Clearly Borges found in Whitman's work a projection of his own literary
idealism, with its imperative to create universalizing structures from contingent realities. He begins "Note on Whitman" on this point: "The practice of
literature sometimes fosters the ambition to construct an absolute book, a
book of books that includes all the others like a Platonic archetype."[73]
Recalling his conception, cited above, of literary genres as "useful Platonic
archetypes," Borges follows this statement with a long list of authors and the
strategies by which they archetypalize their own work. His examples include
Joyce, who presents simultaneously the characteristics of different epochs,
Pound and Eliot, who manipulate anachronisms to "produce an appearance of
eternity," and so on. Naturally, Borges takes Whitman as his central example.

Borges addresses Whitman's pantheism and notices the ways in which
pantheist texts use limited catalogues of endless things—"contradictory and
miscellaneous things"—to describe a ubiquitous God. To elaborate the point,
Borges does the same thing: he provides a "variety of phrases" about a
pantheist God from a welter of seemingly miscellaneous sources: a citation
from the *Bhagavad-Gita*, a fragment from Heraclitus, from Plotinus, from a
twelfth-century Persian poet, from Ralph Waldo Emerson and Stefan
Georg. Recognizing their repeating formulas, Borges writes:

> The prototype of such phrases is this: 'I am the rite, I am the offering, I am
> the oblation to the parents, I am the grass, I am the prayer, I am the libation
> of butter, I am the fire' (*Bhagavad Gita*, IX, 16). Earlier, but ambiguous, is
> Fragment 67 of Heraclitus: 'God is day and night, winter and summer, war
> and peace, satiety and hunger.' Plotinus describes for his pupils an inconceiv-
> able sky, in which 'everything is everywhere, anything is all things, the sun is
> all the stars, and each star is all the stars and the sun' (*Enneads*, V, 8, 4). (p. 69)

A longer list from the *Bhagavad-Gita* is given in the English translation,
which is based on the later version of this essay in Spanish. As Borges revised,
he amplified its elements and heightened their seeming randomness, but in
both versions, the paradoxical relation of parts and wholes symbolizes

universality—here, the universal spirit of the pantheist God. After more examples, Borges generalizes: "Extension of the principle of identity seems to have infinite rhetorical possibilities" (p. 69). The structure of infinite possibility is what Borges admires in Whitman, and what he himself was striving to create in his own hybrid forms. Referring to the pantheists' beautiful lists, Borges writes:

> Walt Whitman renovated that procedure. He did not use it, as others had, to define the divinity or to play with the 'sympathies and differences' of words; he wanted to identify himself, in a sort of ferocious tenderness, with all men. (p. 69)

The parts not only contain the universe but also *generate* it. Borges concludes that Whitman is eternal, and that he is each one of us.

Borges recognizes himself not only in Whitman's enumerations but also in Whitman's narrator, a persona who might mistakenly be confused with the author but who is, Borges reminds us, an archetype rather than an individual. According to Borges, Whitman realized that to write a democratic epic, he would have to avoid the individualized epic hero—an Achilles or Aeneas or Roland or Christ. Rather, he needed a hero "to be innumerable and ubiquitous, like Spinoza's diffuse God. So he came up with a strange creature we have not yet fully understood, and he gave this creature the name Walt Whitman."[74] Whitman, the voice and visionary of the poems, contains Whitman the man, but is not limited by him. Borges continues: this double Whitman now fuses with his reader to become "a triple Whitman, the hero of his epic." So, Borges writes, "Whitman was already plural; the author resolved that he would be infinite" (p. 447). Like the Trinity, the triple Walt Whitman signifies infinity—not in an abstract conceptual sense but in all his disjunctive and contradictory parts.

I have suggested that the dynamic structures resulting from Borges's *ars combinatoria* may be considered in terms of baroque aesthetics. If Borges early abandoned what is frequently referred to as his baroque style, he nonetheless remains a baroque writer in his engagement of mutation, anomaly, and disjunction in the service of a universalizing vision. He also remains baroque in his narrative structures, which are exercises in balance, counterbalance, contradiction, compensation, and sustained ambiguity. His characteristic metaphors—labyrinths, libraries, gardens of forking paths, circular ruins—may seem hermetic and enclosed but they are, in fact, structures of universal inclusion, baroque structures. Without stopping to investigate the fascination with monstrosity that appears throughout the Spanish and Latin American baroque traditions, but hoping that others will, let me say simply that Borges's monsters surely correspond to images and forms in Góngora's *Soledades*, Quevedo's *Sueños*, Sor Juana's *Primero sueño*, Goya's *Caprichios*, and

Valle Inclan's *esperpentos*. They also correspond to Ortega's "core of 'lived' reality, which furnishes the substance, as it were, of the aesthetic body."[75] The "aesthetic body" of Borges's *ficciones* is monstrous in this inclusive, experiential sense, and Whitman's "body electric" is its North American analogue.

Borges's Investigation of Idealism: A Philosophy of Literary Form

Borges often links his unnatural wholes—his monsters and his *ficciones*—to philosophical idealism. As we have observed, he regularly associates Platonic archetypes with both imaginary beings and literary genres. Because references to philosophies and philosophers are ubiquitous in Borges's work, we might think that these references are simply one more feature of his vast, speculative, literary landscape. There is, however, a palpable difference in Borges's narrative approach to idealism. If he often presents philosophical ideas in summary overview—in a kind of minihistory of ideas that verges on parody—his essays on idealism are otherwise. They have a probing quality of personal engagement and aesthetic urgency that, in my view, underlines their centrality to Borges's morphology of genres.

The discussion begins early. In his first volume of essays in 1925, there are two essays devoted exclusively to Berkeleyan idealism, "The Nothingness of Personality" and "The Crossroads of Berkeley."[76] In the volumes that follow in the 1930s, Borges amplified his range of reference and focused his attention on the implications of idealism for literary structure. "The Postulation of Reality," "The Penultimate Version of Reality," and "Narrative Art and Magic," published in *Discusión* in 1932, and in 1936 "A History of Eternity," published in the collection of that name, weigh realist and idealist modes of knowing and writing. Indeed, throughout his career, Borges considers these paired modes under a variety of rubrics: romanticism and classicism, the accidental and the absolute, French philosophy and German philosophy, among others. His most extensive historical survey of the forms of idealism, "Nueva refutación del tiempo" ("New Refutation of Time"), was written in 1946 and collected in *Otras inquisiciones* in 1952. He begins his comprehensive consideration of idealist philosophers with reference to himself and the course of his own life "dedicated to literature and, occasionally, to metaphysical perplexity."[77]

Of the many doctrines recorded by the history of philosophy, idealism is perhaps the most ancient and the most widely divulged. The observation is Carlyle's (*Novalis*, 1829). Without any hope of completing the infinite census, I should like to add to the philosophers he mentioned the Platonists, for whom prototypes are the only reality (Norris, Judah Abrabanel, Gemistus, Plotinus); the theologians, for whom everything that is not the divinity is contingent (Malebranche, Johannes Eckhart); the monists, who make of the universe a vain adjective of the Absolute (Bradley, Hegel, Parmenides). Idealism is as old as metaphysical inquietude. (p. 186)

Borges's early and ongoing engagement with idealist metaphysics provided support for his confrontation with the conventions of Argentine local color in the 1920s and 1930s, and illuminated his investigation of postromantic positions with respect to self, society, and language. Idealist metaphysics assisted him in developing a form of realism that eschews individualized characters in favor of plotted ideas, it encouraged his impulse to make plotted ideas the vehicles of myth and mystery, and it buttressed his refusal to commit to any one system or set of beliefs. If character, plot, setting, and language are presented as dream or otherwise the product of the imagining mind, then all beliefs are real and all imaginary creatures both real and potentially archetypal. In short, idealist metaphysics allowed Borges to affirm that verisimilitude is not necessarily that which conforms to empirical notions of the real but, rather, that which resonates aesthetically and expressively for the reader. Considering the realist/regionalist agenda of Latin American narrative at the time, this was no small gift.

Borges acknowledges this gift by making his most completely imagined world a monument to idealism. In "Tlön, Uqbar, Orbis Tertius" (1944), Borges creates Tlön, a "congenitally idealist" planet, and describes its language and literature in exquisite detail. There are no nouns in the languages of Tlön but only accumulations of adjectives; there is no succession in space, which would imply material objects, but only succession in time; and its literature "is filled with ideal objects, called forth and dissolved in an instant, as the poetry requires."[78] The narrator's extended description of Tlönian idealism moves steadily toward its tongue-in-cheek conclusion: "Century and century of idealism could hardly have failed to influence reality" (p. 77). Nor have centuries of idealism failed to influence Borges's literary forms and figures.

Allegory and the Novel

In his 1948 essay "De las alegorías a las novelas" ("From Allegories to Novels"), collected in *Otras inquisiciones* (1952), Borges compares the history and expressive capacities of these narrative forms in terms of their idealizing potential. The devotion of the novel to individuals and events is contrasted to the affiliation of allegory with abstraction and exempla. Like metaphor and synecdoche, allegory establishes a special relationship between particularity and generality, requiring that the reader draw analogies between the given narrative instance and its hidden "universal" analogue. In this way, allegory and parody (a genre rarely absent from Borges's *ficciones*) are also aligned, for both are texts that mirror an absent text, both depend upon the reader's recognition of that absence, and both imply a hierarchy in which the absent text is, ironically, the more real. In the case of parody, the absent text is the "original"; in the case of allegory, the absent text is presumed to be the repository of larger significance, significance that exceeds the concretions of the literal text.

In this essay, Borges compares allegory and the novel in relation to their capacity to express or contain abstract ideas, and evaluates them accordingly. He writes:

> The allegory is a fable of abstractions, as the novel is a fable of individuals. . . .
> The passage from allegory to novel, from species to individual, from realism
> to nominalism, required several centuries. . . . (p. 157)

Borges's literary idealism is grounded in his efforts to reverse, or at least revise that history.

Using the medieval designations of realism and nominalism (i.e., idealism and realism, respectively) Borges writes: "for realism the universals (Plato would say the ideas, forms; we call them abstract concepts) were fundamental; and for nominalism, the individuals" (p. 157). Again, he historicizes these ways of seeing the world, and implicitly laments the triumph of literalism implied in the modern ascendency of nominalism:

> Nominalism, which was formerly the novelty of a few, encompasses everyone
> today; its victory is so vast and fundamental that its name is unnecessary. No
> one says that he is a nominalist, because nobody is anything else. But we must
> try to understand that for the people of the Middle Ages reality was not men
> but humanity, not the individuals but mankind, not the species but the genus,
> not the genera but God. (p. 157)

If the term magical realism is an oxymoron offered to describe recent incursions of myth and magic into narrative realism, so too literary idealism is an oxymoron in a world such as that described by Borges here. Where literature only describes the real, idealism enters surreptitiously or not at all. No one would have felt this more acutely than Borges as he challenged the reigning positivism in Latin American letters during fully the first half of this century.

"From Allegories to Novels" includes a list—a double list, really—of realists and nominalists, which Borges introduces in this way:

> Coleridge observes that all men are born Aristotelian or Platonist. The latter
> know by intuition that ideas are realities; the former, that they are general-
> izations; for the latter, language is nothing but a system of arbitrary symbols;
> for the former, it is a map of the universe. The Platonist knows that the

universe is somehow a cosmos, an order, which, for the Aristotelian, may be an error or a figment of our partial knowledge. (p. 156)

"A figment of our partial knowledge"—an apt phrase to describe Borges's own generic intentions and procedures. He follows this double list with another of idealists and realists—the "immortal antagonists" whose names, he tells us, change "across the latitudes and the ages" but whose lineage is clear: Parmenides, Plato, Spinoza, Kant, Francis Bradley on one side, and Heraclitus, Aristotle, Locke, Hume, Willliam James on the other. His double list leads Borges to this generalization:

The history of philosophy is not a vain museum of distractions and verbal games; the two theses probably correspond to two manners of intuitively perceiving reality. (p. 156)

Two manners of *intuitively* perceiving reality: thus intuition overarches difference, joining Aristotelians and Platonists and collapsing, at least momentarily, distinction between substantial nature and ideal form.

Complementarity, rather than mutual exclusion, underpins Borges's conception of the reality, and it is G. K. Chesterton, English clergyman and writer of detective fiction, whom Borges singles out as the master of the dual intuition of allegory.[79] Of Chesterton's poetry, Borges writes:

There is something more terrible and marvelous than being devoured by a dragon; it is being a dragon. There is something stranger than being a dragon: being a man. Such elemental intuition . . . shapes all of Chesterton's poems.[80]

Monstrosity and humanity conjoin in this eulogy to Chesterton, "Modes of G.K. Chesterton," written in 1936. Here, as usual, Borges's reference to monstrosity has generic implications. Using Chesterton against Croce in "From Allegories to Novels," Borges writes: "Croce denies the allegorical art; Chesterton vindicates it" (p. 154). According to Borges, Croce refuses the "monstrous" nature of allegory "because it aspires to encipher two contents in one form: the immediate or literal one . . . and the figurative one" (p. 155). Chesterton, on the contrary, embraces this two-headed monster.

For Borges, Chesterton's vindication of allegory is based in his engagement of a multiplicity of signifying forms. Chesterton's work denies "that language is the only way to express reality. . . . With one form of communication declared to be insufficient, there is room for others; allegory may be one of them, like architecture or music" (p. 155). Borges cites verbatim a lengthy passage from Chesterton's 1904 study of the English painter G. F. Watts to affirm his assertion:

Man knows that there are in the soul tints more bewildering, more number-less, and more nameless than the colours of an autumn forest; . . . Yet he seri-ously believes that these tints can every one of them, in their tones and semi-tones, in all their blends and unions, be accurately represented by an arbitrary system of grunts and squeals. He believes that an ordinary civilized stockbroker can really produce out of his own inside noises which denote all the mysteries of memory and all the agonies of desire. (Chesterton, *G.W. Watt*, 1904, p. 88; cited by Borges in "From Allegories to Novels," p. 155)

Chesterton's irony here affirms the position that Borges ascribes to him: signification always exceeds its signifiers, reality is always richer than any of its definitions, being overarches and includes individual lives. Borges agrees so emphatically with Chesterton's allegorical intuition that he cites it in two other essays as well. We find this same passage again in Borges's 1949 essay "Nathaniel Hawthorne," in which he uses it to defend Hawthorne against charges of "allegorism" and to praise Chesterton's intuition "that reality is interminably rich and that the language of men does not exhaust that vertig-inous treasure" (*Other Inquisitions*, p. 50). And again, Borges cites this passage in the concluding paragraph of his 1941 essay, "The Analytical Language of John Wilkins," where he prefaces the passage by saying that "these words by Chesterton are perhaps the most lucid ever written about language" (*Other Inquisitions*, pp. 104–105). So Borges repeatedly celebrates Chesterton's achievement: literary wholes that are inestimably larger than the sum of their linguistic parts.

Borges's Monstrous Persona

We have been tracing the process of generic transformation by which Borges turns realistic narrative parts into ideal wholes. He is well aware of the tension in his own work between Aristotelianism and Platonism, nominalism and realism, romanticism and classicism, or any of the other paired terms with which he describes these "two manners of intuitively perceiving reality."[81] Borges's frequent strategy of setting up this opposition in order to dramatize its tensions belies Mario Vargas Llosa's characterization of Borges's singular devotion to idealism. Vargas Llosa asserts that

[Borges] came to take rather seriously the idealism of Bishop Berkeley, who postulated that reality did not exist, that what existed was only a mirage or cosmic fiction, our ideas or fantasies of reality. He played with that theme, of course, but the game of proclaiming the essential nonexistence of the mate-rial world, of history and objective reality, with dream and fiction as the only reality, became a serious belief and gave to his work not just a recurrent and original theme; it also transubstantiated into his conception of reality.[82] [my translation]

This assessment has the value of emphasizing Borges's idealism, but it is overly simple in its conclusion, for Borges knew that however universalizing his intention and however mythic the resonance of his plots, he—a writer of literary fictions—had to tie his creations to the phenomenological realities of shared human experiences. In contrast to Vargas Llosa's contention, Borges dramatizes the constant intrusions of disorder into all human efforts at order. Indeed, the "elegant hope" for order, as the narrator puts it at the end of "The Library of Babel," is one of Borges's great themes—a theme that Henry Sussman traces in brilliant detail in this volume.

The Borgesian irony between the desire for an ideal order and the knowledge of its impossibility would hardly be so pervasive had Borges embraced idealism as univocally as Vargas Llosa suggests. I have cited Borges's statement in "The Analytical Language of John Wilkins" affirming the human need for systems, despite the knowledge that they are "arbitrary and conjectural." Similarly, in his 1936 "synthetic biography" of Oswald Spengler, Borges contrasts French positivism with German idealism, recognizing ironically the intentions of the latter: "The perfect symmetry of the systems— and not any eventual correspondence with the impure and disorderly universe—constitutes their zealous purpose."[83] In Borges's story "Tlön, Uqbar, Orbis Tertius," the planet of Tlön is so ideally idealistic that parody is certainly intended. The narrator speaks of Tlön's "concept of the universe":

> Hume declared for all time that while Berkeley's arguments admit not the slightest refutation, they inspire not the slightest conviction. That pronouncement is entirely true with respect to the earth, entirely false with respect to Tlön. The nations of that planet are, congenitally, idealistic. Their language and those things derived from their language–religion, literature, metaphysics–presuppose idealism. For the people of Tlön, the world is not an amalgam of *objects* in space. . . . There are no nouns in the conjectural *Ursprache* of Tlön.[84]

The irony is clear: there *are* nouns in the languages of earth. Borges concludes his most concentrated discussion of idealism, "New Refutation of Time," with this wistful recognition: "The world, alas, is real; I, alas, am Borges" (p. 187).

This debate between the ideal poetic persona Borges and the (reluctant) Borges of flesh and blood recalls the archetypal "other Whitman," and it finds its most explicit allegory in "Borges y yo" ("Borges and I"). Although the typical trajectory of Borges's stories is from the particular to the universal, in this *ficción* the slippage also occurs in the opposite direction. The first person narrator tells us that he is trapped in the body of Borges, the archetype of the writer and metaphysician, and he expresses the wistful hope of escaping their shared body, presumably to the freedom of an experiential physical realm now denied him. Like Asterion, the narrator's hybridity—his monstrous composite of two bodies and minds—signals the disjunction between real and ideal, between individuality (personality, corporeality) and the collective outlines of myth. Eduardo González discusses Borges's use of the two-faced Janus in his stories "El Sur" ("The South") and "La muerte y la brújula" ("Death and the Compass") and finds that Janus ushers the protagonists in both stories into a realm of myth and atavistic identity.[85] In "Borges and I" the narrator is himself Janus-like. Despite his wish, he remains fixed, the better to usher others into the realm of myth: "I live, I allow myself to live, so that Borges can spin out his literature, and that literature is my justification."[86] The fable ends: "So my life is a point-counterpoint, a kind of fugue, and a falling away—and everything winds up being lost to me, and everything falls into oblivion, or into the hands of the other man. I am not sure which of us it is that's writing this page" (p. 324). In this same volume, *El hacedor* (1960), Borges includes a poem entitled "Los Borges" (The Borgeses), and four years later, in 1964, he publishes a volume of verse entitled *El otro, el mismo*.

These images of self-division and otherness, when considered along with Borges's conception of monstrosity, may lead critics to consider the traces of homosexuality that abide in Borges's work and in his life. That Borges wrote in praise of monsters—unnatural combinations of natural parts—and sought them out in the world's literature and mythology, and that he celebrates their hybridity and their baroque inclusiveness, would, I think, be the place to begin a discussion of Borges's gendered genres. (In Spanish, as it happens, the word for gender and genre is the same: *género*.) Borges's morphology of genres enables his approach to ideal categories, and it conditions his treatment of gender—also elusive, volatile, and metamorphic. His stories and essays, like his monsters, are presented as wholes that encompass all permutations of human experience.

For my part, I return to Borges's status as Everyman. Surely Borges's monsters are partly responsible. The author's metaphysical mixtures, his disciplinary combinations, and his generic hybrids move his reader from the particular to the universal, from reality to myth, from personality to archetype, from realities to Reality. This universalizing impulse Borges shares with philosophy and with philosophers. It is ironic that Borges's monsters—those most illogical, hence unphilosophical beings—are the beings that impel his work toward universality, hence toward philosophy.

The poet Wallace Stevens, in his extended musings on the shared subjects of poetry and philosophy, finds their most significant conjunction in their sense of "something cosmic":

> [A] sense of the infinity of the world is a sense of something cosmic. It is cosmic poetry because it makes us realize ... that we are creatures not of a

part, which is our every day limitation, but of a whole for which, for the most part, we have as yet no language. This sudden change of a lesser life for a greater one is like a change of winter for spring or any other transmutation of poetry. . . . A realization of the infinity of the world is equally a perception of philosophy and a typical metamorphosis of poetry.[87]

Borges's *ficciones* aspire to the same "realization of infinity" that Stevens finds in philosophy. The methods of philosophers are very different from those of Borges, of course, nor are philosophers' modes of expression necessarily "literary" by any standard definition of the literary. But the universalizing impulse that moves Borges to embed ideal objects—imaginary beings, places, times, texts—in his miniature *ficciones* is surely the same impulse that impels philosophers to propose world hypotheses and universal modes of being. In one of his early ultraist essays, Borges proposes that writers "make manifest the whim transformed into reality that is the mind"; they "add provinces to Being" and "envision cities and spaces of a hallucinatory reality."[88] So, surely, do philosophers. Wallace Stevens may be right that writers probe fortuitously and philosophers deliberately. In any case, and in both, the satisfactions of their readers are commensurate.

Notes

1. *Borges en Sur 1931–1980*, ed. Sara Luisa del Carril and Mercedes Rubio de Sacchi (Buenos Aires: Emecé Editores, 1999); *Borges: Obras, reseñas y traducciones inéditas, colaboraciones de Jorge Luis Borges en la Revista multicolor de los sábados del diario Crítica, 1933–1934*, ed. Irma Zangara (Buenos Aires, Santiago: Editorial Atlántida, 1995); *Textos cautivos: Ensayos y reseñas en El Hogar (1936–1939)*, ed. Enrique Sacerio-Garí and Emir Rodríguez Monegal (Barcelona: Tusquets Editores, 1986). See Mario Vargas Llosa's review of *Borges en Sur*, "Borges, político," *Letras libres* 1, no. 11 (November 1999), pp. 24–26. In English see Eliot Weinberger's invaluable collection *Jorge Luis Borges: Selected Non-Fictions*, ed. Eliot Weinberger, trans. Esther Allen, Suzanne Jill Levine, and Eliot Weinberger (New York: Viking, 1999).
2. *Borges oral: Conferencias* (1979; Buenos Aires: Emecé/Editorial de Belgrano, 1997); *Diálogos: Borges Sábato*, ed. Orlando Barone (Buenos Aires: Emecé Editores, 1996).
3. *Para las seis cuerdas*, illustrated by Héctor Basaldúa (Buenos Aires: Emecé Editores, 1996).
4. Julio Woscoboinik demonstrates how Freudian intuitions permeate Borges's *ficciones*. See Julio Woscoboinik, *The Secret of Borges: A Psychoanalytic Inquiry into His Work*, trans. Dora Carlinsky Pozzi (Lanham, MD: University Press of America, 1998); and by the same author, *El alma de "El Aleph": Nuevos aportes a la indagación psicoanalítica de la obra de Jorge Luis Borges* (Buenos Aires: Nuevo hacer, 1996).
5. Beatriz Sarlo, *Jorge Luis Borges: A Writer on the Edge* (London: Verso, 1993); Beret E. Strong, *The Poetic Avant-Garde: The Groups of Borges, Auden and Breton* (Evanston, IL: Northwestern University Press, 1997).
6. Malcolm K. Read, *Jorge Luis Borges and His Predecessors, or Notes towards a Materialist History of Linguistic Idealism* (Chapel Hill: North Carolina Studies in Romance Language and Literatures, 1993).

7. Eliot Weinberger, "Borges: La biblioteca parcial," *Letras libres* 1, no. 8 (August 1999), pp. 36–38. Weinberger writes: "The first three volumes of the *Complete Works* include less than one hundred essays; the fourth adds another three hundred, which still leaves out some two-thirds of the uncollected work."

8. Sarlo, *José Luis Borges: A Writer on the Edge*, p. 5.

9. Borges, "Epilogue," *Other Inquisitions: 1937–1952*, trans. Ruth L.C. Sims (Austin: University of Texas Press, 1964), p. 189.

10. Floyd Merrell compares Borges and Calvino in his essay "Borges and Calvino: Chaosmos Unleashed?" in *Jorge Luis Borges: Thought and Knowledge in the XXth Century*, ed. Alfonso de Toro and Fernando de Toro (Madrid/Frankfurt: Vervuert/Iberoamericana, 1999), pp. 175–206.

11. There are also three books of poetry from the 1920s and a critical biography: *Fervor de Buenos Aires* (1923), *Luna de enfrente* (1925), *Cuaderno San Martín* (1929), and *Evaristo Carriego* (1930).

12. In his "Autobiographical Essay," Borges refers to these suppressed collections:

> Three of the four essay collections—whose names are best forgotten—I have never allowed to be reprinted. When in 1953 my present publisher—Emecé—proposed to bring out my "complete writings," the only reason I accepted was that it would allow me to keep those preposterous volumes suppressed. This reminds me of Mark Twain's suggestion that a fine library could be started by leaving out the works of Jane Austen, and that even if that library contained no other books it would still be a fine library, since her books were left out. . . . Until a few years ago, if the price were not too stiff, I would buy up copies and burn them.

Borges, "Autobiographical Essay" (1970), in *The Aleph and Other Stories 1933–1969*, trans. Norman Thomas di Giovanni (New York: E.P. Dutton, 1970), pp. 230–231.

13. Rita Guibert, *Seven Voices* (New York: Vintage, 1973), p. 10.

14. Beatriz Sarlo, *Jorge Luis Borges: A Writer on the Edge*, p. 4.

15. See my study of this process, in which I foreground Borges: *The Usable Past: The Imagination of History in Recent Fiction of the Americas* (Cambridge: Cambridge University Press, 1997).

16. Beatriz Sarlo, "Un ultraísta en Buenos Aires," *Letras libres* 1, no. 8 (August 1999), p. 42, my translation.

17. William Wimsatt, Jr., and Cleanth Brooks, *Literary Criticism: A Short History* (New York: Vintage, 1957), p. 665.

18. "El ultraísmo no es quizá otra cosa que la espléndida síntesis de la literatura antigua." Quoted in Strong, *The Poetic Avant-Garde*, p. 80.

19. See David Huerta, "La querella hispánica de Borges," *Letras libres* 1, no. 8 (August 1999), pp. 50–53.

20. Carlos Fuentes, "The Accidents of Time," in *The Borges Tradition*, ed. Norman Thomas di Giovanni (London: Constable, 1995), p. 53. Originally collected in *Geografía de la novela* as "Jorge Luis Borges: La herida de Babel" (Mexico City: Fondo de Cultura Económica, 1993), pp. 32–55.

21. James Woodall, *The Man in the Mirror of the Book: A Life of Jorge Luis Borges* (London: Hodder and Stoughton, 1996), p. 59; Anthony Kerrigan, introduction to José Ortega y Gasset's *The Revolt of the Masses*, trans. Anthony Kerrigan (Notre Dame, IN: University of Notre Dame Press, 1985), p. xix. See also Borges's early essay "Acerca de Unamuno, poeta," in *Inquisiones* (1925; Madrid: Alianza Editorial, 1998), pp. 109–118.

22. David Huerta cites Borges's 1955 essay, "Nota de un mal lector," in which Borges disavows Ortega. Borges writes: "Es posible que yo deba algo a Ortega, autor a quien apenas conozco." (It is possible that I owe something to Ortega, an author

with whom I am scarcely familiar.) Huerta notes "the bad faith" of Borges's statement. "La querella hispánica de Borges," *Letras libres* 1, no. 8 (August 1999), p. 53.
23. Rockwell Gray catalogues Ortega's insulting commentaries on Argentina and Argentines, and particularly notes Borges's aversion to Ortega's seignorial attitudes in *The Imperative of Modernity: An Intellectual Biography of José Ortega y Gasset* (Berkeley: University of California Press, 1989), pp. 117–122 and 176–183. See also José Luis Romero, *El desarrollo de las ideas en la sociedad argentina del siglo XX*, (Mexico City: Fondo de Cultura Económica, 1965), pp. 116–117.
24. José Luis Romero, *El desarrollo de las ideas en la sociedad argentina del siglo XX*, pp. 107–115. See also Luis Gregorich, "La literatura: Creación e industria," in *Buenos Aires: Historia de cuatro siglos*, ed. José Luis Romero y Luis Alberto Romero (Buenos Aires: Editorial Abril, 1983), pp. 365–375. More recently, and more generally, see David William Foster, *Buenos Aires: Perspectives on the City and Cultural Production* (Gainesville: University Press of Florida, 1998).
25. Ortega y Gasset, *Meditations on Quixote*, trans. Julián Marías (New York: W.W. Norton, 1961), p. 113.
26. Ortega, "The Novel as a Sluggish Genre," *The Dehumanization of Art*, pp. 66–67.
27. Ortega y Gasset writes:

> The Renaissance discovers the inner world in all its vast extension, the *me ipsum*, the consciousness, the subjective. *Quixote* is the flower of this great new turn which culture takes. In it the epic comes to an end forever, along with its aspiration to support a mythical world bordering on that of material phenomena but different from it. It is true that the reality of the adventure is saved, but such a salvation involves the sharpest irony. The reality of the adventure is reduced to the psychological, perhaps to a biological humor. (*Meditations on Quixote*, p. 138)

Borges dissagrees with Ortega's preference for psychological fiction over the adventure story in his "Prologue to the *Invention of Morel*."
28. In his chapter "Reality, Leaven of Myth," Ortega asks how

> reality, the actual, can be changed into poetic substance. By itself, seen in a direct way, it would never be poetic: this is the privilege of the mythical. But we can consider it obliquely as destruction of myth, as criticism of myth. In this form reality, which is of an inert and meaningless nature, quiet and mute, acquires movement, is changed into an active power of aggression against the crystal orb of the ideal. The enchantment of the latter broken, it falls into fine, iridescent dust which gradually loses its colors until it becomes an earthy brown. We witness this scene in every novel. So, strictly speaking, it is not reality that becomes poetic or enters into the work of art but only that gesture or movement of reality in which the ideal is reabsorbed. (*Meditations on Quixote*, pp. 139–140)

29. Ortega, "Taboo and Metaphor," *The Dehumanization of Art and Other Essays on Art, Culture, and Literature*, trans. Paul Snodgrass and Joseph Frank (Princeton, N.J.: Princeton University Press, 1968), p. 33.
30. Ortega, "Decline of the Novel," *The Dehumanization of Art*, p. 58.
31. Gray, *The Imperative of Modernity*, pp. 152–153. See also Antonio Rodríguez Huéscar, *José Ortega y Gasset's Metaphysical Innovation: A Critique and Overcoming of Idealism*, trans. Jorge García-Gómez (Albany: State University of New York Press, 1995).
32. Ortega, "Cubism," *The Dehumanization of Art*, pp. 29–30. The translator, Joseph Frank, appends a footnote to Ortega's phrase "ideal object." The footnote reads: "The philosophy to which Ortega refers, but which unfortunately he neglects to name, is obviously Husserlian phenomenology."
33. In the Koran, camels do appear. I am indebted to Verónica Cortínez for pointing out that Borges erroneously attributes this observation to Gibbon when, in fact, Gibbon referred to Mohammed's preference for cow's milk. In this context,

Gibbon notes that Mohammed does not mention the camel. Following his character Pierre Menard, Borges's techniques of "deliberate anachronism and erroneous attribution" are well known.

34. Borges, "The Argentine Writer and Tradition," *Discusión* (1932); in *Labyrinths*, ed. Donald A. Yates and James E. Irby (New York: New Directions, 1962), p. 185.

35. Borges, *The Book of Imaginary Beings*, with Margarita Guerrero; trans. Norman Thomas di Giovanni in collaboration with the author (London: Penguin Books, 1969), p. 14. Originally published as *Manual de zoología fantástica* in 1957, this collection was amplified in *El libro de seres imaginarios* in 1967. See Adriana González Mateo's interartistic discussion of the Mexican painter Francisco Toledo's illustration of Borges's monsters, "Borges y Toledo: zoología fantástica," in *Poligrafías: Revista de literatura comparada*, No. 1 (1996), pp. 151–162.

36. Borges, "Valéry as Symbol," *Other Inquisitions*, p. 74. The entire quote is as follows: "The meritorious mission that Valéry performed (and continues to perform) is that he proposed lucidity to men in a basely romantic age, in the melancholy age of Nazism and dialectical materialism, the age of the augurs of Freud's doctrine and the traffickers in *surréalisme*."

37. Cited by Wimsatt and Brooks, *Literary Criticism: A Short History*, p. 665. Recall that Dr. Johnson was embroiled in a crucial neoclassical debate about the relative nature and value of the general and the particular.

38. T. S. Eliot, "The Metaphysical Poets," in *Selected Essays: 1917–1932* (New York: Harcourt Brace, 1932), p. 243.

39. Borges, "A History of Angels," originally published in *El tamaño de mi esperanza*, 1926); trans. Esther Allen in *Jorge Luis Borges: Selected Non-Fiction*, pp. 18–19.

40. Borges, "The House of Asterion," originally published in 1947 and collected in *El aleph* (1949), was not included in the English translation of *The Aleph*. I cite from *Collected Fictions*, trans. Andrew Hurley (New York: Penguin, 1998), p. 221. (Hereafter *CF*.)

41. Borges, *The Book of Imaginary Beings*, p. 14.

42. Borges, "La metafora," *Historia de la eternidad* (1936); *Obras completas*, I, p. 382.

43. Susan Stewart, *On Longing: Narratives of the Miniature, the Gigantic, the Souvenir, the Collection* (Baltimore: Johns Hopkins University Press, 1984), p. 48.

44. Borges, "Autobiographical Essay," in *The Aleph*, p. 255.

45. Borges, "A Vindication of the Cabala," trans. Karen Stolley in *Borges: A Reader*, p. 23.

46. Borges, "Sobre el doblaje," *Discusión* (1932); *Obras completas* I, p. 283. Not translated into English. My translation.

47. Borges, "After Death," *Discusión* (1932); trans. Suzanne Jill Levine in *Jorge Luis Borges: Selected Non-Fiction*, pp. 253–254.

48. Borges concludes the paragraph that I've cited above:

> I have worshipped the gradual invention of God; Hell and Heaven (an immortal reward, an immortal punishment) are also admirable and curious designs of man's imagination. (255)

About an afterlife, he notes that Argentine Catholics believe in an afterlife but are not interested in it; he, on the contrary, is interested but does not believe.

49. Borges, "The Doctrine of Cycles," published in *A History of Eternity* (1936); trans. Esther Allen in *Jorge Luis Borges: Selected Non-Fiction*, p. 117. Fifty years later, Borges was to select Cantor's book to appear in Spanish translation with his prologue in his series Biblioteca Personal, Borges's last project (1985 and 1986). The prologues are published in *Obras completas*, volume IV.

50. Borges, "Personality and the Buddha," published in *Sur* in 1950; never reprinted in Spanish, and not collected in *Obras completas*; I cite from *Jorge Luis Borges:*

Selected Non-Fictions, pp. 348–349. I am indebted to José Ricardo Chaves for his insights in his unpublished essay, "Borges y el Buddhismo."

51. Borges, "Pascal's Sphere" (1951); collected in *Otras inquisiciones* (1952); trans. Eliot Weinberger in *Jorge Luis Borges: Selected Non-Fictions*, p. 352.

52. Borges, "The Detective Story," collected in *Borges oral*, 1979; trans. Esther Allen in *Jorge Luis Borges: Selected Non-Fictions*, p. 491.

53. See Jacques Derrida, *Of Grammatology*, trans. Gayatri Chakravorty Spivak (Baltimore: Johns Hopkins University Press, 1976), p. 18, where Derrida asserts that the "book" is a closed, logocentric structure and the "text" is its opposite. The refusal of closure—*différence*, or deferred meaning—characterizes most of Borges's *ficciones*, most explicitly in his recurring proposal that the dreamer is dreamed, and "the Almighty is also in search of Someone." "The Approach to al-Mu'tasim," in *The Aleph*, p. 50.

54. See Hayden White, who distinguishes between the open-ended list that is the medieval annal, or chronicle, and history, which has been "narrativized" with a beginning, middle, and end. "The Value of Narrativity in the Representation of Reality," *Critical Inquiry*, 7, no. i (1980), p. 5.

55. Umberto Eco, "The Poetics of the Open Work," in *The Role of the Reader: Explorations in the Semiotics of Texts* (Bloomington: Indiana University, 1984), pp. 47–66.

56. Borges, "Autobiographical Essay," in *The Aleph*, p. 238.

57. Borges, *A Universal History of Infamy*, trans. Norman Thomas di Giovanni (1935; London: Penguin, 1970), p. 15.

58. Borges, "The Zahir," *CF*, p. 286.

59. Ibid.

60. "Pascal's Sphere," trans. Eliot Weinberger, in *Jorge Luis Borges: Selected Non-Fiction*, p. 353.

61. Borges, "The Challenge," published in *La nación* in 1952 and collected in *El hacedor* (1960); collected in English in *The Aleph*, p. 143.

62. Borges, "The Aleph," published in September 1945 in *Sur*; collected in *El aleph* (1949); *The Aleph*, p. 26.

63. Borges, Commentary on 'The Aleph,'" *The Aleph*, p. 264.

64. Borges, "The Circular Ruins," published in December 1940 in *Sur*; collected in *CF*, p. 99.

65. Borges, "The Analytical Language of John Wilkins," published in *La nación* in 1941; collected in *Otras inquisiciones* (1952); *Other Inquisitions*, p. 103.

66. Michel Foucault, *The Order of Things: An Archaeology of the Human Sciences* (1970; New York: Vintage, 1973), p. xvii.

67. Borges, "The Concept of an Academy and the Celts" (1962), trans. Eliot Weinberger, in *Jorge Luis Borges: Selected Non-Fictions*, p. 461.

68. Borges, "Autobiographical Essay" (1970), in *The Aleph*, p. 217.

69. Borges coins the phrase to describe his own intention with his list in "The Aleph." Commentary on "The Aleph," *The Aleph*, p. 264.

70. Borges, "La nadería de la personalidad," first published in *Proa* in 1922; collected in *Inquisiciones* (1925); trans. Esther Allen as "The Nothingness of Personality," in *Jorge Luis Borges: Selected Non-Fictions*, pp. 3–9. Several times in this essay Borges repeats the phrase "There is no whole self." He then mentions Whitman, stating that Whitman "was the first Atlas who attempted to make this obstinacy a reality and take the world upon his shoulders. He believed he had only to enumerate the names of things in order to make their unique and surprising nature immediately palpable" p. 7.

71. Borges, "Camden, 1892," in *El otro, el mismo* (1964); *Obras completas*, II, p. 291

72. Borges, "Prólogo: *Hojas de hierba*." Prologue to Borges's translation of *Leaves of Grass*, published in 1969 and reprinted in *Prólogos con un prólogo de prólogos*, 1975.

See the prologue in English: "Walt Whitman, *Leaves of Grass*," trans. Esther Allen, in *Jorge Luis Borges: Selected Non-Fictions*, pp. 445–449.
73. Borges, "Note on Walt Whitman," originally published in *Discusión* (1923); *Other Inquisitions*, p. 66.
74. Borges, "Walt Whitman, *Leaves of Grass*," trans. Esther Allen, in *Jorge Luis Borges: Selected Non-Fictions*, p. 447.
75. Ortega y Gasset, "Invitation to Understanding," *The Dehumanization of Art*, p. 24.
76. "La nadería de personalidad" and "La encrucijada de Berkeley," in *Inquisiciones* (Madrid: Alianza Editorial, 1998).
77. Borges, "New Refutation of Time," originally published in pamphlet form in 1947, collected in *Otras inquisiciones* (1952); *Other Inquisitions*, p. 180.
78. Borges, "Tlön, Uqbar, Orbis Tertius," in *CF*, p. 73.
79. For an overarching comparison of Chesterton and Borges, see Elmar Schenkel, "Circling the Cross, Crossing the Circle: On Borges and Chesterton," in *Jorge Luis Borges: Thought and Knowledge in the XXth Century*, ed. Alfonso de Toro and Fernando de Toro (Madrid/Frankfurt: Vervuert/ Iberoamericana, 1999), pp. 289–302.
80. Borges, "Modes of G.K. Chesterton," published in *Sur* in 1936, not included in the *Obras completas*; trans. Mark Larsen, in *Borges: A Reader*, p. 91.
81. Borges, "From Allegories to Novels," originally published in *La nación* (1949), collected in *Otras inquisiciones* (1952); trans. Ruth L. C. Sims, in *Borges: A Reader*, p. 232.
82. Mario Vargas Llosa, "Borges, político," *Letras libres*, 1, no. 11 (November 1999), p. 24.
83. Borges, "Oswald Spengler: A Capsule Biography," published in *El hogar* in 1936; trans. Karen Stolley in *Borges: A Reader*, p. 87.
84. Borges, "Tlön, Uqbar, Orbis Tertius," in *CF*, pp. 72–73.
85. Eduardo González, *The Monstered Self* (Durham, NC: Duke University Press, 1992), pp. 39–42.
86. Borges, "Borges and I," first published in *El Hacedor* (1960); in *Collected Fictions*, p. 324.
87. Stevens, "The Collect of Philosophy," in *Opus Posthumous*, p. 271.
88. Borges, "After Images," published in *Proa* in 1924, collected in *Inquisiciones* (1925); trans. Suzanne Jill Levine, in *Jorge Luis Borges: Selected Non-Fiction*, p. 11.

5

JORGE J. E. GRACIA

Borges's "Pierre Menard": Philosophy or Literature?[1]

In a letter to his wife, to whom he dedicated the Eighth Symphony, Mahler wrote:

> It is a peculiarity of the interpretation of works of art that *the rational element in them (that which is soluble by reason) is almost never their true reality*, but only a veil which hides their form. Insofar as a soul needs a body—which there is no disputing—an artist is bound to derive the means of creation from the natural world. But the chief thing is still the artistic conception. . . . [In *Faust*] everything points with growing mastery toward his final supreme moment— which, *though beyond expression, touches the very heart of feeling.*[2]

Mahler's point concerns what is peculiar to works of art: They defy rationality and expression. By this, I take him to mean that works of art are not reducible to ideas and, therefore, cannot be effectively translated.

If works of art are idiosyncratic in this way, then it would be expected that this is also what distinguishes them from works of philosophy. Whereas art is irreducible to ideas and defies translation, philosophy is reducible to ideas and can be translated.

This is the standard modernist view of philosophy and art—and, by extension, of literature—which has been one of the points of attack by post-modernists. The argument is not just that art and literature are irreducible to ideas and therefore untranslatable, but that there is no distinction in this respect between art and literature on the one hand and philosophy on the other. Philosophy is also art.[3]

Postmodernism has found a receptive audience in Latin America, particularly in literary circles and especially on this point. Indeed, the view that there is no distinction between literature, in particular, and philosophy is often treated as dogma. I quote from a recent source: "[I]n fact, there is no substantial difference between philosophical discourse and literary discourse" in spite of "the boundaries that have been traditionally claimed to separate both discourses."[4]

An author who, more than any other, is cited as proof of the absence of boundaries between philosophy and literature is Jorge Luis Borges.[5] And with reason, for Borges is widely known outside the Hispanic world and it would be very difficult to claim that his thought is not philosophical. The short story, "Pierre Menard, the Author of the *Quixote*," in particular seems to address a set of very interesting and even profound philosophical questions. Indeed, many authors from different philosophical traditions have used it as a point of departure for discussions that are generally regarded as philosophical. We need mention only Michel Foucault and, more recently and from a different philosophical tradition, Gregory Currie, to give credibility to this claim.[6] I wish, then, to address the question of the distinction between philosophy and literature in the context of Borges and particularly "Pierre Menard." Is "Pierre Menard" philosophy or literature? And, more generally, what distinguishes philosophy and literature if, indeed, there is a distinction between the two?[7]

To ask these two questions in the way I have done, however, is confusing, for the terms "philosophy" and "literature" are used in ordinary language to mean a variety of things. It is common to speak of philosophy, for example, as a discipline of learning, as an activity, as the thought of an author, and so on.[8] And we find a similar variety of meanings for the term "literature." Moreover, because our ultimate aim is to establish whether Borges's "Pierre Menard" is philosophy or literature, and "Pierre Menard" is both a work and a text, to facilitate our task I propose to reformulate the general question we are trying to answer as follows: What distinguishes literary works from philosophical works and literary texts from philosophical texts? The more specific question about Borges turns out something like this: Is Borges's "Pierre Menard" a work of philosophy or of literature, and is it a philosophical or a literary text?

My thesis about Borges's "Pierre Menard" in particular is that it is a literary work and text rather than a philosophical one. My thesis about philosophy and literature in general is that literary works are distinguished from philosophical ones in that their conditions of identity include the texts through which they are expressed. Moreover, literary texts are distinguished from philosophical ones in that they express literary works.[9]

As will become clear, this is an ontological rather than an epistemological or a causal claim. I assume that the question, concerning the identity conditions of works and texts, is not logically the same as the question concerning the conditions under which works and texts are known or are produced. This means that in principle, knowing a work or text may entail certain conditions that are not part of the identity conditions of the work or text, and vice versa. And the same could be said concerning the conditions of their production. But I shall argue that some of the conditions of identity of literary works that are not conditions of identity of philosophical ones are nonetheless necessary conditions, in context, of knowing philosophical works. This is one of the important elements of distinction between my position and the standard modernist view and has significant implications that I shall point out later.

Texts and Works

Let me begin by introducing a distinction between works and texts. This is, of course, a much disputed topic. Because I have no space to engage in a discussion of the relative merits of various current views in this matter, I shall proceed instead by presenting my own position.[10] This will not be sufficient to establish it fully, but I hope it will at least clarify how I use it to articulate my view concerning the nature of literary and philosophical works and texts.

A text is a group of entities used as signs, selected, arranged, and intended by an author to convey a specific meaning to an audience in a certain context.[11] The entities in question can be of any sort. They can be ink marks on a piece of paper, sculpted pieces of ice, carvings on stone, designs on sand, sounds uttered by humans or produced by mechanical devices, actions, mental images, and so on. These entities, considered by themselves, are not a text. They become a text only when they are used by an author to convey some specific meaning to an audience in a certain context. Ontologically, this means that a text amounts to these entities considered in relation to a specific meaning. The marks on the paper on which I am writing, for example, are not a text unless someone mentally connects them to a specific meaning. The situation is very much like that of a stone used as a paperweight. The stone becomes the paperweight only when someone thinks of it as a paperweight or uses it as a paperweight.

A work, on the contrary, is the meaning of certain texts. Not all texts have meanings that qualify as works. "The cat is on the mat" is a text as judged by the definition given, but no one thinks of its meaning as a work. By contrast, *Don Quixote* is both a text and a work. On the difficult question of which texts have corresponding works, and which do not, there is much disagreement in the literature. The matter does not seem to depend on length, style, authorship, or the degree of effort involved in the production of the text. Fortunately, there is no need to resolve the question at this juncture.[12] The pertinent point for us is that texts and works are not the same thing: A text is a group of entities considered in relation to a specific meaning, whereas works are the meanings of certain texts. I leave the notion of meaning open, for what I am going to say later does not depend on any particular conception of meaning.

In the case we are discussing here, namely, "Pierre Menard," the text is the marks on the page I am looking at, the sounds I hear when someone reads "Pierre Menard" to me, certain images I imagine when I think about the marks on the page or the sounds uttered by someone reading, and so on, as long as the marks, sounds, or images in question are considered as signs intended to convey a specific meaning. In contrast, the work "Pierre Menard" is the meaning those marks, sounds, or images are intended to convey.

This way of looking at texts and works, by the way, allows us to understand one of the main points Borges makes in "Pierre Menard." We can say that the entities that constitute the texts of Cervantes' *Don Quijote* and Pierre Menard's *Don Quijote* are the same, but the work of Cervantes and the work of Pierre Menard are different.[13] Indeed, as Borges so well puts it: "The Cervantes text and the Menard text are verbally identical, but the second is almost infinitely richer."[14] This point will be relevant later, as we shall see.

Three Popular Views on Philosophy and Literature

Philosophers have not shied away from giving answers to the more general question concerning the distinction between philosophy and literature we have posed. Indeed, the number and variety of opinions in this matter are staggering and the positions frequently conflicting. In part this reflects a general confusion about the nature of literature, if not also about the nature of philosophy. It is not surprising to find claims to the effect that what distinguishes literature from other disciplines is that it is concerned with life whereas others claim that it is not about life but about itself.[15] Again, some authors claim that literature is about reality, contradicting others who say that literature is always fictional.[16] Others make a distinction in terms of the noncognitive nature of literature.[17] And more recently some have argued that literature, *qua* text, refers only to other texts or to itself (self-referential view), whereas others object that literature is not about texts at all but about nontextual reality.[18] These and other views of literature are used to contrast it with philosophy. For example, the literary concern with life is contrasted with the philosophical concern with ideas; and the fictional character of literature is set against the nonfictional character of philosophy;[19] philosophy, some say, is concerned with truth whereas literature is not,[20] whereas others argue just the opposite.[21] Today, however, I ignore most of the many views that have been offered in this matter, limiting the discussion to three answers that are widely held but that appear to be inadequate. I discuss these because their inadequacy and popularity may have helped to undermine the belief in the distinction between philosophy and literature. The first I call the *institutional* view; the second, the *interpretational view*; and the third, the *particularist view*. After I present these views, I turn to the position I favor.

The *institutional view* may be presented as follows: There is no feature or set of features common to literary works and texts that distinguishes them from philosophical works and texts. Indeed, the same work or text has at different times been considered literary or philosophical, so it would be futile to attempt to find this distinction in anything that characterizes the work or text itself. Literary and philosophical works and texts are cultural creations, and it is the culture that creates them that determines how they are regarded. Moreover, because this kind of task is usually left to an institutionalized segment of society, it is clear that it is the institution in question that determines, through its members, whether particular works and texts are literary or philosophical.[22] Hence, whether "Pierre Menard" is a literary or philosophical work or text depends on the institution or institutions in society that determine such questions and, to know the answer to the question, we need go no further than to pose the question to well-established members of the pertinent institution who are known for their agreement with institutional views. In fact, because the question has to do with philosophy, we might just as well ask any bona fide philosopher or literary critic whether Borges's "Pierre Menard" is a literary or philosophical work or text.

I suspect, however, that if we were to follow the procedure just suggested, we would get as many different answers to the question as persons asked. Some would answer yes, some no, some both, and some neither, but in all cases there would be so many qualifications that it would be difficult to find full agreement between any two answers. But perhaps this is unfair to the institutional view. Perhaps it is not bona fide philosophers, or literary critics, who should be asked. And yet, if not them, then who should be asked? Moreover, who determines who should be asked? Indeed, I suspect that if we were to pose these questions to the readers of this essay we would again receive as many different answers to them as we would receive concerning the earlier question.

I imagine that by now the thrust of my objection is clear: The institutional view leads to a vicious circle or an infinite regress. It does so because it does not identify the feature or set of features that makes something literary or philosophical. To say that it is philosophers and literary critics who determine what is literary or philosophical is either to postpone the question, which can again be asked and postponed *ad infinitum*, or to force us to return to literary and philosophical works and texts. But neither of these paths leads to closure. The institutional view is very popular today, and is favored by many of the most fashionable and well-established philosophers and literary critics in connection with various issues that have to do with aesthetics, but it certainly does not help us answer the particular question we are seeking to answer here.

The second view I wish to consider briefly here is the *interpretational view*. According to it, literary works and texts are distinguished from philosophical ones because the meaning of the first is never completely clear—there are always ambiguities in them—whereas philosophical works and texts, like scientific ones, do not have this feature. *Don Quixote*, for example, is literary and not philosophical because there can never be a definitive interpretation of it; there can never be interpretative closure with respect to it. Philosophical texts and works, by contrast, have definite and unambiguous meanings that can be identified.

This is a well-entrenched view of the distinction between literary works and texts and philosophical ones. I heard it expressed for the first time in high school many more years ago than I would like to acknowledge, and have heard it voiced repeatedly ever since. Naturally, this view has also found its way into professional discussions of this issue.[23] Moreover, it has some backing from experience, for it looks as if, indeed, most literary works and texts have the kind of openness to interpretation that this position confers on them.

The problem this position encounters is not so much with what it holds concerning literary works and texts, but with what it holds concerning philosophical ones, for it cannot easily be claimed with a straight face that philosophical works and texts have definitive interpretations and lack ambiguity and openness. It is perhaps *prima facie* possible to argue that some scientific works and texts are this way, but can we really say the same concerning philosophical ones? Do not interpreters of Aristotelian works and texts, for example, argue endlessly about what Aristotle meant by them? Consider the meetings of the American Philosophical Association. How many different interpretations of Aristotle's works and texts are presented every year in them? And what about Plato? In short, ambiguity and openness of meaning do not seem to be demarcating criteria between philosophical and literary works and texts.

The third view is the *particularist*. It finds the distinction between philosophical texts and works on the one hand and literary texts and works on the other in that the content of the first is abstract and universal whereas the content of the second is concrete and particular. Philosophy deals with common experience whereas literature deals with individual experience. This is why literature always tells a story or presents a picture from an individual point of view. Philosophy, on the contrary, never tells a story and always seeks a perspective common to everyone.

Again, this is an often repeated position, and one that appears to have some basis in experience.[24] Novels and short stories, for example, always deal with individual lives and events. And even poetry, so the argument goes, when not concerned with individual lives or events, is nonetheless concerned with personal experiences.

Now, it is quite true that much literature is like this, but it is false that all literature is so. Moreover, it is also true that much philosophy is abstract and universal, but again it is false that all philosophy excludes the concrete and particular. There are many examples that could be cited to substantiate these claims. Much Enlightenment literature, for example, ignores the concrete and particular. Think of Alexander Pope. True, he is not a very popular writer these days, and some would even say that his works are not very good, but preference or even quality should not be confused with nature. It would be hard to deny Pope a place in English letters and to consider his works not literary.

On the other hand, even the most universalist and abstract philosophers frequently engage in story telling to illustrate their claims or even to raise questions that otherwise would be very difficult to raise. Indeed, in certain areas of philosophy such as the philosophy of law, cases are never too far from the discussion and often direct it.[25] In short, it makes no sense to say that the distinction between philosophy and literature amounts to a distinction in terms of the abstract and universal on one hand and the concrete and particular on the other.

Clearly there are serious problems with the three theories of the distinction between literary and philosophical works and texts we have examined. Does this mean, then, that the postmodernist position is correct? Is there no distinction between philosophy and literature because in fact philosophy is literature?

Literary and Philosophical Texts and Works

The answers to both questions are negative; the postmodernist position is not correct and there is a distinction between works and texts of literature on the one hand and works and texts of philosophy on the other. A literary work is distinguished from a philosophical one in that its conditions of identity include the text of which it is the meaning. This is to say that the signs of which the text is composed, the entities of which these signs are constituted, and the arrangements of the signs and the entities that constitute the signs are essential to the literary work in question. This is the reason why no work of literature can ever be, strictly speaking, translated. It is in the nature of a literary work that the text that expresses it be essential to it. This is not the case with philosophical works. It should not really matter whether I read Kant's *Critique of Pure Reason* in German or English (in fact, many believe it is better to read it in English). What should matter is that I get the ideas. The work is not essentially related to German, whereas Shakespeare's *Hamlet* could have been written only in English and Cervantes' *Don Quixote* could have been written only in Spanish.

Note, however, that the impossibility of translation may have various origins and, therefore, it is possible that a philosophical, and indeed even a scientific, work may not be translatable, but if it is not—and this is my contention—it would not be because the conditions of identity include its text. For example, "$0 + 1 = 1$" may not be translatable into the language of a culture that has no concept of zero. But this has nothing to do with its literary quality, that is, with its text.[26]

So much, then, for the distinction between literary and philosophical works. Now we can turn to the distinction between a literary text and a philosophical one. But this proves not to be difficult: A literary text is a text that is essential to the work it expresses, whereas a philosophical text is not essential to the work it expresses.

But perhaps I have gone too fast. After all, I have just stated my view and have not given any arguments for it. I could be wrong in holding that literary texts and works are distinguishable from philosophical ones. And even if not wrong about this, I could be wrong about the basis of the distinction. After all, there are plenty of philosophers who do hold, or have held, both views.

To provide the kind of substantiation that this objection implies would take more space than I have at my disposal here, but I do need to say something in response to it. As a compromise, I will offer some evidence to support my position, even if limited and sketchy.

First, let me point out that those who oppose the distinction between philosophical and literary works and texts do so from at least two different perspectives. According to some, philosophical and literary works and texts are not distinguishable from each other because all philosophical works and texts are also literary works and texts. The distinction between them is artificial and based on a misunderstanding of the nature of works and texts. This is the kind of position that is quite popular these days in certain philosophical circles. All works and texts, and particularly philosophical ones, are to be viewed as literary or aesthetic ones; they are aesthetic or literary artifacts.[27]

Others, however, although also rejecting the distinction between philosophical and literary works and texts, do so because they hold that all works and texts are philosophical to the extent that they express ideas and philosophy is about ideas. Thus there is really no essential distinction between philosophical and literary works and texts, but not because philosophical texts are literary, but rather because literary texts are philosophical. This kind of position is not very popular these days, but echoes of it can be found in the history of philosophy beginning with Plato and his followers.[28]

Now, what evidence can be supplied against these positions? I offer three pieces of evidence. The first is that in practice we do make distinctions between at least some philosophical and literary works and texts and we treat them differently. That is, what we do with philosophical works and texts differs from what we do with works and texts we regard as literary. This is a kind of pragmatic argument. The *Critique of Pure Reason* is studied in different academic departments, by different specialists, and in different ways than *Hamlet*. We do act as if these works and texts were quite different in function and aim, and we use them for different purposes. Moreover, when we study them, we apply different methodologies to them. In the case of the *Critique of Pure Reason*, historians of philosophy and philosophers are concerned with the understanding of the ideas it proposes, with the arguments it provides, and with the truth value of the ideas and the validity and soundness of the arguments it contains. We do pay attention to the language and the way Kant expresses himself, but the study of this language and the way Kant uses it is secondary to the main purpose of the study, which is determining the cognitive meaning and value of what Kant said. On the contrary, what we do with *Hamlet* is quite different. Here there may still be some concern about ideas, but there is no concern about arguments. No literary critic I know has ever tried to apply logic to discourses contained in the play. Moreover, the overriding preoccupation seems to be with the overall significance of the work and text. And by significance I mean the impact of the text on ourselves, others, society, and culture.[29]

Still, it is obvious that although we do use at least philosophical and literary texts and works in different ways, we could be wrong about this. Someone could argue that we do so simply because we are following certain modernist traditions and customs well entrenched in our society, and that there is nothing in the works or texts themselves that justifies the different ways in which we treat them.

To this I respond with a second piece of evidence, namely, the case of poetry. Here is a kind of work or text that seems clearly to fit the distinction I have drawn between philosophical and literary texts and works. There are aspects of a poem that make it quite different from prose, and although some philosophy has been presented in poetic form, most philosophy has not. The fact is that poetry involves certain structures, punctuation, and rhythm that stand out in contrast with the form of expression generally used in philosophical texts and works. Moreover, it seems that in poetry, such factors are as essential for the identity of the work or text as the ideas expressed by the text.

But even if this piece of evidence were to convince us that at least poetic works and texts can be distinguished from philosophical ones, in that poetic texts are essential to works, whereas this is not so with philosophical ones, the problem we still face is that not all literary works and texts are poetic. So what do we make of prose works and texts that are literary? How are we to distinguish them from philosophical ones, and vice versa?

My contention is that there is still a sense in which the identity of prose literary works depends on the texts they express, a fact that does not apply to philosophical works and that also affects the identity conditions of literary texts and works. The reason is not controversial. Indeed, it is generally accepted that the majority of terms that constitute the vocabularies of different languages are not equivalent in meaning or function. Still, many people would hold that in a large number of cases formulas can be found in one language that would get across the meaning of the terms used in the other language. My point is that this is possible in principle in the case of philosophical works, but that it can never be in the case of literary works. But we may ask, why is this so? What are the differences between literary and philosophical texts and works that make literary meaning to be dependant on the text, whereas this is not so for philosophical meaning?

There are many differences at stake here, but I shall refer only to five to make my point. Consider first the nature of the vocabulary used in literary and philosophical texts, how that vocabulary is used, and how the meaning of that vocabulary is treated. Philosophical vocabulary is overwhelmingly technical. This does not mean only that the terms used in philosophy are not generally used in ordinary discourse, whether spoken or written. It means that even when terms that are commonly used are employed by philosophers, most of these terms acquire meanings different from those involved in common usage.[30] Moreover, even when the meanings are not changed completely, philosophers circumscribe and limit the meanings of the terms they use. A word such as "substance," for example, which is commonly used in ordinary English, is a technical term in philosophy. Indeed, it is a technical term for most philosophers who use it, because they determine a particular sense in which they use it. The terms used in ordinary language, on the other hand, have meanings that are frequently open-ended both because there are no strict criteria for their use and because their connotations vary. So much, then, for philosophy.

The situation with literature is very different from that in philosophy. In literary works and texts, terms are used primarily in an ordinary sense and their open-endedness is usually regarded as a good thing. Writers of literature do not generally define their terms or explain what they mean. They thrive on suggestion and connotation, leaving much leeway for the audience.

This brings me to a second difference that explains why the text is necessarily a part of the identity conditions of the work in literature but not so in philosophy. Most terms used in philosophy are rare, not because they do not occur frequently in common speech—if that were the case many pieces of literature would be indistinguishable from philosophy insofar as they too use words not commonly used in everyday speech—but because they are abstruse terms, which have meanings not directly related to common human experience. By contrast, literature is precisely founded on common experience, which is one reason why the appeal of most literature is broad and takes little for granted in audiences and why some philosophers have been led to believe that it is in the nature of literature to be about common experience, as we saw earlier.

The order of the words is also very important in literature, because literature aims to cause a certain effect on audiences that does not consist in the pure intellectual grasp of ideas. Literature is highly rhetorical. Each language has developed certain syntactical structures that produce certain effects in the audience that speaks the language of the text and that are impossible or produce very different effects in audiences unfamiliar with that language.

The audience plays a very special role in the case of literary works and texts.[31] The Latin periodic sentence, the epitome of elegance in that language, is generally a failure in English. In Latin, it is not only a sign of elegance, but is intended to produce a certain effect. Reading these clauses and subclauses, not yet having arrived at the verb that puts it all together, is supposed to develop a sense of anticipation in the reader that culminates in the grasp of meaning and in the relief that is achieved when the verb is reached at the end. In English, it is impossible to put the verb at the end of a sentence in most cases, and the use of long periods of subordinated clauses, instead of causing anticipation, tends to produce confusion and frustration in audiences. A translation from Latin, then, that tries to reproduce the Latin period in English is bound to have an entirely different effect on the English audience than the Latin had on the original Latin audience for which the Latin text was intended.

This brings me to style. Style is largely a matter of word choice, syntax, and punctuation. But style also depends very much on historical circumstances. Consider, for example, that a literary piece may be regarded as having an archaic style at a certain time, but as not having it at another time. A book written in the twentieth century in the style of Cervantes is considered archaic, but a book Cervantes wrote in the seventeenth is not considered to have an archaic style.[32] Style is always historically relative. It is also contextual insofar as it is relative to an audience. Now style is of the essence in literature. The style of an author is fundamental to the consideration of the author and his or her work. But this is not so important, and some would say not important at all, when it comes to philosophy. What matters in philosophy is not the style of the author or the piece in question, but the philosophy, that is, the ideas the piece contains or, if you will, the claims it makes.[33] In this sense, although a text of philosophy may have a certain style, generally the work has little to do with it. This is a reason why the elements constitutive of texts are not part of the identity conditions of works of philosophy, whereas they are in a literary work.

Of course, it may be argued that because philosophy is expressed in texts, there is no way of avoiding style. And indeed, there are some philosophers who have insisted that the only way to present philosophy is in a particular format. This was certainly the case with Plato, for whom the proper philosophical form of discourse was the dialogue.[34] And many other philosophers' writings can be and are characterized stylistically, for example, Russell and Hume. Indeed, even those philosophers who avoid stylistic peculiarities, like Aquinas, can be said to have a certain style that is clear or obscure, direct or indirect, and so on. Moreover, they use certain genres in their writing, such as the article form, the *quaestio* form, the commentary, and so on, and genre is bound up with style even if it is not the same thing. So it is difficult to argue that philosophy does not care for style, although it can be argued that it does not care for a particular style.

Still, the point I am making is not that philosophical writing lacks style, or even that the style is always unrelated to meaning. My point is that philosophers do not generally think that what they are doing is essentially related to the style they use. Of course, not all philosophers have thought this way. The mentioned case of Plato is a clear exception. But this attitude is rather the exception than the rule.[35]

Finally, let me turn to the use of cultural symbols and icons. In literature, these are most important; they are essential for both the work and the text of literature. These symbols and icons are particular to a society and are supposed to speak to us in ways that are not always expressible in discourse. But this is not generally the case with philosophy. The language of philosophy is supposed to be transcultural and universal. Philosophers aim to communicate with the whole world independently of elements peculiar to particular cultures.

"Pierre Menard"

All this sounds too general and theoretical, so an illustration is in order. Let us take a look at "Pierre Menard" and see whether it can put some flesh on the bones of my theory. To avoid the accusation that I concentrate only on certain passages of the text that particularly suit my view, I shall simply turn to the first two sentences of it to show how a translation of "Pierre Menard" into English does not do justice to the text or work "Pierre Menard" in Spanish. The point of all this will be to show that in "Pierre Menard" in particular, and in all literary texts and works in general, elements of the text are essential to the meaning.

In the very first sentence of the translation I am using, there are at least three English words that fail to carry the full meaning of the words in Spanish.[36] The full sentence reads as follows:

La obra visible que ha dejado este novelista es de fácil y breve enumeración.

The *visible* work left by this novelist is easily and briefly enumerated.

The first two words of the English translation that create difficulties are "easily" and "briefly"; they translate *fácil* and *breve*. The Spanish words in question are adjectives whereas the English words are adverbs. This changes the force of what is being said in subtle ways. For one thing is to do something in a certain way—the adverbial modification—and another is to have something that is easy and brief. There is also a problem with the word "easily" insofar as the English term has no negative connotation. If anything, it has a positive one: to do something easily is a good thing. But in Spanish to say that something is *fácil* sometimes carries the notion that in English is expressed by the term "facile." Things that are *fácil* are not always good things. Now, insofar as Borges is one of the greatest ironists of the Spanish language, it would be expected that for him words such as *fácil* will carry all possible ambiguity.

Another word that creates difficulty is "enumerated," which translates the Spanish *enumeración*. The English term is a verb form, but the Spanish term is a substantive. This again paints a different picture for us, we might even say a different ontological picture. In one case, an action, or the remains of an action at least, are involved; in the other, we have a more substantial entity. But this is not all, for again the connotations of the English and Spanish terms are different, first because the use of the Spanish term in a context such as this is not unusual. Indeed, the very term *enumeración* in Spanish is not an unusual term. But "enumeration" is rare and rather pedantic in English. When was the last time you said that you were enumerating anything? For English speakers, this is a word of foreign origin, a learned term derived from Latin; they prefer to count, not enumerate. We, in Spanish, *enumeramos* as much as *contamos* (the counterpart of "counting").

The second sentence also presents us with difficulties.

Son por lo tanto, imperdonables las omisiones y adiciones perpetradas por Madame Henri Bachelier en un catálogo falaz que cierto diario cuya tendencia protestante no es un secreto ha tenido la desconsideración de inferir a sus deplorables lectores—si bien éstos son pocos y calvinistas, cuando no masones y circuncisos.

Impardonable, therefore, are the omissions and additions perpetrated by Madame Henri Bachelier in a fallacious catalogue which a certain daily, whose *Protestant* tendency is no secret, has had the inconsideration to inflict upon its deplorable readers—though these be few and Calvinist, if not Masonic and circumcised.

The first area of difficulty with this sentence is its length: it is approximately six lines long, depending on the type that is used. This, by English standards, is an abomination. But by Spanish standards, which often derive from Latin, it is not particularly long. Moreover, in English, the sentence is rather convoluted and confusing, calling for certain modifications in the translation—note, for example, the addition of a comma after "secret." For a Spanish audience, on the contrary, the sentence is quite elegant, revealing the dexterity in the language that one would expect in the writer of the piece.

The second source of difficulty concerns the first word in the sentence. The first word in the English translation is "Impardonable" and in Spanish it is *Son*. The emphases of the two sentences, then, are quite different. In English, the character of the omissions and additions is paramount; the position of the adjective suggests that this is a great fault. In Spanish, the use of

98 Jorge J. E. Gracia

the form of the verb "to be" at the beginning suggests no such force, particularly because in Spanish *imperdonables* could have been placed first. Of course, the English translator had to place "Impardonable" at the beginning, for he could not very well have begun with "Are," not so much because it is ungrammatical as because it is inelegant, and this sentence is, without doubt, intended to be "elegant."

The word "fallacious" in English creates a different problem, for although it does accurately translate the word *falaz*, the latter is a more common word in Spanish and one whose connotation is not as technical and narrow as fallacious. Generally, when people use "fallacious" in English, they are thinking of arguments of some sort, but in Spanish the word *falaz* is often used to mean simply false or incorrect. The translation of *desconsideración* by "inconsideration" also poses problems. *Desconsideración* is a rather common word in Spanish, but the English cognate is rare. Again, it smacks of learning and pedantry. Finally, there is the subjunctive translation of *son* as "be." Borges is saying that the readers are in fact few, etc., but the subjunctive introduces a certain hesitation that is missing in the original text.

In short, the translation of the two sentences of "Pierre Menard" we have before us misses much that is essential to the work of the Spanish text. And yet, the translation is very good indeed. In many ways, it is so good that it cannot be improved. Now, if we were trying to be faithful merely to the ideas expressed by the text, I am sure we could find circumlocutions that would do the trick. Or we could add learned notes that would make it possible for us to understand precisely what the Spanish says. But if we do this, we lose "Pierre Menard"; we lose tone, emphasis, elegance, irony, rhythm, and particular connotations, to mention just a few essential elements to it. Indeed, to do this would be like putting a commentary or gloss in place of "Pierre Menard," or to use another example, to put St. John of the Cross' *Commentary on the Spiritual Canticle* in place of the *Spiritual Canticle*. And this will not do, which suggests that "Pierre Menard" is a literary text and work rather than a philosophical one. But is this right and, more important still, is the general thesis of the distinction between philosophical texts and works, and literary texts and works, that I have presented defensible?

Identity, Identification, and Causation

According to my thesis, the difference between literary works and philosophical works is that for the former the texts that express them are part of their identity conditions, whereas for the latter they are not. With respect to texts, I have proposed that those that are philosophical differ from those that are literary in that philosophical texts do not have corresponding works in which the texts are part of the identity conditions of the works, whereas literary texts do.

The particular thesis concerning the work "Pierre Menard" is that it is literary because its text is part of its identity conditions, with the result that it cannot be successfully translated. Its translations are more or less close approximations, rather than faithful renderings of the original. Moreover, the text of "Pierre Menard" is literary because the work it expresses depends on it essentially.

At this point two questions arise: First, is this anything more than the stale, Platonic-based, position that philosophy is independent of the medium in which it is presented, whereas literature is not?[37] Second, is not the criterion for philosophy being used so strong that most of what we call philosophy is left out? These are good questions that must be addressed if my view can claim any originality and credibility.

The answer to the first question is that, indeed, my position has much in common with the position described, provided that position is understood clearly. However, even then, there are elements in my position that do not coincide with it. I do not claim, for example, as some Platonists do, that the ideas philosophy is all about are independent from the texts that express them in the sense that their ontological status is independent of those texts. Perhaps they are, but nothing I have said requires such a claim. My position is more modest. I merely claim that philosophical works, unlike literary ones, are not supposed to be tied to particular texts. In principle, philosophical works, unlike literary ones, ought to be able to be presented or expressed, or conveyed, if you wish, through different texts, and the different texts should not alter their identity as works. In short, the translation of philosophical works into other languages should be possible, whereas it should never be possible for a literary work.[38] Indeed, the styles and genres used by philosophers are usually those that make possible translation, whereas the literati use forms and structures so bound up with their meaning that any attempt at translating becomes impossible. The philosophical text, then, is not entirely superfluous or merely instrumental to the work. It is essential insofar as a certain type of text is conducive to the independence of the work, whereas others are not.

Moreover, no work does or can exist unless there is a text that expresses it, and this is quite contrary to the Platonic position. To my knowledge, there are no works, ideas, meanings, or the like floating around anywhere.

Finally, I hope it is quite obvious that the elements that constitute texts are essential both for philosophical and literary texts. German words are essential to the text of the *Critique of Pure Reason*, just as Spanish words are essential to the text of *Don Quixote*. But German words are not necessary for the work *Critique of Pure Reason*, whereas Spanish words are for the work *Don Quixote*. Particular literary contents are inseparable from particular forms; particular philosophical contents should be separable in principle from particular forms, even though they are not separable from all forms.

The answer to the second question, namely, Is not your criterion of philosophy so strong that most of what we call philosophy is left out?, is as follows: If applied strictly, the criterion I have suggested appears to disqualify much that is considered philosophy and make it literature. Indeed, as stated at the beginning, I believe this is one of the reasons some philosophers wish to see philosophy as literature. If we were to apply strictly the criterion I have suggested, we might have to leave out of the philosophical canon many works that are part of it. Out would go such works as Pascal's *Pensées*, Montaigne's *Essays*, and even perhaps Descartes' *Discourse on Method* and Wittgenstein's *Philosophical Investigations*. And not only this, but we might have to develop a technically precise language to be used in all philosophical texts. Yet I do not think any of us, except for a very small group of ideological purists, would want to do this. The time of the Vienna Circle and the search for an ideal scientific language in philosophy is over, at least for the moment. So what do we do?

Part of the problem arises because so far we have not distinguished between identity, identification, and causation. Thus far, I have been speaking of conditions of identity, and these conditions concern the identity of philosophical and literary texts and works considered apart from the knowledge we may have of those texts and works and the causes that bring them about. But we can also speak of the conditions under which we know philosophical and literary texts and works and of the conditions under which they are produced. The distinction between identity, identification, and causation is standard, and I trust does not need much elaboration. I assume that the conditions of being X, the conditions of knowing X, and the conditions of there being an X are not necessarily the same. One thing is to be human, another to know that something is human, and still another to cause something human.

The application of this distinction to philosophical texts and works allows us to draw certain important inferences. First, by keeping causal conditions separate from conditions of identity and identification, we can understand how the distinction between literary works and texts can still be made in terms of the character of the texts and works themselves in spite of the fact that the causes that produce them include factors other than the texts and works. Consider that a text is a human artifact. A text is a group of entities *used* as signs, which are *selected, arranged,* and *intended* by an author *to convey* a specific meaning *to* an audience *in* a certain context. This means, of course, that a text is causally dependent on its author, audience, and context. It depends on the author because the author is the one who does the using, selecting, arranging, and intending. It depends on the audience at least insofar as the audience is the target of the communication and, therefore, determines to some extent the choices the author makes (its dependence on the audience may actually be stronger, but this is another issue). And it depends on the context because the context alters the conditions of receptivity for the text. The entities that constitute a text by themselves are not a text. The lines, sounds, and whatever that an author uses to compose a text are by themselves not a text. To be a text they have to be used for a definite purpose that is related to an audience and a context. This means that the conditions of the existence of a text involve factors outside the text, for a text does not come to be by itself. The conditions of being a text and the conditions required to bring a text into being are not the same. And something similar can be said about meaning. The meaning of a text is determined by factors that are other than the entities that constitute the text, for the meaning is not naturally tied to those entities. It becomes tied to them through the use the author and the audience make of it in context.[39]

This has important consequences for the issue we are addressing here. It entails that the distinction between literary and philosophical texts and works in general, and of particular literary and philosophical texts and works, can be made in terms of the texts and works themselves. But it also allows us to hold that these distinctions are caused by what authors and audiences do in particular contexts. For it is the uses and practices of authors and audiences that are responsible for texts and works and for the connection between particular meanings and the entities that constitute the texts. That the identity conditions of the meaning (i.e., works) of certain texts necessarily includes reference to the entities that constitute the texts, whereas in others it does not, is a result of the actions of authors and audiences in context. Moreover, that there are some texts that express works like these, and others that do not, again is a result of the actions of authors and audiences in context. But this does not reduce the conditions of identity of texts and works to their causes. It is a mistake, then, to reject the distinction between philosophical and literary texts and works based on the consideration of their character because texts and works are artifacts, that is, the results of human activity and design. The conditions that make a coat hanger what it is are logically independent of the fact that someone invented and made the coat hanger.

Now let us turn to the distinction between identity and identification. This distinction is important for our purposes because, when applied to texts and works, it explains how, although it is essential for the *identity* of a literary work to include the corresponding text and this is not so for a philosophical one, there is no reason why the conditions of the *knowledge* of a philosophical work cannot include precisely the conditions of identity of a literary work, at least in some cases. Indeed, I propose that they do for many reasons, at least three of which I would like to mention. First, many philosophical claims and issues are too profound and abstract to be grasped without heuristic devices that make them clear. We need to give them flesh and blood, as it were; that is, we need to make them concrete in order to render them intelligible. Second, humans are not mere rational faculties; they are complex entities with passions and feelings. This make-up influences their capacity to understand, so that often they need to have their feelings and emotions moved in order for them to understand. Third, all works are known through texts, and texts are made up of linguistic entities and structures that are cultural in nature, and this has repercussions for our understanding.

In short, the conditions of our knowledge of philosophical works include textual elements, for without some of these elements we might not be able to know them at all, or if we are, at least we might not be able to know them effectively. So although philosophical works do not in principle include these conditions among their conditions of identity, they can and often do include them among the conditions of their being known.

This looks fine at first sight, for it amounts to a distinction between a philosophical work and how we know it. But there is a difficulty. The philosophical work, as I have proposed, is the meaning of a certain text, and now we have found that in order to know the philosophical work, the text must include elements that are characteristic of literary rather than philosophical texts. Moreover, because every literary text expresses a literary work, it turns out that those philosophical works that require the inclusion of literary devices in their texts in order to be known entail the existence of literary works as well as texts.

Consider Descartes' *Discourse on Method*. If what has been said is correct, then in Descartes' *Discourse on Method* we have (1) a work of philosophy, (2) a text of philosophy, (3) a work of literature, and (4) a text of literature. This creates two problems, one of which is ontological. Now it appears that Descartes' *Discourse on Method* is two works and two texts rather than one work and one text. The other problem is epistemological: We cannot easily determine who is to separate them or how they are to be separated. In the face of these difficulties, why not give up the whole thing? Why not go with the postmodernists or the Platonists after all?

At least two responses can be given to the ontological difficulty. One, which I call the Two-Text/Two-Work Alternative, is that to say that Descartes' *Discourse on Method* is two works and two texts is not such a bad thing after all. The philosophical work is a certain meaning that does not include a text among its conditions of identity. The philosophical text is the text whose meaning the philosophical work is. The literary work is a certain meaning that includes a text among its conditions of identity. And the literary text is the text whose meaning the literary work is. Presumably, then, only the philosophical work is translatable; the literary one is not. This sounds a bit strange, but it does make sense to this extent: It allows us to maintain that there is something about the *Discourse on Method* that is translatable and something that is not. And this is, indeed, something that anyone familiar with the French text knows quite well. Moreover, it allows us to hold that what is translatable is the philosophy, whereas what is not is the literature. And this, again, makes sense in terms of our common intuitions and practices.

A second response, which I call the One-Text/One-Work Alternative, is that there are in fact only one work and one text in Descartes' *Discourse on Method*, for the literary textual devices required for the knowledge of the philosophical work are merely ancillary and do not form part of the identity conditions of a separate literary work. And, of course, if there is no literary work, there is no literary text. This ancillary relationship is similar to the relationship that exists between an English sentence written on a white paper and the color of the ink in which it is written. The color is black in order to make the sentence visible, but the color is not part of the sentence or its meaning.

This response has at least two advantages over the first: It is more economical and it solves the epistemological problem we raised. If there are not two works and two texts, then we need not devise a way of distinguishing them. All the same, even if we adopt this second alternative, we are still left with an epistemological problem, albeit a different one. For how can we tell when we have a philosophical work expressed by a philosophical text accompanied by literary devices, or a literary work and a literary text? That is, how can we tell when the literary devices are not essential to the work and when they are? The answer is that it is probably a matter of degree. There are some works that have so little relation to anything textual that clearly they are philosophical. This is the case of Suárez's *Metaphysical Disputations* and Kant's *Critique of Pure Reason*. At the other extreme there are some works that are so tightly related to their texts that clearly they are literary. This is the case of Shakespeare's *Hamlet* and St. John of the Cross' *Spiritual Canticle*. So what is accidental and what is essential in these? It does not really make sense that the ideas of a work such as Shakespeare's *Hamlet* are accidental, and only the textual elements are essential to the work. Moreover, there are many works that fall in between, and here it is not clear whether we have a philosophical work or a literary one. This is the case of Montaigne's *Essays* and Pascal's *Pensées*. Surely, this does not undermine the distinction we have drawn between the literary and the philosophical, just as the existence of gray does not undermine the distinction between black and white, although it does put into question the One-Text/One-Work Alternative.

What should we say about Borges's "Pierre Menard," then? Is it like Kant's *Critique of Pure Reason*, Shakespeare' *Hamlet*, or Montaigne's *Essays*? I tend to think it is more like Shakespeare's *Hamlet*, but this is not an incontestable conclusion. I am not absolutely certain of it. And if I am right, it turns out that there are two works "Pierre Menard," the literary, which we have, and the philosophical, which is implicit in, or part of, the literary. The first is the "Pierre Menard" that includes elements of its text as essential; the second is one concerned only about ideas and translatable. And we also have two texts: the literary, which corresponds to the literary work and that we have; and the philosophical, which is the text that expresses the philosophical work. The

philosophical work is implicit in the literary one, and therefore produced by
Borges, but the philosophical text is what readers interested in the philosophy in "Pierre Menard" construct.[40] But I am quite certain of at least two
things as a result of the foregoing reflections, and regardless of whether one
adopts the Two-Text/Two-Work Alternative or the One-Text/One-Work
Alternative: First, the uncertainty about the literary or philosophical nature
of "Pierre Menard" does not undermine the distinction between philosophical works and texts on the one hand and literary ones on the other. And
second, we need not reject the distinction between philosophy and literature
in order to make room in the philosophical canon for such works and texts as
Montaigne's *Essays* or Pascal's *Pensées*. [41]

Notes

1. A shorter, and in some important ways, different version of this essay appeared in
   The Journal of Aesthetics and Art Criticism 59, no. 1 (Winter 2001), pp. 45–57.
2. Quoted by Jack Diether, in "Notes to the Program," Carnegie Hall, Tuesday
   Evening, November 4, 1997, p. 19.
3. Still another view of this relation sees philosophy as sharing a method of knowledge with both literature and science. This is why it is not possible to distinguish
   philosophy from literature strictly speaking. See Christiane Schildknecht, "Entre
   la ciencia y la literatura: Formas literarias de la filosofía," trans. José M. González
   García, in *Figuras del logos: Entre la filosofía y la literatura*, ed., María Teresa López
   de la Vieja (Mexico City: Fondo de Cultura Económica, 1994), pp. 21–40.
4. José Luis Gómez Martínez, "Posmodernidad, discurso antrópico y ensayística latinoamericana. Entrevista," *Dissens, Revista Internacional de Pensamiento Latinoameri-
   cano* 2 (1996), pp. 46 and 45. In the Anglo-American world, similar views have
   been expressed by Richard Rorty and others. See Rorty, *Consequences of Pragmatism* (Hussocks, Sussex: Harvester, 1982), pp. 92–93, and the essay by Knight in
   this volume.
5. Gómez Martínez, p. 45; Pedro Lange-Churrión and Eduardo Mendieta, "Philosophy and Literature: The Latin American Case," *Dissens* 2 (1996), pp. 37–40.
6. Michel Foucault, "What Is an Author?" trans. Donald F. Bouchard and Sherry
   Simon, in *Language, Counter-Memory, Practice: Selected Essays and Interviews*, ed.
   Donald F. Bouchard (Ithaca, NY: Cornell University Press, 1977), pp. 113–138;
   and Gregory Currie, "Work and Text," *Mind* 100 (1991), pp. 325–339.
7. Keep in mind, then, that in this essay I am staying away from several other questions that are under discussion today concerning philosophy and literature. For
   example, I will not discuss issues concerned with the morality, value, or use of
   literature, or questions that have to do with the cognitive or noncognitive nature
   of the knowledge we derive from literary texts. These are issues that have received
   considerable attention recently. See, for example, Martha Nussbaum, *Love's
   Knowledge: Essays in Philosophy and Literature* (New York: Oxford University Press,
   1990).
8. For other uses, see the essays by Irwin and Knight in this volume.
9. For other attempts at distinguishing literary texts and works from philosophical
   ones, and at exploring the relations between philosophy and literature, see, for
   example, S. Halliwell, "Philosophy and Literature: Settling a Quarrel?" *Philosophical Investigations* 16, no. 1 (1993), pp. 6–16; George Dickie, *Art and the Aesthetic:
   An Institutional Analysis* (Ithaca, NY: Cornell University Press, 1974); Susan L.

Anderson, "Philosophy and Fiction," *Metaphilosophy* 23, no. 3 (1992), p. 207;
Peter Lamarque and Stein H. Olsen, *Truth, Fiction, and Literature: A Philosophical Perspective* (Oxford: Clarendon Press, 1994), chapters 15 and 16; Anthony Quinton, *The Divergence of the Twain: Poet's Philosophy and Philosopher's Philosophy* (Warwick: University of Warwick, 1985); Mark Edmundson, *Literature against Philosophy, Plato to Derrida: A Defense of Poetry* (Cambridge: Cambridge University Press, 1995); and the essay by Irwin in this volume.

10. For a discussion of other views, see Jorge J. E. Gracia, *A Theory of Textuality: The Logic and Epistemology* (Albany, NY: State University of New York Press, 1995), pp. 59–70.
11. Ibid., p. 4.
12. For some suggestions in this direction, see ibid., pp. 59–70.
13. "Same" applies to the type, not tokens, of course.
14. In the new translation by Andrew Hurley, in Jorge Luis Borges, *Collected Fictions* (New York: Penguin Books, 1999), p. 94.
15. Cf. Stephen Halliwell, "Philosophy and Literature: Settling a Quarrel?," pp. 7, 12, and 13.
16. Cf. Daniel Innerarity defends the fictional nature of literature in "La verdad de las mentiras: Reflexiones sobre filosofía y literatura," *Diálogo Filosófico* 24 (1992), pp. 367–380.
17. For the controversy, see J. R. Searle, "The Logical Status of Fictional Discourse," in *Expression and Meaning* (Cambridge: Cambridge University Press, 1979), pp. 58–75. For the basis of the noncognitive position, see G. Frege, "On Sense and Reference," in *Translations from the Philosophical Writings of Gottlob Frege*, ed. and trans. P. Geach and M. Black (Oxford: Blackwell, 1952). Opposing the noncognitivists is G. Gabriel, "Sobre el significado en la literatura y el valor cognitivo de la ficción," trans. María Teresa López de la Vieja, in *Figuras del logos*, ed. María Teresa López de la Vieja, pp. 57–68.
18. See Halliwell, "Philosophy and Literature: Settling a Quarrel?," pp. 7, 12, and 13, and Innerarity, "La verdad de las mentiras."
19. Innerarity, "La verdad de las mentiras."
20. See Halliwell, "Philosophy and Literature: Settling a Quarrel?," pp. 6, 7, and 15–16, and Susan L. Anderson, "Philosophy and Fiction," *Metaphilosophy* 23, no. 3 (1992), p. 207.
21. See Ermanno Bencivenga's essay in this volume. Note that his position is complex and involves the notion of liberation as well.
22. For a defense of the institutional view of art in general, see George Dickie, *Art and the Aesthetic: An Institutional Analysis* (Ithaca, NY: Cornell University Press, 1974).
23. Most recently in Anderson, "Philosophy and Fiction," p. 207.
24. Cf. Halliwell, "Philosophy and Literature," pp. 6, 7, and 15–16. The position that philosophy is about universals and not about individuals goes back at least to Aristotle and the conception of science he presented in *Posterior Analytics* I.
25. For various ways in which fiction is used in philosophy, see Anderson, "Philosophy and Fiction," pp. 204–207.
26. Carolyn Korsmeyer and Lois Parkinson-Zamora suggested to me that perhaps it would be better to speak of paraphrase rather than translation here. The suggestion is intriguing, but I am not convinced it works. My point is that there are things we call translations of literary works, but they are not strictly speaking translations, but rather more or less close approximations. Translations of literary works are works different from the originals that share some of the same properties of the originals. And their authors are the translators, not the original authors. Thus the author of the English translation of the *Coplas por la muerte de su padre* of

Jorge Manrique is Henry Wadsworth Longfellow, not Manrique, even though Longfellow tried very hard to duplicate the work of Manrique.

27. Cf. Hans-Georg Gadamer, "Plato and the Poets," in *Dialogue and Dialectic: Eight Hermeneutical Studies in Plato*, trans. P. Christopher Smith (New Haven, CT: Yale University Press, 1980), p. 46 ff., and "Goethe and Philosophy," in *Literature and Philosophy in Dialogue: Essays in German Literary Theory*, trans. Robert H. Paslick (Albany, NY: State University of New York Press, 1994), pp. 18–19.

28. Cf. Renford Bambrough, "Literature and Philosophy," in *Wisdom: Twelve Essays*, ed. Renford Bambrough (Oxford: Blackwell, 1974), pp. 274–292.

29. Cf. E. D. Hirsch, Jr., "Objective Interpretation," *PMLA* 75 (1960), pp. 463–479, and *Validity in Interpretation* (New Haven, CT: Yale University Press, 1967), p. 62; also Gracia, *A Theory of Textuality*, pp. 18–19.

30. This has led some philosophers, such as Deleuze, to claim that it is in the nature of philosophy to create concepts. See his "The Conditions of the Question: What Is Philosophy?" *Critical Inquiry* 17 (1981), pp. 471–473.

31. Arthur C. Danto, "Philosophy as/and/of Literature," in *Literature and the Question of Philosophy*, ed. Anthony Cascardi (Baltimore, MD: The Johns Hopkins University Press, 1987), p. 7. Danto goes too far, however, when he argues that literature, in contrast with philosophy, is a kind of mirror, and finds its subject only when it is read (p. 19). First, it is not just literary texts that require an audience, all texts do; second, that texts require an audience does not mean that they are about the audience. For my discussion of these issues, see Jorge J. E. Gracia, *Texts: Ontological Status, Identity, Author Audience* (Albany, NY: State University of New York Press, 1996), chapter 4.

32. A point made by Borges in "Pierre Menard," p. 94 in the translation cited earlier.

33. Indeed, some argue that it is precisely the opposition to style that distinguishes philosophy from literature. Cf. Dalia Judovitz, "Philosophy and Poetry: The Difference between Them in Plato and Descartes," in *Literature and the Question of Philosophy*, ed. Anthony J. Cascardi (Baltimore, MD: The Johns Hopkins University Press, 1987), pp. 24–51.

34. Plato, *Phaedrus* 276–277a.

35. Some have gone so far as to argue not only that philosophy has style, but that its style and that of literature are similar. Cf. Tom Conley, "A Trace of Style," in *Displacement: Derrida and After*, ed. Mark Krupnick (Bloomington: Indiana University Press, 1983), p. 79.

36. I am using the following edition and translation: "Pierre Menard, Autor del *Quijote*," in *Prosa completa* (Barcelona: Bruguera, 1980), vol. 1, pp. 425–433; "Pierre Menard, Author of the *Quixote*," in *Labyrinths: Selected Stories and Other Writings*, eds. Donald Yates and James E. Irby (New York: New Directions Books, 1964), pp. 36–44. I use this older translation for this analysis because it is the most widely available. The terms emphasized in the translation were also emphasized in the Spanish original.

37. Plato, *Republic* 601a–b. Some literary people agree to the extent that they believe literature is not about ideas. Recent textualists accept this, but the position goes back to much earlier times. Danto quotes a text from Flaubert to this effect (Danto, "Philosophy as/and/of Literature," p. 13).

38. Note that this does not imply a disagreement with Nussbaum's view that "if the writing is well done"—and I think this applies to both literature and philosophy— "a paraphrase in every different form and style will not, in general, express the same conception." See Nussbaum, *Love's Knowledge*, p. 3.

39. The role of use and practice in this context is discussed by Lamarque and Olsen, *Truth, Fiction, and Literature*, particularly chapters 2, 10, and 17. See also my defense of cultural function as determining textual meaning in Gracia, *A Theory of Textuality*, chapter 4.

40. Henry Sussman raised the intriguing question, which I cannot take up here, of the status of the philosophical work in literary works: Are they works as such, or are they fragments?

41. I would like to express my appreciation to the audience present at a session of the Capen Symposium where I read a version of this essay for their questions and objections. I am particularly grateful to William Eggington, Peter Hare, Anthony Cascardi, Henry Sussman, Carolyn Korsmeyer, Lois Parkinson Zamora, and Rosemary Feal.

6

ANTHONY J. CASCARDI

Mimesis and Modernism:
The Case of Jorge Luis Borges

For Sylvia Molloy

> "Ignoro si la música sabe desesperar de la música y si el mármol del mármol, pero la literatura es un arte que sabe profetizar aquel tiempo en que habrá enmudecido, y escarnizarse con la propia virtud y enamorarse de la propia disolución y cortejar su fin."[1]
>
> ("I do not know whether music can give up hope in music, or marble in marble, but literature is an art that is able to foresee the moment when it will have grown silent, to scorn its own virtue, to become enamored with its own dissolution and to court its own death.")

> "It is self-evident that nothing concerning art is self-evident anymore, not its inner life, not its relation to the world, not even its right to exist."[2]

During the years that have followed the publication of John Barth's provocative essay "The Literature of Exhaustion," the reading public has come to accept the fact that the writings of certain late and postmodernist authors—Borges, Calvino, and Eco among them—could not be measured by the same yardsticks of creative "originality" that served their romantic predecessors so well.[3] This may have come as no surprise, as it was modernist practice itself that helped solidify the critique of romantic ideals. What greater challenge to the desires that supported romantic creativity than the deflationary gestures of minimalism, irony, parody, and pastiche? What is surprising is that so many "high modernist" writers continued to make a large investment in the principle of artistic innovation. Indeed, a central imperative of high modernist art was to "make it new." But just how to "make it new" was a very difficult question, given the realities of literary history and social circumstances. Nonetheless, the task could not be set aside by the heirs to the high modernist tradition. And so among many such writers, and Borges most prominently for my concerns, the great modernist call to innovation had to be answered in the face of some very sobering facts: that in the literary past everything seemed already to have been said, done, thought, and even felt; and that the social circumstances in which literature was produced seemed to deprive it of the very powers to which it once laid claim—if not to conjure a world, as the quasi-magical incantations of poetry might once have been thought capable of doing, then at least to transform the world, and especially to undertake a transformation of the social world: to act as a shaping force rather than simply as one among the many conditioned elements of a reality whose motor springs lie outside of our control. If the history of art in the culture of modernity corresponds to the gradual erasure of what Walter Benjamin famously called the "aura," then modernism took one of its challenges to be a search for whatever factors might be able to establish the artwork's irreducible difference in a world that seemed to have grown indifferent to its very existence. To be sure, the dissolution of "aura" might well seem to consign art to the role of the mere repetition of the *déjà dit*, or to relegate art to nostalgic glances at the past. And yet this is not necessarily the case. By thinking of the artwork's particular difference as a matter of inflection within a world seemingly bereft of originality or aura, I hope to draw the discussion of Borges away from the tendency to regard his works as the repetition of familiar philosophical problems, such as the "problem of fictional worlds," the ontology of texts, or the question of personal identity, interesting and important though those questions may be.[4] My more constructive hope is to identify the particular modes of inflection that allow Borges to imagine and articulate difference within historical conditions that might well be called the "age of mimesis as mechanical reproduction."

Although we may credit modernism with having brought such issues to the foreground, some of the news about the modernist predicament is not in fact all that new. It is part of a received tradition of literary and philosophical thinking about the status of art in the modern world. Already in the nineteenth century Hegel's *Lectures on Aesthetics* confronted something like the problem of the "end of art." And yet when Hegel proclaimed that art had become "a thing of the past" he was not necessarily prophesying a future in which no new artworks would be ever produced. Nor was he envisioning that art would be confined to a secondary or peripheral role within the spectrum of human culture. Rather he was suggesting that art could serve a reflective function—that it could afford the chance for us to recall how sensuous forms could (and once did) play a role in the shaping and disclosure of the truth.[5] To understand the reflective function of art in this way is to recognize the very conditions of art's situation in the modern world, as standing at a distance from, but nonetheless as remembering, such powers. To bring this reflexivity to full self-consciousness, to claim the recollection of the loss of aura as art's most authentic mode of consciousness while nonetheless forging ahead with some version of art, was one of modernism's principal achievements. Indeed, it would have been just as false for art to forget its world-making powers as it would have been for it to think that it could ever reclaim their full force. Flaubert knew one side of this problem quite well—the side that leads to a resigned skepticism, if not to a full-blown cynicism, about modern art's apparent inability to escape the cycle of repetition to which it seemed to be consigned. Witness the story of Bouvard and Pécuchet, the summary account of which I draw from an essay on Flaubert written by Borges himself ("Vindicación de Bouvard et Pécuchet"). Two copyists, bordering on the age of fifty, develop a close friendship. An inheritance allows them to leave their regular jobs and take up residence in the country-side. There, they try out gardening, archaeology, hydrotherapy, veterinary medicine, history, philosophy, politics, and religion; in short, they explore the full array of the arts and sciences known to man, hoping in each case to find satisfaction. Yet each of these endeavors individually, and all of them together, leave them unfulfilled and so, after twenty years of trying, they decide to return to their "old" jobs as copyists. The return to copying is a repetition of their past, but it is also a return to writing as a means of mechanical reproduction and as a repetition of what "literature" once was as it was practiced by scribes and clerks.[6]

To be sure, Hegel was quite a bit more optimistic and "progressive" in his thinking, and quite a bit less cynical in his overall vision than Flaubert.[7] This is largely because Hegel maintained that the "exhaustion" of one mode of spirit's self-expression in the world—art—would eventually lead it to another, higher, form: to a full flowering of philosophical ideas. Which leads me all but directly to Borges. If Borges's fiction can be taken as a provocative model for thinking about mimesis and repetition in the context of modernity, this is in part because Borges seems to accept the possibilities marked out by Hegel and Flaubert while giving both yet another turn of the screw. On the one hand, Borges's fictions seem to veer away from literature as such to critical and philosophical reflections about it, for all intents and purposes certifying the exhaustion of the kind of original creativity that would meet "romantic" ideals. Indeed, some of Borges's most important works seem to forsake the desire to imagine a world, choosing instead to limn the possibility of alternative worlds in concept and thought. The Borgesian imagination often yields to discursive ruminations on issues such as the nature of time and space, the question of causality, and the problem of personal identity. But we should not be too quick to say *either* that Borges forsakes the world-making ambitions of imaginative literature for the speculations of philosophy, *or* that he leads us to a place where the distinctions between literature and philosophy can be declared null and void. After all, Borges couches his fictions in familiar literary genres (the detective story, the mock-essay), and some of his most interesting and important works are engagements of literature's central concerns: the nature of authorship and originality, the power of reading and criticism as modes of engagement of the past, and the problem of fictional worlds. Moreover, there is throughout Borges's texts the commitment to a distinctive verbal inflection of ideas that marks them as irreducible to whatever notional content they may convey. Indeed, to regard Borges as a philosopher *manqué* is to overlook the excess of language and feeling over what mere thought would require. Likewise, to see Borges as a writer who has resigned himself to a vision of mimesis as the endless repetition of the same is to miss his sustained fascination with fabulation even while he thinks about the limits of fiction making, or to ignore his efforts to speak in a distinctive voice even in the face of worries that authoring is at bottom nothing more than a vehicle for the "mechanical reproduction" of ideas. Rather than confine this discussion to the question of literature and its exhaustion, or its possible supersession by philosophy, it may be more insightful to frame those issues in terms of the larger question of mimesis and/as repetition that shapes the modernist predicament. Doing so may allow us better to respond to the self-reflective qualities of a body of work that took shape at a historical moment when literature's continued existence as an autonomous discourse seemed to be in doubt.

One of Borges's most often-cited texts, "Pierre Menard, Author of the *Quixote*," raises these questions incisively. Pierre Menard, a relatively minor French author, dedicates his efforts to what Borges describes as "repeating a pre-existing book in a foreign language" ("repetir en un idioma ajeno un libro preexistente"). Menard rewrites Cervantes' text exactly and completely. But although Menard's *Quixote* is "verbally identical" to Cervantes' novel it is also said to be "richer" and "more subtle." How is this possible? In essays in the present volume, Deborah Knight and William Irwin treat this question as an instance of the problem of indiscernibles and the ontology of texts: if texts are identical in their constitution then are they the same?[8] But the problem of Menard's *Quixote* in relation to Cervantes' is that they are at once identical and different. That is why my attention is drawn to what the question of indiscernibles leaves out. What is it that an understanding of mimesis as repetition fails to take into account? Borges's "Pierre Menard" raises a question that is at once a philosophical puzzle and a modernist predicament: how to account for the kind of difference that literature can make when art seems obliged simply to repeat the past.[9] One prong of an answer seems clear enough: to bring the limits of mimesis to consciousness, to make those limits explicit in discourse and in practice, is already to shift the terms of discourse and to add something "new" to what has already been said. Menard's *Quixote* is just as much *like* Cervantes' "original" as it is *un*like it, and Borges's text is of course identical to neither one: "The Cervantes text and the Menard text are verbally identical, but the second is almost infinitely richer. (More *ambiguous*, his detractors say—but ambiguity is richness)."[10] The result—wherein two apparently identical passages are reproduced within Borges's text—may well involve a form of "repetition," but Borges's commentary renders the conventional literary distinction between "original" and "copy" of relatively little use in describing it.

"Pierre Menard" addresses the questions of identity and difference with all the literary self-consciousness characteristic of modernist texts. To that "literary" self-consciousness Borges adds a philosophical spin that becomes further apparent in other texts. Consider "Funes, El Memorioso" as a case in point. For Ireneo Funes (the character with the prodigious memory who is the subject of the story), memory is a form of cognition that requires a full and complete correspondence with the world. It is also a form of mimesis, by which Funes repeats the world not just in conceptual or verbal terms, but sensuously and materially. He grasps the world by means of an internal mimesis that reproduces it in minute physiological detail rather than merely in concept or outline. In Funes's mind "every visual image was linked to muscular sensations, thermal sensations, and so on."[11] Moreover, his reconstruction of the world in memory is conceived to be complete. It leaves no gaps: "He was able to reconstruct every dream, every daydream he had ever had. Two or three times he had reconstructed an entire day; he had never once erred or faltered, but each reconstruction had itself taken an entire day." He is said to have remarked: "*I, myself, alone, have more memories than all mankind since the world began.*"[12] Memory is a talent that grants Funes enormous power, and yet it immobilizes him. Funes is godlike "as monumental as bronze—older than Egypt, older than the prophecies and the pyramids"[13]— but he is also a vanishing and ghostlike figure, as impotent as he is powerful. His memory is at once excessive and inadequate. Its contents are wholly unfiltered (he himself describes it as "like a garbage heap" ("*como un vaciadero de basuras*"), and its structure renders him "incapable of general, platonic ideas" ("*incapaz de ideas generales, platónicas,*" *F,* p. 125). This mimesis of the world in memory treats everything as different and new and so undermines the very criteria by which what is "new" might be distinguished from what is familiar and old. Little wonder, then, that there is scant room for Funes' own identity to take root: he remains unable to establish continuity with himself over time ("his own face in the mirror, his own hands, would surprise him each time anew"[14]). And so, at the age of only twenty-one, Funes dies what might best be described as a minor death, having suffered first from insomnia and then from a pulmonary infection.[15] There is a certain pathos in this detail that does not escape the narrator's notice. It is worthy of further remark because of the affinity between Funes's burdensome memory and the "memorial" work of narrative itself. Indeed, the narrator insists on this conjuncture from the very beginning of the text:

> I recall him (though I have no right to speak that sacred verb—only one man
> on earth did, and that man is dead) holding a dark passionflower in his

hand. . . . I recall him—his taciturn face, its Indian features, its extraordinary
remoteness—behind the cigarette. I recall (I think) the slender, leather-
braider's fingers. I recall near those hands a *mate* cup, with the coat of arms of
the Banda Oriental. . . . I clearly recall his voice. . . . My first recollection of
Funes is quite clear. (*CF*, p. 131)

Lo recuerdo (yo no tengo derecho a pronunciar ese verbo sagrado, sólo un
hombre en la tierra tuvo derecho y ese hombre ha muerto) con una oscura
pasionaria en la mano, ... Lo recuerdo, la cara taciturna y aindiada y singu-
larmente *remota*, detrás del cigarillo. Recuerdo (creo) sus manos afiladas de
trenzador. Recuerdo cerca de esas manos un mate, con las armas de la Banda
Oriental; . . . . Recuerdo claramente su voz. . . . Mi primer recuerdo de Funes
es muy perspicuo. (*F*, p. 118)

If we were to follow some of the dominant directions in contemporary
literary theory we might attempt to explain the erasure of personal identity,
or the recursive structure of certain of Borges's texts, as socially embedded
and conditioned. That Borges seems almost studiously to refuse to acknowledge the weight of the social world might serve simply to increase suspicions
about its importance. And at some level we do indeed want to know what
kind of a world might have provoked such careful avoidance on Borges's part,
what material conditions of existence his fictions might have sought to refuse
by wandering off into the maze of ideas. If there is indeed a historical transformation in the nature of mimesis that corresponds to what Benjamin
described as the "loss of aura," then we might well want to know the circumstances surrounding Borges's case.

There are compelling reasons to link Borgesian "fabulation" to certain
social forms of rationalization, including some that can be tied to the role of
the avant garde in the globalization of culture. Indeed, Borges saw himself
not only as a modernist writer but also as a cosmopolitan man of letters able
to "transcend" local and national culture. This is at least one way to explain
the range of his literary and philosophical interests, which embrace Homer,
the presocratic thinkers, Shakespeare, the Icelandic sagas, the poetry of
Quevedo, and the Jewish Cabala. Borges's philosophical preoccupations are
likewise played out in universal terms; themes like the cyclical nature of time
and the eternal return of the same are designed to defy the limits of history
and place. And yet Borges's "cosmopolitanism" is laden with details drawn
specifically from the Río de la Plata. The final story of Borges's most famous
collection, *Ficciones*, is set in Buenos Aires in 1871; "El Aleph" takes place in
the house of one Carlos Argentino Daneri on the Calle Garay; the back alleys
and knife fights of Buenos Aires form the fabric of "Hombre de la esquina
rosada," published in the *Universal History of Infamy*. Funes himself appears
to be of creole blood.[16]

More important, any approach to Borges's works that appeals strictly to the pressures of commodity capitalism, the conditions of bureaucratic organization, or the globalization of culture in the twentieth century flies in the face of what I take to be certain essential Borgesian insights about the ability of literature to exceed the bounds of socially encoded and enforced forms of rationality.[17] To be sure, stories such as "The Lottery in Babylon" or "The Library of Babel" acknowledge the conditions of rationalization and reification that prevail in modern bureaucracies. Those texts are all but unintelligible unless regarded as reflections of the systematic imposition of organizational controls. But seen only in such terms it would be impossible to account for the moments in which the systems they describe draw attention to their own flaws; likewise it would be difficult to give an account of the distinctive pathos and irony that color the narrator's voice at crucial moments in their development. "Like all the men of Babylon," writes Borges in "The Lottery in Babylon," "I have been proconsul; like all, I have been a slave. I have known omnipotence, ignominy, imprisonment. Look here—my right hand has no index finger. Look here—through this gash in my cape you can see on my stomach a crimson tattoo."[18] Is this one of those characteristic instances in Borges's works where the uniqueness of personal identity seems to be lost in the wake of repetition? Perhaps. Remember Herbert Ashe, a figure mentioned in "Tlön, Uqbar, Orbis Tertius," whose very name bespeaks his anonymity ("in life, Ashe was afflicted with unreality, as so many Englishmen are; in death, he is not even the ghost he was in life").[19] Ashe is said to resemble all Englishmen, just as the narrator of "The Lottery in Babylon" is said to be all men. Such figures are nearly lost in sameness, and yet in each case there are certain distinguishing marks (in the case of the narrator of "Lottery in Babylon" the missing finger and the tatoo), and each is presented with the force of the new; each one impresses itself upon consciousness through the subtle insistence of the narrator's voice: not only "look" but also "look again." And so there is still wonder in this world of repetition and sameness, even if this is a diminutive wonder that derives from repetition itself.

As far as the lottery itself is concerned, this dubious institution appears to give us a world in which the dutiful fulfillment of administrative obligations rules out the possibility either of establishing meaningful differences or of identifying any deep, structural coherence lying beneath them. We are in a social structure that marries the conditions of Pierre Menard (the repetition of identity) to that of Funes (the proliferation of difference). Behind the ostensible perfection of the lottery's administrative rationality is said to lie mere chance. Stray matter and unpredictable events foil its administrative efficiency. In one instance, the narrator notes that "the purchasor of a dozen amphorae of Damascene wine will not be surprised if one contains a talisman, or a viper."[20] And yet it seems that such flaws serve a positive and constructive goal: by defeating the semblance of a perfect order, they help secure the reality of the real. There is, it seems, a crack in the otherwise sealed system, a flaw in the social structure of repetition for which we might in the end be grateful. Borges continues: "the scribe who writes out a contract never fails to include some error; I myself, in this hurried statement, have misrepresented some splendor, some atrocity—perhaps, too, some mysterious monotony."[21]

I take this passage and others like it as evidence of a peculiarly Borgesian way of marking difference through a process of self-reflection that asks us to go beyond the claim that modernist literature is condemned to practice mimesis as mere repetition. On such occasions, the articulation of the significant difference that "makes it new" comes about through what Adorno might call the process of a "second reflection" on the place of mimesis within a socially conditioned framework of repetition. In contrast to mere repetition, "second reflection" allows the work of art to reassert its claim to be something more or other than a mimesis of the world, in part by reflecting on the impossibility of it ever being a full and complete mimesis of the world. "Second reflection" grants art its autonomy; it acknowledges the status of art as not just as *like* the world it resembles but as definitively *unlike* it. There is a passage from Novalis that Borges cites in the essay "Avatars of the Tortoise" that makes the point in a compelling way—by suggesting that the *imperfections* in the work of artistic "creation" ensure the artwork's claim to truth: "The greatest wizard would be the one who could bewitch himself to the point of taking his own phantasmagorical creations as autonomous apparitions. Would that not be our case? I conjecture that it is so. We (that is, the undivided divinity that is at work in us) have dreamed a world. We have dreamed it resistant, mysterious, visible, ubiquitous in space and fixed in time; *but we have consented to the presence of tenuous and eternal interstices of irrationality in its architecture in order to know that it is false.*"[22] This admission is the paradoxical key to a discovery of the artwork's claim to truth. The "flaws" that prove it false, like the extraneous elements that intervene in the perfectly administered society, are imperfections that suggest how art remembers what it was like to *be* a world, and not just to *be like* the world.

ADORNO: "Art is actually the world once over, as like it as it is unlike it."[23]

BORGES: "Mirrors and copulation are abominable, for they multiply the number of mankind."[24]

Borges is himself so subtle and compelling on such points that rather than turn further to someone like Adorno or Benjamin for elucidation of the relations of mimesis, repetition, and difference, I want to proceed by reconstructing what I think of as the archaeology of their relations using some of

Borges's own texts for the purpose. Said in other terms, I think that Borges himself provides models for the process out of which his distinctive mode of fiction-making emerges. This is, admittedly, a speculative or mythopoetic account that involves a reflection upon origins—speculative because such origins are accessible only through the powers of memory and desire, as the counterfactual, fictional, or "fantastic" image of conditions that would be ungraspable in a more disenchanted world. But it is nonetheless a Borgesian account, and so consistent with the material under scrutiny. It begins from Borges's interest in certain archaic forms of mimesis that are related to what I call "fabulation" and it proceeds from there to include various forms of reflection—both literary and philosophical—on the fate of art as both *like* the world and categorically *unlike* it. It leads to some of the distinctively Borgesian ways of marking the transformation from mimesis to repetition and then of articulating difference within repetition, of which we have already seen some examples.

Fabulation: this Borgesian version of what Horkheimer and Adorno in *Dialectic of Enlightenment* speculatively called the moment of "myth" provides a point of reference for the reconstruction of what Benjamin described as the power of the "mimetic faculty" in art. Unlike certain forms of philosophy, which give us notional worlds, fabulation is mimetic in the more archaic and potentially powerful sense. It works by nonsensuous similarities rather than by conceptual representations. Unlike other forms of world- or image-making (architecture and building, for example), or creature-fashioning (the kind involving sex and childbirth), fabulation dreams of creation at a safe and clean distance, without sweat or labor; it would proceed purely, exactly, and absolutely. Correspondence and sympathy are its archaic modes, a familiarity with which Borges draws from James Frazer's *Golden Bough*, although it could just as well have been from Benjamin's essay "On the Mimetic Faculty."[25] For instance, Borges suggests that sympathy "postulates an unavoidable link between different things, either because its figure is the same—imitative magic, homeopathy—or because of some previous contiguity—contagious magic. An illustration of the second was the curative ointment of Kenelm Digby, which was applied not to the bandaged wound, but rather to the guilty steel that inflicted it—while the wound, without the rigor of barbarous cures, was forming a scar. . . . The redskin Indians of Nebraska dressed up in bison skins . . . and danced wildly on the desert day and night to make the bison arrive."[26] Mimesis in this archaic form has the power to establish connections remotely, as in certain instances of superstition and magic: "For the superstitious person, there is a necessary connection not just between a bullet and a dead person, but between a dead person and a tortured effigy of wax or the prophetic breaking of a mirror or the salt that one throws over the shoulder."[27] The subtlety of Borges's development of this point—easily the match for anything that Horkheimer and Adorno or Benjamin might have to say—lies in his ability to identify the rational kernel of causality in magic just as well as he locates the kernel of magic within the seemingly rational relations of the causal world: "Magic is the crowning moment or the nightmare of causality," he writes, "not its contradiction. Miracles are no less alien in that universe than in the work of astronomers. All the laws of nature govern it, as well as other, imaginary laws."[28] The coherence of a novel also recalls the sympathetic correspondences of the archaic world: "The worry that a fearful event may be caused by its mere mention is impertinent or useless in the asiatic disorder of the real world, but not in the novel, which must be an exact play of vigilances, echoes, and affinities. Every episode in a carefully crafted story is a projection from outside."[29]

Among the most powerful accounts of the mimetic origins of fiction in Borges is the dream-like mode of creation imagined in "The Circular Ruins." In this text, Borges imagines that a dreamer sets out to fashion a person, a purpose characterized as "not impossible, though supernatural." His hope is for creation by means of a complete and total mimesis. He proposes to create a set of correspondences that would be full and exact, "to dream a man . . . in minute entirety and impose him on reality."[30] But here the labor of making real involves arduous work: "This magical objective had come to fill his entire soul; if someone had asked him his own name, or inquired into any feature of his life till then, he would not have been able to answer." "He understood that the task of molding the incoherent and dizzying stuff that dreams are made of is the most difficult work a man can undertake, even if he fathom all the enigmas of the higher and lower spheres—much more difficult than weaving a rope of sand or minting coins of the faceless wind."[31]

Borges's fable of creation proceeds in detail, and the contours of narrative itself mime the meticulous labor required for it. The dream is nonplatonic in some crucial ways. Borges tells of the fabrication not just of a structure that would serve as a template for further production or repetition, but of the creation of the specific, differentiated, irreducibly particular being—the creation not just of "Being" as such, but of *this* being, of a being whose concrete particularities and points of difference from Being as such attest to the authenticity of its creator's powers:

> He dreamed the heart warm, active, secret—about the size of a closed fist, a garnet-colored thing inside the dimness of a human body that was still faceless and sexless; he dreamed it, with painstaking love, for fourteen brilliant nights. Each night he perceived it with greater clarity, greater certainty. He did not touch it; he only witnessed it, observed it, corrected it, perhaps, with his eyes. He perceived it, he *lived* it, from many angles, many distances. On the fourteenth night, he stroked the pulmonary artery with his forefinger, and then the entire heart, inside and out. And his inspection made him

proud. He deliberately did not sleep the next night; then he took up the heart again, invoked the name of a planet, and set about dreaming another of the major organs. Before the year was out he had reached the skeleton, the eyelids. The countless hairs of the body were perhaps the most difficult task. The man had dreamed a fully fleshed man—a stripling—but this youth did not stand up or speak, nor could it open its eyes. Night after night, the man dreamed the youth asleep. (*CF*, p. 98)

Lo soñó activo, caluroso, secreto, del grandor de un puño cerrado, color granate en la penumbra de un cuerpo humano aun sin cara ni sexo; con minucioso amor lo soñó, durante catorce lúcidas noches. Cada noche, lo percibía con mayor evidencia. No lo tocaba: se limitaba a atestiguarlo, a observarlo, tal vez a corregirlo con la mirada. Lo percibía, lo vivía, desde muchas distancias y muchos ángulos. La noche catorcena rozó la arteria pulmonar con el índice y luego todo el corazón, invocó el nombre de un planeta y emprendió la visión de otro de los órganos principales. Antes de un año llegó al esqueleto, a los párpados. El pelo innumerable fué tal vez la tarea más difícil. Soñó un hombre íntegro, un mancebo, pero éste no se incorporaba ni hablaba ni podía abrir los ojos. Noche tras noche, el hombre lo soñaba dormido. (*F*, pp. 62–63)

The narrator continues:

Under the pretext of pedagogical necessity, he drew out the hours of sleep more every day. He also redid the right shoulder (which was perhaps defective). . . . His days were, in general, happy; when he closed his eyes, he would think *Now I will be with my son*. Or less frequently, *The son I have engendered is waiting for me, and he will not exist if I do not go to him.* Gradually, the man accustomed the youth to reality. Once he ordered him to set a flag on a distant mountaintop. The next day, the flag crackled on the summit. He attempted other, similar experiments—each more daring than the last. He saw with some bitterness that his son was ready—perhaps even impatient— to be born. That night he kissed him for the first time, then sent him off, through many leagues of impenetrable jungle, many leagues of swamp, to that other temple whose ruins bleached in the sun downstream. But first (so that the son would never know that he was a phantasm, so that he would believe himself to be a man like other men) the man infused in him a total lack of memory of his years of education. (*CF*, pp. 99–100)

Con el pretexto de la necesidad pedagógica, dilataba cada día las horas dedicadas al sueño. También rehizo el hombro derecho, acaso deficiente. . . En general, sus días eran felices; al cerrar los ojos pensaba: *Ahora estaré con mi hijo*. O, más raramente: *El hijo que he engendrado me espera y no existirá si no voy.* Gradualmente, lo fué acostumbrando a la realidad. Una vez le ordenó que embanderara una cumbre lejana. Al otro día, flameaba la bandera en la cumbre. Ensayó otros experimentos análogos, cada vez más audaces. Comprendió con cierta amargura que su hijo estaba listo para nacer—y tal vez impaciente. Esa noche lo besó por primera vez y lo envió al otro templo cuyos despojos blanquean río abajo, a muchas leguas de inextricable selva y de ciénaga. Antes (para que no supiera nunca que era un fantasma, para que se creyera un hombre como los otros) le infundió el olvido total de sus años de aprendizaje. (*F*, p. 64)

There is more than just a trace of the Promethean desire to appropriate cosmic creative energies in a passage such as this. But there is also a purposeful weakness in the Borgesian version of creation, a flaw in the mimetic pattern that in turn confers a semblance of consciousness upon it. It seems that Borges's dreamer cannot himself endure the complete repression of origins that he imagines or wishes for his creature. The dreamer may well be able to conceal the contingency of existence from his creature, but he cannot repress the fact that his own existence may be feigned. He is himself rather stunned and humiliated by this possibility: "To be not a man, but the projection of another man's dream—what incomparable humiliation, what vertigo! Every parent feels concern for the children he has procreated (or allowed to be procreated) in happiness or in mere confusion" (*CF*, p. 100). "With relief, with humiliation, with terror, he realized that he, too, was but appearance, that another man was dreaming him" (*CF*, p. 100).[32] With this admission comes the awareness that mimesis has an edge or a fold at the very core of its creation. (Think of all the seam-like scars that mark the body of the monster in the 1994 Kenneth Branagh film, *Mary Shelley's Frankenstein.*) With it, Borges opens the door to a panoply of further reflections on the problem of mimesis and/as repetition.[33]

Always, the question "why" is prominent in Borges's thinking: not just why such resemblances should be imperfect, but why the conditions giving rise to them should affect us so. In a text entitled "Partial Enchantments of the *Quixote*," published in *Otras inquisiciones*, Borges asks: "Why does it make us uneasy to know that the map is within the map and the thousand and one nights within the book of *A Thousand and One Nights*?" And also "Why does it disquiet us to know that Don Quixote is a reader of the *Quixote*, and Hamlet is a spectator of *Hamlet*?" He offers a speculative response that most readers would recognize as the source of a constant preoccupation in his texts: such inversions suggest that if the characters in a story can be readers or spectators, then we, their readers or spectators, may likewise be fictitious.

Borges shares Nietzsche's suspicion that "philosophy" may have its origins not in wonder but in anxiety, in the desire to quiet the fear that comes from this abandonment of reality's metaphysical grounds. And because Borges also shares the view that there may be no final quieting of this anxiety, no reducing the basic contingency of the world, he is inclined to regard philosophical discourse as a series of puzzles to be enjoyed, in their multifarious versions and inversions, rather than as presenting definitive solutions to problems. Indeed, what often is recognized as "philosophy" within Borges's texts frequently takes the form of "baroque" reflections on the embedding of worlds within worlds, or the doubling of the self. Philosophy in this "baroque" guise revels in the enigma. It takes an intellectual, bookish, even literary delight in the paradox. Here we think of such Borges texts as "New Refutation of Time," "Avatars of the Tortoise," or "The Next-to-Last Version of Reality." In "An Examination of the Work of Herbert Quain" Borges comments on a book purportedly entitled *April March*. It is said to have all the features of games—among them "symmetry, arbitrary rules, tedium."[34] As yet another kind of game, philosophy helps relieve the boredom of a world ruled by repetition. A short passage from the important and elaborate story "Tlön, Uqbar, Orbis Tertius" captures the point especially well: "The fact that every philosophy is by definition a dialectical game, a *Philosophie des Als Ob*, has allowed them to proliferate. There are systems upon systems that are incredible but possessed of a pleasing architecture or a certain agreeable sensationalism. The metaphysicians of Tlön seek not truth, or even plausibility—they seek to amaze, astound. In their view, metaphysics is a branch of the literature of fantasy."[35] Why? The answer lies in the suggestion that the world may itself be the product of an aberrant mimesis. "Tlön, Uqbar, Orbis Tertius" attributes the origins of a fantastical world, Uqbar, to "the conjunction of a mirror and an encyclopedia" (*CF*, p. 68). The encyclopedic Enlightenment project may be every bit as exhausted in Borges as it is in Flaubert, and yet here it becomes the source of a new productivity. The terror it produces is worthy of special remark ("mirrors and copulation are abominable").

In the "mimetic" universe of doubled worlds, the heated debates among philosophers, all ostensibly in search of some final truth, become rather like rhetorical "points" in a process of argumentation that never ceases to unfold, ultimately substituting its discursive folds for the world it attempts to fathom.[36] We think of Borges's observation that in the land of Tlön "century upon century of idealism could hardly have failed to influence reality."[37] As for Uqbar, it is a place where entire schools of thought collide and conflict, although always inconclusively. One school of thought denies time whereas another declares that everything has already taken place and that our lives are but repetitions of the past; some theorists propose that the history of the universe was written by a demiurge, whose secret script we must seek to decipher, whereas others gesture toward a different secret: that each person's existence is doubled by someone living on the other side of the earth. Moreover, it turns out that the very text containing these seemingly irreconcilable, "baroque" speculations is enfolded within yet another text; what we are reading is eventually disclosed to be the citation—the repetition in writing— of an essay supposedly drawn from a forty-volume work entitled *Anthology of Fantastic Literature.*

Borges remains fully aware that the modernist engagement with mimesis as repetition poses special problems for narrative. To recognize that the world may be the product of a prior mimesis is to acknowledge its indifference to human action, and yet to engage in narrative at all is to accept the demands of plot. And so, just as personal identity is subject to the laws of a certain "erasure" in Borges, so too Borgesian plots attempt to register the contingency of action. Instead of the grand climax, the astonishing reversal, or the resolution of "suspense," Borges is drawn to the subtleties of the witty conclusion, to the odd concurrence, and to coincidental events. Insofar as action is itself subject to the rules of repetition, plot is the product of a combinatory matrix. And yet Borges frames his own resistance to plot by those narrative genres, such as the detective story, that tempt us to locate the consequences of agency within a determinate chain of events.

To take what may be the most outstanding example of the Borgesian refashioning of "plot" so as to reflect the contingency of the world and the vertiginous nature of actions and their consequences within it, consider "The Garden of Forking Paths," where Ts'ui Pen's labyrinth-book is governed by the possibility of permutations and combinations rather than by the linear structure of time. In what the narrator describes as this "chaotic novel," plot embraces various possible future times; there are several outcomes of a given sequence of events, not just one: "In all fictions, each time a man meets diverse alternatives, he chooses one and eliminates the others; in the work of the virtually impossible-to-disentangle Ts'ui Pen, the character chooses— simultaneously—all of them. *He creates*, thereby, 'several futures,' several *times*, which themselves proliferate and fork. That is the explanation for the novel's contradictions."[38] Such contradictions can be resolved only if one accepts the fiction of a "total book":

> Unlike Newton and Schopenhauer, your ancestor did not believe in a uniform and absolute time; he believed in an infinite series of times, a growing, dizzying web of divergent, convergent, and parallel times. That fabric of times that approach one another, fork, are snipped off, or are simply unknown for centuries, contains *all* possibilities. In most of those times, we do not exist; in some, you exist but I do not; in others, I do and you do not; in others still, we both do. In this one, which the favouring hand of chance has dealt me, you have come to my home; in another, when you come through my garden you find me dead; in another, I say these same words, but I am an error, a ghost.[39]

A diferencia de Newton y de Schopenhauer, su antepasado no creía en un tiempo uniforme, absoluto. Creía en infinitas series de tiempos, en una red creciente y vertiginosa de tiempos divergentes, convergents y paralelos. Esa trama de tiempos que se aproximan, se bifurcan, se cortan o que secularmente se ignoran, abarca *todas* las posibilidades. No existimos en la mayoría de esos tiempos; en algunos existe usted y no yo; en otros, yo, no usted; en otros, los dos. En éste, que un favorable azar me depara, usted ha llegado a mi casa; en otro, usted, al atravesar el jardín, me ha encontrado muerto; en otro, yo digo estas mismas palabras, pero soy un error, un fantasma. (*F*, pp. 109–110)

Whether reality is one or many, there remains the possibility that the structures of repetition can disclose the possibility for what might be called a "knowing wonder."[40] Neither the baroque philosophical speculations of a text like "Tlön, Uqbar" nor the labyrinthine structure of Ts'ui Pen's novel in "The Garden of Forking Paths" precludes the possibility of an aesthetic reflection on the predicament in which everything seems to be *either* a mere repetition *or* a failed mimesis. At the edge of representation, at the limits of verisimilitude, standing in the space that is cleared by literature's apparent exhaustion, there lies a new and subtle pleasure that Borges knows well how to savor. Indeed, what Borges seems to appreciate is that forsaking the ambition to fashion anything radically new affords the possibility of an affective relationship to reality—as evidenced in the momentary awe we might feel at the vertiginous structure of resemblances, in the pathos that marks the narrator's response to the erasure of personal identity, or in the abjection of the character Stephen Albert, whose life is given up so that the name of a British city can be revealed to the Germans ("*abominably*, I have won'"[41]). To forsake the possibility of radical creation suggests that the weight of "novelty," such as it is to be found in Borges's texts, will fall most heavily on the adjectival moments of thought.[42] And so it is often the case at the semantic level, where adjectives seem to qualify "substantive" reality in baffling and unfathomable ways, each time rendering it both more precise *and* less graspable. I am put in mind of the "asiatic disorder" of "Tlön, Uqbar," the "atrocious variety" of the "Lottery in Babylon," the "innumerable contrition and tiredness" of "The Garden of Forking Paths," as well as of the "unanimous night" of creation and of the creature's "innumerable hair" in "The Circular Ruins." There is in each of these phrases the reflection of a loss that is at once tragic and sublime, a moment of pathos and sympathy that exceeds representation. Such inflections establish differences and validate the artwork's claim to truth, marking it as being both *like* and *unlike* the world.

This is Borges's aesthetics and also his philosophical stance. His is a position that takes the challenge of literary modernism as its point of departure and finds solutions consistent with the philosophical work of figures whose names could well have been more prominent in the foregoing remarks. His work meets Adorno's description of art all too well. As Adorno writes in the passage from *Aesthetic Theory* cited in one of the epigraphs above, "art is actually the world once over, as like it as it is unlike it" (*AT*, p. 336). I think that Borges proves the point.

Notes

1. Jorge Luis Borges, "La supersticiosa ética del lector" (1930), in *Discusión* (Buenos Aires: Emecé Editores, 1970; henceforth abbreviated as *D*), pp. 49–50.
2. Theodor W. Adorno, *Aesthetic Theory* (henceforth *AT*), trans. Robert Hullot-Kentor (Minneapolis: University of Minnesota Press, 1997), p. 1.
3. John Barth, "The Literature of Exhaustion," *The Atlantic* 220, no. 2 (August 1967), pp. 29–34. See also Barth's palinode, "The Literature of Replenishment: Postmodernist Fiction," *The Atlantic* 233, no. 3 (January 1980), pp. 65–71.
4. The project is consistent with the view sketched by William Irwin in "Philosophy and the Philosophical, Literature and the Literary, Borges and the Labyrinthine," in this volume.
5. This view derives from Martin Heidegger, "The Origin of the Work of Art," in *Poetry, Language, Thought*, trans. Albert Hofstadter (New York: Harper & Row 1971), pp. 17–81.
6. In "Philosophy and the Philosophical, Literature and the Literary, Borges and the Labyrinthine" Willian Irwin (this volume) describes this as a "secondary meaning" of the word "literature," but I would argue that it has *become* secondary; it remains prior, if not primary, in the historical sense.
7. Throughout all this Flaubert displays a discernible sympathy toward his heroes, and thus introduces a mode of articulation that the rhetoric of repetition would not of itself allow. I would suggest that sympathy may be regarded as a form of mimesis concentrated in, or displaced to, the affective domain.
8. See Irwin, "Philosophy and the Philosophical, Literature and the Literary, Borges and the Labyrinthine," and Knight, "Intersections: Philosophy and Literature, or Why Ethical Criticism Prefers Realism," both in this volume.
9. Cf. Borges's self-conscious repetition of the problem of the Eternal Return in "El tiempo circular": "Yo suelo regresar eternamente al Eterno Regreso," *Historia de la Eternidad* (Madrid: Alianza, 1971), p. 97.
10. *Collected Fictions*, trans. Andrew Hurley (New York: Penguin Books 1998) p. 94 (henceforth, *CF*). "El texto de Cervantes y el de Menard son verbalmente idénticos, pero el segundo es casi infinitamente más rico. (Más ambiguo, dirán sus detractores; pero la ambigüedad es una riqueza)" in *Ficciones* (Buenos Aires: Emecé Editores 1956), p. 54 (henceforth, *F*).
11. *CF*, p. 135. "Cada imagen visual estaba ligada a sensaciones musculares, térmicas, etc." (*F*, p. 123).
12. *CF*, p. 135. "Podía reconstruir los sueños, todos los entresueños. Dos o tres veces había reconstruído un día entero. . . . Me dijo: *Más recuerdos tengo yo sólo que los que habrán tenido todos los hombres desde que el mundo es mundo*" (*F*, p. 123).
13. *CF*, p. 137. "Monumental como el bronce, más antiguo que Egipto, anterior a las profecías y a las pirámides" (*F*, p. 127). The passage echoes Horace, *Odes*, III, 30.
14. "Su propia cara en el espejo, sus propias manos, lo sorprendían cada vez" (*F*, p. 125).
15. Cf. The character Herbert Ashe in "Tlön, Uqbar, Orbis Tertius," who dies from an aneurism (*F*, p. 21). In Funes' case, the name suggests remembrance and death

(funereal), and also that which goes up in smoke (*humo*). On matters relevant to the erasure of character in Borges, see Sylvia Molloy, *Las Letras de Borges* (Buenos Aires: Editorial Sudamericana, 1979).

16. For a related discussion, see Daniel Balderston, *Out of Context: Historical Reference and the Representation of Reality in Borges* (Durham, NC: Duke University Press, 1993).

17. As for the Argentine literary tradition itself, Borges addresses the matter in an essay published in *Discusión* ("El escritor argentino y la tradición").

18. *CF*, p. 101. "Como todos los hombres de Babilonia, he sido proconsul; como todos, esclavo; también he conocido la omnipotencia, el oprobrio, las cárceles. *Miren*: a mi mano derecha le falta el índice. *Miren*: por este desgarrón de la capa se ve en mi estómago un tatuaje bermejo" [*F*, p. 67 (emphasis added)].

19. *CF*, p. 70. "En vida padeció de irrealidad, como tantos ingleses; muerto, no es ni siquiera el fantasma que ya era entonces" (*F*, p. 17).

20. *CF*, p. 105. "El comprador de una docena de ánforas de vino damasceno no se maravillará si una de ellas encierra un talismán o una víbora" (*F*, p. 74).

21. *CF*, p. 105. "El escribano que redacta un contrato no deja casi nunca de introducir algún dato erróneo; yo mismo, en esta apresurada declaración, he falseado algún esplendor, alguna atrocidad. Quizá, también, alguna misteriosa monotonía" (*F*, p. 74).

22. "El mayor hechicero . . . sería el que se hechizara hasta el punto de tomar sus propias fantasmagorías por apariciones autónomas. ¿No sería ése nuestro caso? Yo conjeturo que así es. Nosotros (la indivisa divinidad que opera en nosotros) hemos soñado el mundo. *Lo hemos soñado resistente, misterioso, visible, ubicuo en el espacio y firme en el tiempo; pero hemos consentido en su arquitectura tenues y eternos intersticios de sinrazón para saber que es falso*" ("Avatares de la tortuga," *D*, p. 136).

23. Adorno, *AT*, p. 336.

24. *CF*, p. 68. "Los espejos y la copulación son abominables, porque multiplican el número de los hombres," "Tlön, Uqbar, Orbis Tertius" (*F*, p. 13).

25. See Shierry Weber Nicholson, *Exact Imagination, Late Work: On Adorno's Aesthetics* (Cambridge, MA: MIT Press, 1997), pp. 139–145.

26. "Ese procedimiento o ambición de los antiguos hombres ha sido sujetado por Frazer a una conveniente ley general, la de la simpatía, que postula un vínculo inevitable entre cosas distantes, ya porque su figura es igual—magia imitativa, homeopática—ya por el hecho de una cercanía anterior—magia contagiosa. Ilustración de la segunda era el ungüento curativo de Kenelm Digby, que se aplicaba no a la vendada herida, sino al acero delincuente que la infirió—mientras aquella, sin el rigor de bárbaras curaciones, iba cicatrizando. De la primera los ejemplos son infinitos. Los pieles rojos de Nebraska revestían cueros crujientes de bisonte . . . y machacaban día y noche sobre el desierto un balie tormentoso, para que los bisontes llegaran" (*D*, pp. 88–89).

27. "Para el supersticioso, hay una necesaria conexión no sólo entre un balazo y un muerto, sino entre un muerto y una maltratada efigie de cera o la rotura profética de un espejo o la sal que se vuelca o trece comensales terribles" (*D*, 89).

28. "La magia es la coronación o pesadilla de lo casual, no su contradicción. El milagro no es menos forastero en ese universo que en el de los astrónomos. Todas las leyes naturales lo rigen, y otras imaginarias" (*D*, p. 89).

29. "Ese recelo de que un hecho temible puede ser atraído por su mención, es impertinente o inútil en el asiático desorden del mundo real, no así en una novela, que debe ser un juego preciso de vigilancias, ecos y afinidades. Todo episodio, en un cuidadoso relato, es de proyección ulterior" (*D*, p. 90).

30. *CF*, p. 97. "Quería soñar un hombre . . . con integridad minuciosa e imponerlo en la realidad" (*F*, p. 60).

31. *CF*, pp. 97, 98. "Ese proyecto mágico había agotado el espacio entero de su alma; si alguien le hubiera preguntado su propio nombre o cualquier rasgo de su vida anterior, no habría acertado a responder." "Comprendió que el empeño de modelar la materia incoherente y vertiginosa de que se componen los sueños es el más arduo que puede acometer un varón, aunque penetre todos los enigmas del orden superior y del inferior: mucho más arduo que tejer una cuerda de arena o que amonedar el viento sin cara" (*F*, pp. 60, 62).

32. "No ser un hombre, ser la proyección de otro hombre ¡qué humillación incomparable, qué vértigo! A todo padre le interesan los hijos que ha procreado (que ha permitido) en una mera confusión o felicidad"; "Con alivio, con humillación, con terror, comprendió que él también era una apariencia, que otro estaba soñándolo" (*F*, pp. 65, 66).

33. Among the prominent literary issues this raises is the question of verisimilitude: how to make narrative seem *like* the world while acknowledging that its powers are but secondary and "degraded" forms of magic. There is a Borges text published in the collection "Discusión," "El arte narrativo y la magia," that speaks directly to the point. Borges begins from a consideration of the 1867 text by William Morris, *The Life and Death of Jason*. The "problem" of such a narrative is finding the means by which to produce what Borges describes, following Coleridge, as "una fuerte apariencia de veracidad . . . [la] espontánea suspensión de la duda" (*D*, p. 82). The problem of how to conjure a world becomes the question of how to produce the effect of belief. Insofar as Borges shares the historical self-awareness of modernism, the issue is complicated by the need to take history into account. How to establish the plausibility of the mythological world when a belief in, for example, centaurs or sirens is historically impossible? Borges is fascinated by Morris because he works as if by insinuation; he derives world-making powers from the suggestiveness of language. In one instance Morris simply introduces centaurs, without comment, among natural wild animals—bears and wolves ("Where bears and wolves the centaurs' arrows find," *D*, p. 82, is a first reference). Then, on a second occasion, he introduces a minimal qualifier ("quick-eyed centaurs," p. 82), as if to suggest that their existence has now been taken for real. The ploy is of course purely rhetorical, but equally telling is the fact that Borges names it as such. "Morris puede no comunicar al lector su imagen del centauro ni siquiera invitarnos a tener una, le basta nuestra continua fe en sus palabras, como en el mundo real" (*D*, p. 83).

34. "La simetría, las leyes arbitrarias, el tedio" (*F*, p. 79).

35. *CF*, p. 74. "El hecho de que toda filosofía sea de antemano un juego dialéctico, una *Philosophie des Als Ob*, ha contribuído a multiplicarlas. Abundan los sistemas increíbles, pero de arquitectura agradable o de tipo sensacional. Los metafísicos de Tlön no buscan la verdad ni siquiera la verosimilitud: buscan el asombro. Juzgan que la metafísica es una rama de la literatura fantástica" (*F*, p. 23).

36. Cf. the narrator's comment on Ts'ui Pen's labyrinthine book in "The Garden of Forking Paths," that "la controversia filosófica usurpa buena parte de su novela" (*F*, p. 108).

37. *CF*, p. 77. "Siglos y siglos de idealismo no han dejado de influir en la realidad" (*F*, p. 27).

38. *CF*, p. 125. "En todas las ficciones, cada vez que un hombre se enfrente con diversas alternativas, opta por una y elimina otras; en la del casi inextricable Ts'ui Pen, opta—simultáneamente—por todas. Crea, así, diversos porvenires, diversos tiempos, que también proliferan y se bifurcan. De ahí las contradicciones de la novela" (*F*, p. 107).

39. *CF*, p. 127. "A diferencia de Newton y de Schopenhauer, su antepasado no creía en un tiempo uniforme, absoluto. Creía en infinitas series de tiempos, en una red

creciente y vertiginosa de tiempos divergentes, convergents y paralelos. Esa trama de tiempos que se aproximan, se bifurcan, se cortan o que secularmente se ignoran, abarca *todas* las posibilidades. No existimos en la mayoría de esos tiempos; en algunos existe usted y no yo; en otros, yo, no usted; en otros, los dos. En éste, que un favorable azar me depara, usted ha llegado a mi casa; en otro, usted, al atravesar el jardín, me ha encontrado muerto; en otro, yo digo estas mismas palabras, pero soy un error, un fantasma" (*F*, pp. 109–110).

40. I borrow this phrase from Lawrence Weschler, from a talk on the work of Tobias Rheberger presented at the Berkeley Art Museum in September 1999.

41. "'*Abominablemente* he vencido'" [*F*, p. 111 (emphasis added)].

42. One of the languages of Tlön is built around adjectives, not verbs; nouns are in turn built of adjectives: "la célula primordial no es el verbo, sino el adjetivo mono-silábico. El sustantivo se forma por acumulación de adjetivos" (*F*, p. 21).

7

ELIZABETH MILLÁN-ZAIBERT

A Method
for the New Millennium:
Calvino and Irony[1]

Analyses of the relationship between philosophy and literature should be framed within the context of a more general issue that, echoing Arthur Danto, we may call *the problem of philosophy*.[2] The problem of philosophy is the question of how to define what philosophy is. And I take it that knowing the *goals* and concomitant *methods* of philosophy is crucial to the task of defining it. To say something about philosophy's goals is to be on our way toward offering some sort of definition of philosophy. Much can be gleaned about philosophy's goals by examining the methods that philosophers choose to develop their systems. In what follows, I shall take this path; I shall examine different philosophical methods with the hope of gaining insights into the problem of philosophy and ultimately into the relationship between philosophy and literature.

The history of the relationship between literature and philosophy is filled with examples of philosophers scornfully rejecting what they consider artistic "imitations of reality." The stereotype has it that philosophers are interested in reality and artists in appearances.[3] This stereotype has led many mainstream philosophers to identify themselves more closely with the community of scientists and shun the company of artists. Attempts to establish the boundaries that would define the field of philosophy have often been mapped in exclusionary terms, creating borders that keep the artists out of philosophical territory. Such protectionism, if based upon uninformed prejudice, only promotes intolerance. It does not help us to address the problem of philosophy. What is needed is an open-minded, unprejudiced investigation of philosophy and its boundaries.

In *Philosophy and Literature*, Italo Calvino offers the sketch of just such an investigation.[4] While observing that "[p]hilosophy and literature are embattled adversaries," he also notes that there is more to their relationship than mere hostility. They share a common bond: comedy. This fertile insight is eloquently expressed in the following:

[The relationship] between literature and philosophy first became explicit in the comedies of Aristophanes, and was destined to continue to move behind the shield of comedy, irony, and humor. It is no coincidence that what in the eighteenth century were called *contes philosophiques* were in fact lighthearted acts of revenge against philosophy executed by means of the literary imagination.[5]

Calvino is rather laconic and admits that this insight is something "for which [he] cannot claim to provide any general explanation."[6] Yet, it is worthwhile to develop possible explanations for his claim. By turning our attention to what I shall call the "aesthetic method" (and away from the scientific methods), I hope to provide an explanation for Calvino's claim that philosophy and literature share a common bond in comedy, an explanation that amounts to a redefinition of philosophy itself.

It is hard to present a full-blown definition of "aesthetic method." I shall not attempt to do that. Rather, I shall examine what I consider to be the best example of a philosophical system that displays this method, and I shall try to gather from this presentation some important, if not defining, characteristics of this method. And I shall attempt to show that a result of embracing this method is that philosophy and literature turn out to be intimately connected. After this rough outline of the aesthetic method, I shall examine the different ways in which the boundaries between philosophy and literature have been traditionally drawn. I shall pay special attention to the diverse ways in which philosophers have tried to keep philosophy and literature separate. I shall conclude with a discussion of irony and the "completion of philosophy in literature."

Early German Romanticism and the Aesthetic Method

On first approximation, it makes sense to define the aesthetic method by contrasting it to what it is not. It is not a method of verification or of deduction or of pure analysis. It is something more like a hermeneutical method, in which reading and historical understanding play a role. Most importantly, it is a method in which the issue of representation and the problems involved therein become thematized. Irony is a mimetic device that serves to make the frame of representation apparent, and so it is a crucial element of the aesthetic method.

There is a strong connection between the shield of irony that Calvino presents as a metaphor for illuminating the relation between literature and philosophy and an important philosophical movement. Not coincidentally, the philosophical dimension of this movement has rarely been recognized. Part of the reason for this neglect is that these thinkers defined philosophy in terms of its relation to art. The movement I have in mind is early-German

Romanticism.[7] I shall show that early-German Romanticism was indeed a philosophical movement and provided an excellent alternative model to the mainstream systems of philosophy based upon the methods of mathematics and the natural sciences. Moreover, the alternative that they presented was deeply rooted in that concept that is so central to Calvino's view of the relationship between literature and philosophy: irony.

The early-German Romantics, more than any other group of thinkers, moved "behind the shield of comedy, irony, and humor." And as they carried out their "lighthearted acts of revenge against philosophy," against a philosophy defined in terms of nonaesthetic methods, the traditional boundaries between literature and philosophy shifted tremendously; indeed, the very definition of the field changed so drastically that the battlefield disappeared, and these "embattled adversaries" became united.[8]

Because the members of this group—among others, Friedrich Schlegel, Friedrich von Hardenberg (Novalis), and Friedrich Hölderlin—were gifted writers and poets, there has been a tendency to classify their movement as merely literary.[9] They were poet-philosophers, and as such often were refused entry into the territory of the philosophers. Because of this, their attempt to develop an "aesthetic method" is not acknowledged. Right or wrong, it was their view that art could show us a standard of truth. As long as philosophers stubbornly deny that there are any philosophical views to be found in the early-German Romantic movement, the Romantics' views concerning the role of aesthetic method within philosophy are neither affirmed nor denied: they are simply ignored. Although it falls beyond the scope of this investigation to show that their view is correct, I do wish to present the view as a *viable* alternative to the venerable methods of philosophy—and one that explains Calvino's fertile insights concerning the common bond of philosophy and literature that we find in irony.

To understand what the "aesthetic method" of the early-German Romantics amounts to, we must have a clear understanding of their call for a new connection between philosophy and literature, and the new literary forms required to heed this call, and how this is connected with their abandonment of first principles and with the "longing for the infinite" that guides our search for knowledge in the wake of this abandonment. Moreover, we must also understand the central role of irony, the irony they thought they had discovered in Socrates, Shakespeare, and Cervantes.

The main goal of the early-German Romantics was to question the feasibility of a philosophy based on first principles. Hence, their project was obviously not merely a literary one. By questioning philosophy's need for first principles, the early-German Romantics were questioning foundationalism, that is, the view that in order to secure knowledge, philosophy needs a set of absolutely certain propositions from which all else can be deduced. The romantic abandonment of first principles was part of a rejection of the mathematical methods that had dominated the modern period. This antifoundationalism opened space for the development of a new method in philosophy.

The new method called for new literary forms. In *Athenäum* fragment #53 Schlegel writes: "It is just as fatal for the spirit to have a system and not to have a system. Some way of combining the two must be reached."[10] The literary form that the early-German Romantics favored for this sort of combination was the fragment. The use of the fragment was in keeping with the early-German Romantics' desire to call foundationalism into question. If philosophy no longer departs from a single, absolute first principle, how can a system be created at all? The fragment was Schlegel's solution to the problem of having and not having a system—with the use of fragments he thought he could combine both.[11] This we may call a "romantic combination."

Few philosophers are hospitable to a conception of philosophy that entails an intimate relation with art, and most would be suspicious of Schlegel's "romantic combination." Stanley Cavell is a recent exception. Cavell was made aware of various writings from the journal *Athenäum* (1798–1800) and has written about his discovery of early-German Romanticism.[12] In particular, Cavell is impressed by Schlegel's call for a new relation between philosophy and literature, and he reflects upon the relevance and acceptance such a call finds in the philosophical climate of today. He writes:

> I guess such remarks as "poetry and philosophy should be made one" would not in themselves have been enough even in my day to have gotten one thrown out of most graduate programs in philosophy, but their presence, if used seriously, as a present ambition, would not have been permitted to contribute to a Ph.D. dissertation either; and like vestigial organs, such ideas may become inflamed and life-threatening.[13]

Cavell is a twentieth-century philosopher whose work can be labeled "romantic" in the sense that he does not fear that attention to the literary elements of philosophy or the poetic aspects of reality threaten to undermine philosophy.

The most comprehensive account of Schlegel's meaning of the term "romantic" is found in *Athenäum* Fragment #116. This fragment can best be read as a kind of romantic manifesto. Here we find Schlegel's announcement that

> [R]omantic poetry is a progressive, universal poetry. It alone can become, like the epic, a mirror of the whole circumambiant world, an image of the age. And it can also—more than any other form—hover at the midpoint between the portrayed and the portrayer, free of all real and ideal self-interest, on the wings of poetic reflection again and again to a higher power, can multiply it in an endless succession of mirrors.[14]

Romantic poetry is an ideal, a poetry that is progressive because it is always in a state of becoming, never reaching completion.[15] A poetry that hovers at the midpoint between portrayer and portrayed, on the wings of poetic reflection, is created by a poet who has discovered the secret and value of lightness and is not bound to simply producing copies of what there is in the world, but is able to use the wings of poetic reflection to reflect upon how what there is in the world is represented in the first place, and then reflect on this reflection, and reflect upon the reflection of the reflection, etc., ultimately creating "an endless succession of mirrors."

In fragment #116, we receive many clues that help us to understand the new method initiated by the early-German Romantics. The group of thinkers that contributed to *Das Athenäum* were introducing, via the term "romantic," a new, revolutionary description of an ideal not only of poetry, but of reality in its boundlessness: a new philosophical category. Gone from this scheme were the paradigmatic methods of mathematics and the natural sciences, which were rooted in some first principle or another. If one were to be a Romantic, one would have to give up the security of absolute first principles and the firm foundations supplied therewith.

For the early-German Romantics, philosophy was a search for truth that begins with a feeling, a longing for the infinite.[16] This feeling is a result of realizing our own finitude and of the realization that the scope of knowledge is infinite.[17] In other words, the longing comes with the realization of the inherent incompleteness of knowledge. Accordingly, philosophy, defined in terms of a search for knowledge, also becomes inherently incomplete.

This new way of understanding the nature of philosophy gave rise to the need for a new method. This method, which I indistinctly call the "romantic" or "aesthetic method," was not deductive; rather it involved a kind of hovering "between the portrayed and the portrayer," with the philosopher as the portrayer and reality as the portrayed. Only a philosophy that is rooted in irony has the agility and lightness necessary to hover between reality and the philosopher. This sort of philosophy is intimately related to poetry; indeed, it finds its completion in poetry.

Irony, Agility, and the Philosophical Method

In spite of the fact that Calvino does not provide an explanation for his thesis regarding the bond between philosophy and literature, such an explanation is tacitly expressed in many of his essays. The explanation is implicit as a leitmotif throughout his essays on the nature of literature: the relationship between "the phantom lightness of ideas and the heavy weight of the world."[18] In the final days of his life, Calvino wrote a confessional series of memos concerning his work and his view of literature. In the first of these, he states:

> Were I to choose an auspicious image for the new millennium, I would choose the sudden agile leap of the poet-philosopher who raises himself above the weight of the world, showing that with all his gravity he has the secret of lightness.[19]

This image of the poet-philosopher sounds much like Schlegel's romantic poet who can "hover between the portrayer and the portrayed" on the wings of poetic reflection. And the point behind Calvino's scenic image is related to just what Schlegel was addressing: representation. Schlegel uses the relation between the portrayer and the portrayed in order to discuss representation. Calvino's reference to "the weight of the world" is a reference to the portrayed, and the poet-philosopher, the portrayer, is able to use a reflection on the very structure of representation to soar above that which is portrayed (reality) and gain a new perspective of reality. This is done in and through irony. The poet-philosopher who uses irony knows how to play with reality and to reveal its structure to us in a multiplicity of ways. A poet-philosopher who demonstrates this sense of playfulness can be said to have the secret of lightness.

The view of the value of lightness brings Calvino into close company with the early-German Romantics. Schlegel, in particular, was well aware of the value of irony and the lightness it granted to the representation of ideas. Hence, his views on irony will help to explain the insight that Calvino presents in such an admittedly sketchy fashion. The form of irony that inspired Schlegel was Socratic irony. Plato's Dialogues provide many examples of the sort of irony that leaves one wondering what the words used to express an idea really mean; the reader is left suspended between the portrayer, Socrates, and the portrayed, his claims, never quite sure that the meaning has been captured.

For example, in the *Phaedrus* when we are given a scathing critique of the written word, this is given in writing. But after we have been told that the written word is deceptive, on what grounds can we accept written claims against the written word?[20] Ironically, to understand irony itself, we must already have the sort of agility that irony requires. As Schlegel expresses this paradox: "Socratic irony is the only involuntary and yet completely deliberate dissimulation. In this sort of irony, everything should be playful and serious, guilelessly open and deeply hidden."[21] Irony became the cornerstone of Schlegel's romantic philosophy, reflecting a view of philosophy as an infinite task, as a kind of longing for the infinite that could never be expressed by using the unplayful method of the natural sciences, but only by uniting philosophy with literature.

Philosophers can hardly make any sudden, agile leaps if such leaps are not part of the goals of what they believe philosophy is all about. What kind of goal must a philosopher have to join the leaping order of the poet-philosophers? What sort of method will enable the philosopher to reach that goal?

The Traditional Boundaries between Philosophy and Literature

Often, a position becomes most clear amidst the most inhospitable audience. For there is no operative principle of charity, and each point must be clarified and defended with great ardor. So, let us further clarify the nature of the aesthetic method by looking at those philosophers who were most certainly not interested in joining the ranks of the poet-philosophers, and who would have viewed the "sudden agile leaps" of the poet-philosophers as mortal leaps into an abyss of meaninglessness. It is not difficult to find such groups, for the traditional boundaries of philosophy have excluded poetry, art, and literature.

A fine contemporary example of the way in which the boundaries between philosophy and anything aesthetic have been drawn in exclusionary terms can be found in Carnap's article, "The Overcoming of Metaphysics through the Logical Analysis of Language."[22] In this article, Carnap defines philosophy as a method of logical analysis. The task of philosophy is to eliminate meaningless words and nonsensical pseudopropositions (philosophy's negative application) and to clarify meaningful concepts and sentences so that they can serve as the logical foundation or basis for the natural sciences and mathematics (philosophy's positive application). Carnap wrote this article partly as a response to what he considered to be Heidegger's meaningless claims regarding metaphysics. Metaphysicians, according to Carnap, can do nothing more than express feelings, much in the way musicians (dreaded artists) do. Rather acrimoniously, he defines metaphysicians as "musicians without musical talent."[23]

According to Carnap, the domain of art belongs to the poets and the domain of theory belongs to the philosopher. And, for Carnap, to confuse these two distinct domains is to confuse art with theory. To produce theories, philosophers support their statements with arguments, claim assent to the content of these arguments, and polemicize against philosophers of divergent persuasions by attempting to refute their assertions. Poets, on the other hand, "do not try to refute in their poem statements in a poem by another poet, for they know they are in the domain of art and not in the domain of theory."[24] Clearly, then, for Carnap a poet-philosopher would be a strange, deformed creature, who might have the ability to leap with agility, but not in any way that would further the goals of philosophy as presented by the method of logical analysis. The leaps of the poet-philosophers would only be leaps beyond what could be verified and so journeys to the realm of nonsense. Philosophy defined in terms of the method of logical analysis proposed by Carnap is not one that will give birth to a philosophy with any kind of relation to literature—there are no poet-philosophers amongst the logical positivists.

Richard Rorty began his career with great sympathy for the conception of philosophy outlined by the logical positivists and their emphasis on linguistic method. Yet, this changed. It is hard to imagine that the same philosopher who edited *The Linguistic Turn* in 1967 would publish something like *Philosophy and the Mirror of Nature* in 1979 and eventually develop a conception of philosophy that would lead to statements like the following:

> Logical positivists such as Ayer [or Carnap] trained students to brush past romance and to spot nonsense. In the space of two generations, Ayer and dryness won out over Whitehead and romance. Philosophy in the English-speaking world became "analytic"—antimetaphysical, unromantic, highly professional, and a cultural backwater.[25]

The only way out of this stagnant water is to see that "Philosophy is best seen as a kind of writing. It is delimited, as is any literary genre, not by form or matter, but by tradition—a family romance involving, e.g., Father Parmenides, honest old Uncle Kant, bad brother Derrida."[26] Linguistic analysis, the method that Rorty had taken so seriously at the beginning of his career, is not a method that goes along with a conception of philosophy as a kind of writing. If philosophy is seen as a kind of writing, then the act of reading takes on new significance, and issues concerning literary forms and historical context become an important part of understanding texts. Once we begin to see philosophy as a "family romance," issues of "honest old Uncle Kant's" relation to "Father Parmenides" and "bad brother Derrida" may arise and with these, the act of comparing various stages of this family romance with other stages. In this way, philosophy becomes a historical, comparative study. The hermeneutical dimension of philosophy becomes more prominent and issues of representation and interpretation move into focus. Rorty's conception of philosophy as a kind of writing goes hand in hand with certain aesthetic methods that involve issues of interpretation and historical contextualization. Under the definition of philosophy as a kind of writing, there is room again for the sudden, agile leaps of the poet-philosophers.

Rorty's response to a narrow view of philosophy as a method of linguistic analysis leads him to emphasize the literary dimensions of philosophy. And here he is in the company of "bad brother Derrida," who is famous for his controversial claim that philosophy *is* literature. This has made Derrida the black sheep of the philosophical family. His postmodern views on the nature of philosophy and literature have been the object of much attention both in the United States and in Europe.[27] And that should not come as a surprise, for his postmodern view draws a radically new map of philosophy and literature, allegedly eradicating all boundaries between the two.

One important debate concerning the ramifications of Derrida's views centered on Calvino's novel *If on a Winter's Night a Traveler*. Calvino's novel became the center of the debate insofar as this novel was understood to represent postmodern literature. In this novel Calvino presents life as a kind of reading, and two prominent German thinkers, Hans Robert Jauß and Jürgen Habermas, discussed the implications of a view of literature like the one presented in Calvino's novel.[28] Let us examine Habermas' conception of philosophy as it was developed in his criticism of postmodern literature.

In this debate, Habermas, who is far from being a logical positivist and has a view of philosophy that is, in many ways, at odds with Carnap's, expresses views concerning the nature of relationship between philosophy and literature that are remarkably similar to Carnap's. Habermas opposes any attempts to level the difference between philosophy and literature. Although philosophy *and* literature do share important commonalities, philosophy cannot be understood *as* literature. His argument against understanding philosophy *as* literature rests upon the following three theses: (1) there is a qualitative difference between literature and philosophy (*Gattungsunterschied*); (2) philosophical discourse is propositional (*Wahrheits-different*) whereas literary discourse represents only feeling; and (3) the speech-acts of a novel have no illocutionary force and so literature demands of the reader only commentary whereas philosophy demands critique.

Habermas's conception of philosophy is far broader than Carnap's, yet the same cannot be said of his conception of literature. Whereas Carnap drew the boundaries between philosophy and literature by narrowing the definition of philosophy to a method of logical analysis, Habermas draws clear boundaries between the two by presenting a narrow view of literature as a modification of reality that eludes method and truth, an absolutely subjective thing, one not open to critique or justification.[29] Once literature is defined as something cut off from objective reality, it is not difficult to mark sharp boundaries between philosophy and literature.

Habermas, like Carnap, draws a clear line between the domain of the philosophers and that of the poets. Habermas does not deny that there is a relation between philosophy and literature or that important critics and philosophers can also be writers of rank. He locates the bond between literature and philosophy in the rhetorical achievements they share; both literature and philosophy use rhetorical elements and count upon them to make certain points. But acknowledging a bond here does not amount to leveling the distinction between literature and philosophy. Quite the contrary, for the rhetorical elements used in philosophy serve the ends of arguments, whereas in literature, rhetoric serves what we might call a poetic function.[30] Like Carnap, Habermas views philosophy and literature as belonging to two distinct domains—one guided by truth and argument and the other by something more akin to feeling.

Habermas, like Carnap, develops a view of philosophy according to which it has a method at odds with literature. The only characteristic philosophy shares with literature results from the fact that philosophy *has* to take place in language, it *has* to be written and read, and so it must resign itself to the low company of literature. Philosophy and literature are related, because philosophy is carried out in writing, but it is more than just writing, it is a method of argument. Habermas' conception of philosophy and its method are clearly at odds with Rorty's endorsement of philosophy as a kind of writing.

Habermas emphasizes the different purposes of philosophy and of literature to make a case against those who want to dissolve the borders between the two fields. Philosophers want to convince and prove, whereas poets merely want to suggest and elicit sentimental feelings. And here again Habermas is in close company with Carnap, for to prove a point, to build a theory, the rules laid down by logic must guide the discourse of the philosopher; they cannot give way to rhetoric. Philosophy has the duty to solve problems; and the substance of philosophy is to be found in its power of critique. For both Carnap and Habermas, the power of philosophy, be this a power to clarify or to critique, is undermined by the very notion of a poet-philosopher and the conception of philosophy as a kind of writing.

For Habermas, to locate the critique of reason that defines philosophy in the realm of rhetoric amounts to undermining the power of critique itself, and so of philosophy. He writes:

> Whoever moves the radical critique of reason to the area of rhetoric in order to weaken the paradox of its self-reference, silences the bells of the critique. The wrongful pretension to level the distinction between philosophy and literature cannot escape this aporia.[31]

Habermas wants to distance philosophy from the position in rhetoric that he alleges deconstruction reduces it to, for he believes that this position leaves us with powerless discourse. According to this reading, the deconstructionists hold that the linguistic signs of poetic discourse refer to themselves rather than to objective reality. Habermas goes along with this understanding of literary discourse, claiming that aesthetic considerations for presenting the subject matter become more important than any commitments to presenting objective reality. Ultimately, the language of poetry degenerates into a narcissistic self-portrayal, with no connection to the objective world or its discourse partners. Habermas works with the assumption that the inexhaustibility of meaning that is found in literary texts must certainly disqualify this discourse from clarity (hence poetic discourse is obscure, close to Carnap's diagnosis of it as nonsensical) and from a relation to the world (hence it has no truth-value, no communicative power). Habermas' move from an endorsement of the myth of the nonreferentiality of poetic discourse, to the dismissal of literature as having any productive relation with philosophy, is predictable. This move is also based on a prejudiced view of the nature of literature as having nothing to do with objectivity or with correspondence to an independent reality.

We can compare any well-known mainstream views, from philosophers ranging in diversity from Carnap to Habermas, with Calvino's. From the inexhaustibility of meanings found in literature, Calvino retrieves quite another conclusion regarding literature's connection with reality. Modern and postmodern literature do present a highly sophisticated level of multiplicity—of discourse, methods, and levels of meaning—but this multiplicity, far from severing literature from reality, enables it to present itself as a method of knowledge, a network of connections between the events, the people, and the things of the world. Calvino writes:

> Knowledge as multiplicity is the thread that binds together the major works both of what is called modernism and of what goes by the name of the postmodern, a thread—over and above all the labels attached to it—that I hope will continue into the next millennium.[32]

The inexhaustible meaning that is present in literature is not the result of a narcissistic self-mirroring. Poets do not leap irresponsibly away from reality, while philosophers maintain a dignified commitment to it. That is why for Calvino the notion of a poet-philosopher is not a contradiction of terms, the way it would have to be for Carnap and Habermas.

Calvino's reference to knowledge as multiplicity has a resonance with an observation made by Arthur Danto. In *The Transfiguration of the Common Place*, Danto talks about the various ways in which the mimetic function of art has been regarded.[33] After discussing Socrates and his "aversion to mirror images and mimesis," Danto moves to what may have been overlooked by Socrates' narrow view of what artistic representation entailed, namely, that "mirrors and then, by generalization, artworks, rather than giving us back what we already can know without benefit of them, serve . . . as instruments of self-revelation."[34] To illustrate the mirror functioning of art as a mode of self-revelation, Danto discusses Shakespeare's *Hamlet* and the play within the play meant to "catch the conscience of the king." In Shakespeare's play, we have two different representations of the murdered King of Denmark: the character that Shakespeare creates, who is present to us only as a memory and possibly as a ghost, and the player-king in the play that Hamlet has arranged to have staged. This double mirroring makes the issue of representation a theme of the play. Hamlet uses a play, a representation of what he believes transpired between his dead father and his Uncle Claudius, to demonstrate to his uncle that he knows the truth about the circumstances surrounding his father's death. The play put on by Hamlet (call this Hamlet's play) is a play within Shakespeare's play, and is consciously used by Hamlet as a mirror to reflect the circumstances surrounding his father's death and so to "catch the conscience" of his uncle, to see his uncle's (Claudius) face cloud with guilt as it becomes clear that Hamlet knows the truth about Claudius's deeds. Before Hamlet's play is over, Claudius rises and leaves the performance; he cannot stand to see such a story represented. We can conclude that Hamlet has indeed used his play to catch successfully the conscience of the King. This sort of maneuver, a kind of revelation of the mimetic function of art, reflects the great power of literature and art in general.

There is nothing "narcissistic" about these representations. Although Hamlet's intention with his play might have been exclusively to elicit feelings of guilt in his uncle, clearly, Shakespeare's intentions with his play are not merely to elicit sentimental reactions in us. Shakespeare's play leads us to reflect upon the nature of art and representation. Moreover Shakespeare's play forces us to give *rational consideration* to human emotions and character traits. When reading Shakespeare's play, we reflect rationally about the nature of, say, betrayal; we do not *feel* betrayed.[35] Art can represent reality. And an artist can make the act of representation visible in the work of art. This is done through the use of irony.

Irony and the Completion of Philosophy in Literature

For both Schlegel and Calvino, irony is linked to lightness and agility, and they both found this agility exemplified in the age of Cervantes and Shakespeare. Schlegel remarks:

> This is where I look for and find the Romantic—in the older moderns, in Shakespeare, Cervantes, in Italian poetry, in that age of knights, love, and fairy–tales where the thing and the word originated.[36]

Calvino, for his part, locates the secret of the agility of the poet-philosopher in the *characters* of Shakespeare, Cervantes, and the age of knights, love, and fairy-tales.[37]

> Don Quixote and Hamlet opened up a new relationship between the phantom lightness of ideas and the heavy weight of the world. When we speak of the relationship between literature and philosophy we must not forget that the whole question begins there.[38]

Why should the whole question of philosophy's relation to literature begin with Cervantes' *Don Quixote* and Shakespeare's *Hamlet*? The reason why both Schlegel and Calvino are drawn to such works is that they lead us directly to irony, where the root of the relationship between literature and philosophy is to be found. Calvino speaks of "that particular and existential inflection that makes it possible for Shakespeare's characters to distance themselves from their own drama."[39] This is one function of irony, a kind of distancing device that enables the characters to reflect on the power of the mirroring that is one central aspect of art, namely, representation. Irony is a mimetic device that enables Shakespeare's characters to make the issue of the power of representation explicit. In a review, Schlegel discusses the importance of acknowledging that over and above being an artist who can represent a full spectrum of feelings to an audience, Shakespeare is one of the "most intentional artists" (*einer der absichtsvollsten Künstler*).[40] That is, the play within the play that we find in Hamlet occurs neither by accident nor simply to intensify the intellectual joys associated with the great sorrow we may feel as we read of Hamlet's plight. The play within the play is ironic; it is an intentional mimetic structure that is put into the play by one of the "most intentional artists" to make us reflect upon the very nature and power of art (in addition to reflecting on such lofty things as human suffering, revenge, loyalty, etc.).

For Schlegel, "Irony is the clear consciousness of eternal agility, of an infinitely teeming chaos."[41] Irony is not irony if it is not part of the intention of the author; irony requires that the author *know* that he is moving from a representation of a given subject to a reflection on the nature of that representation. This is related to the agility that Calvino alludes to when he invokes the image of the poet-philosopher who has the secret of lightness. The use of irony requires that the author know how to move from a representation of the subject matter at hand to a reflection of the representation of that subject matter, creating a kind of frame in which the subject matter is seen at a different level. This makes the subject matter move between two levels of meaning or even more if we are to take Schlegel's reference to "an infinitely teeming chaos" seriously.

As mentioned at the outset, Schlegel's model for irony is drawn from Socratic irony. Irony is the device that joins Socrates with Shakespeare. In the same fragment in which Schlegel discusses the paradox of irony discussed earlier, he goes on to tell us that irony "contains and arouses a feeling of indissoluble antagonism between the absolute and the relative, between the impossibility and the necessity of complete communication."[42] Irony makes us aware of the tensions between our limitations and the infinite nature of the Absolute, between what we can know and what there is to know. Any attempt to completely communicate the Absolute or the infinite is futile. Yet the philosopher has a duty to make this impossibility apparent, and the philosopher does this by revealing the limitations of philosophy itself.

The limitations of philosophy give rise to the necessity of literature in general, although Schlegel speaks specifically about poetry. In a private lecture of 1807, Schlegel explains the relation between philosophy and poetry:

> It should be brought to mind that the necessity of poetry is based on the requirement to represent the infinite, which emerges from the imperfection of philosophy.[43]

This leads him to conclude that "Where philosophy ends, poetry must begin."[44]

Irony belongs to poetry as a mode of representation. Yet it also belongs to philosophy, the result of philosophy's inability to represent the Absolute. Nothing is complete, and irony is the tool used to make the inherent incompleteness of human experience apparent.

Romantic irony is playful and irreverent, but it is not the result of any lack of respect that the early-German Romantics had for the world and reality. It is rather the result of a deep respect for and commitment to *understanding* reality. Romantic irony makes no mockery of the world; it is not a disparaging attitude toward the world. Calvino, it should be noted, was no fan of mockery either. In his essay, "Definitions of Territories: Comedy," he tells us that

> One component of satire is mockery. I would like [mockery] to remain foreign to me, partly because I do not appreciate [it] in others. [A]nyone who goes in for mockery thinks he is smarter—or, rather, he believes that things are simpler than they appear to be to others.[45]

Schlegel's use of irony is not used to mock anyone or to place himself above others; rather, romantic irony is the ultimate show of humility; it is used to show how little humans, all humans, know.[46] Romantic irony is part of the general romantic vision of reality as essentially incomplete, as an approximation toward the distant and unreachable goal of the infinite. As Schlegel puts it:

> Pure thinking and cognition [*Erkennen*] of the highest can never be represented [*dargestellt*] adequately—this is the principle of the relative unrepresentability [*Undarstellbarkeit*] of the highest.[47]

This difficulty of representing the highest or the infinite is overcome when philosophy gives up its haughty independence and turns to art for help.[48] The infinite can be alluded to only indirectly, and this is possible only if art is able to go beyond what it represents, by alluding ironically to what it does not succeed in saying. For this reason Schlegel claims that

> Philosophy is the real homeland of irony, which one would like to define as logical beauty: for wherever philosophy appears in oral or written dialogues—and is not simply confined into rigid systems—there irony should be asked for and provided.[49]

Philosophy that is the product of a mathematical or scientific deductive method is a philosophy confined to rigid systems. The dialogue form, like the fragment, is a literary form that is part of a philosophical "system" that combines having and not having system; this "romantic combination" is part of a philosophy informed by the aesthetic method, and here we find irony. Irony is a literary tool that lifts the rigid confines of language.

Irony is a sort of play that reveals the limitations of a view of reality that presumed to have the last word. With the use of romantic irony, the early-German Romantics showed that there was no last word. And once we give up a last word, aesthetic methods become sensible alternatives to the methods of mathematics and the natural sciences. Thus the "embattled adversaries," philosophy and literature, disappear and in their stead we find that philosophy needs poetry to reach its goal of understanding the nature of reality.

Epilogue: The Poet-Philosopher

As several contributions in this volume illustrate, Calvino was a most philosophical teller of tales.[50] I have tried to show that he offers us a new way to view philosophy, for a philosophy rooted in irony is a flower of a different kind than the one rooted in the deductive or inductive methods of mathematics or empirical science.

And when we are dealing with a philosophy rooted in irony, Calvino and his literature and Schlegel and his philosophy are not "embattled adversaries," they are more like friends in an ongoing conversation with each other. Thus, it is no coincidence that both thinkers valued irony and the lightness with which it endowed language and thought. Each thinker observed the important and beautiful plant born of this common root.

In *Six Memos for the Next Millennium*, Calvino uses the first memo to present the value of lightness. He confesses that

> My working method has more often than not involved the subtraction of weight. I have tried to remove weight, sometimes from people, sometimes from heavenly bodies, sometimes from cities; above all I have tried to remove weight from the structure of stories and from language.[51]

Calvino turns to a myth to explain more fully the value of lightness. Perseus, with his winged sandals, was the hero who finally killed Medusa and rid the world of her petrifying gaze. How did Perseus do this? Calvino explains that "Perseus' strength lies in a refusal to look directly, but not in a refusal of the reality in which he is fated to live."[52] Perseus looks at a mirrored surface to escape the petrifying gaze. A look at a mirrored surface is not an escape from our reality; such a gaze can serve as an instrument of self-revelation. Irony is a mode of presentation used to make the referential frame obvious to the reader, to force the reader to be aware of his or her limits and yet to look away from those very limits to that which is without limits. Hence, it can be said that with irony we refuse to look directly but do not refuse the reality to which we are fated.

The early-German Romantics realized that we were fated to our condition of being finite creatures with a longing for the infinite. Irony was the tool used to make this condition apparent. Now, Carnap with his conception of philosophy as a kind of linguistic analysis would have convicted the early-German Romantics of irrationality or nonsensical flights of fancy precisely because of their poetic approximation to reality. Calvino never would have made this mistake. He realized that certain flights reconfigure our view of reality and provide us with a new, fresh method for understanding it.

> Whenever humanity seems condemned to heaviness I think I should fly like Perseus into a different space. I don't mean escaping into dreams or into the irrational. I mean that I have to change my approach, look at the world from a different perspective, with a different logic and with fresh methods of cognition and verification.[53]

Calvino was well aware that a change of approach, a flight into a different space, was not necessarily an escape into some nonsensical or irrational sphere. Not all flights need be dizzying flights of fancy that do not inform us of our reality or seek to escape reality.

Romantic irony is not vague and haphazard; it has that precision and determination that Calvino associates with lightness.[54] Understanding philosophy through irony is a way to approach philosophy through lightness, with the winged feet of Perseus. And this approach brings us to the poet-philosopher. I return now to an insight that I presented at the beginning of the essay, Calvino's call to follow the image of agility and lightness symbolized in the figure of the poet-philosopher:

> Were I to choose an auspicious image for the new millennium, I would choose the sudden agile leap of the poet-philosopher who raises himself above the weight of the world, showing that with all his gravity he has the secret of lightness.[55]

At the dawn of a new millennium, the time has come to heed Calvino's call, to think seriously about what the poet-philosopher is and what a poetic philosophy entails. Once philosophy is characterized within this sort of aesthetic framework, and once the traditional framework of the natural sciences is removed, so is the battlefield upon which literature and philosophy met as adversaries—in its place we find a common meeting ground, we find poetic philosophy.

Notes

1. With thanks to Jorge J. E. Gracia, Carolyn Korsmeyer, Leo Zaibert for valuable suggestions on earlier drafts.
2. Arthur Danto refers to the issue of defining what philosophy is as "The Problem of Philosophy." See Danto, "Philosophizing Literature," in *The Philosophical Disenfranchisement of Art* (New York: Columbia University Press, 1986), esp. p. 167.
3. We see this sort of critique of the poets in Plato. See *Republic*, Book X, esp. 595a–602b and 607b–d. Plato's views on the nature and importance of poetry are infused with Socratic irony and so it would be unfair to read him as an enemy of art, yet his criticisms of art are part of a tradition that has informed Western philosophy. The "ancient quarrel between philosophy and poetry" to which Socrates makes reference in Book 10 (607b–c) of *The Republic* was settled in favor of a philosophy modeled on the methods of the natural sciences. This is most clearly seen in the Modern period. In Continental Europe, Descartes, Spinoza, and Leibniz turned to mathematics as a model that would ensure absolute and necessary truths.
4. Calvino, "Philosophy and Literature," in *The Uses of Literature*, trans. Patrick Creagh (New York: Harcourt Brace, 1982).
5. Calvino, "Philosophy and Literature," p. 46.
6. Ibid.
7. Early-German Romanticism (1794–1803) was centered alternatively in Jena and Berlin. Among early-German Romantics are August Wilhelm Schlegel and his brother Friedrich Schlegel, Ernst Daniel Schleiermacher, Friedrich von Hardenberg (Novalis), Ludwig Tieck, Caroline Veit Schlegel, and Dorothea Schlegel Schelling. Early-German Romanticism must be distinguished from two other periods of Romanticism in Germany, middle or high Romanticism and late Romanticism. High Romanticism (1808–1815) was shaped by the work of poets, artists, and thinkers, such as Achim von Arnim, Clemens Brentano, Caspar David Friedrich, and Adam Mueller, among others. This movement was more clearly literary. Finally, the members of late Romanticism (1816–1830) included Franz Baader, E. T. A. Hoffmann, Johann von Eichendorff, and also the elder Friedrich Schlegel and Friedrich Schelling.
8. Calvino begins his essay "Philosophy and Literature" with the claim that "Philosophy and literature are embattled adversaries" (p. 39).
9. *Loci classici* of works dealing with the literary strengths of early-German Romanticism are Ernst Behler, *German Romantic Literary Theory* (Cambridge: Cambridge University Press, 1993); Rudolf Hayn, *Die Romantische Schule* (Hildsheim: Georg Olm Verlagsbuchhandlung, 1961); Richarda Huch, *Die Blütezeit der Romantik— Ausbreitung, Blütezeit und Verfall der Romantik* (Tübingen: R. Wünderlich, 1951); Georg Lukács, *Soul and Form*, trans. Anna Bostock (Cambridge, MA: MIT Press, 1971).
10. Schlegel's fragments have been translated by Peter Firchow in *Friedrich Schlegel. Philosophical Fragments* (Minneapolis: University of Minnesota Press, 1991), and I have used, with minor modifications, his translations. All references to Schlegel's original work are to *Friedrich Schlegel Kritische Ausgabe* (*KA*), in 35 volumes, edited by Ernst Behler et al. (Paderborn: Ferdinand Schoenigh, 1958 ff.). *KA* II, p. 173, *Athenäum* Nr. 53, Firchow translation, p. 24.
11. See Rodolphe Gasché, "Ideality in Fragmentation," foreword to Peter Firchow's translation of Schlegel's *Philosophical Fragments* (Minneapolis: University of Minnesota Press, 1991), pp. vii–xxxii. According to Gasché, fragmentation constitutes the properly Romantic vision of the system (p. xiii). His analysis takes its theoretical starting point from the work of Walter Benjamin (*Der Begriff der*

Kunstkritik in der deutschen Romantik) and Lacoue-Labarthe/Nancy (*The Literary Absolute*), yet goes beyond these in finding a common thread between "idea" and the "fragment" and tracing this to Kant's discussion of representation (*Vorstellung*) and presentation (*Darstellung*) in the *Critique of Judgment*. He concludes that fragments are ideas in presentation. Azade Seyhan's "Fractal Contours: Chaos and System in the Romantic Fragment" [in *Beyond Representation. Philosophy and Poetic Imagination*, ed. Richard Eldridge (Cambridge: Cambridge University Press, 1996)], also discusses the philosophical importance of the fragment. According to Seyham, the romantic fragment reflects the circumstance of human subjects as in the process of becoming without ever quite reaching completion. The best source of these fragments was a journal that Schlegel edited with his brother, August Wilhelm. In 1798 the Schlegel brothers founded *Das Athenäum*, a journal that became a major vehicle for the articulation of the ideas of the early-German Romantics. The journal appeared between 1798 and 1800 and was in part a reaction against what Schlegel viewed as the conservative mood of the journals of the period.

12. Translated and interpreted by Phillipe Lacoue-Labarthe and Jean-Luc Nancy in *The Literary Absolute* (Albany, NY: SUNY Press, 1988).
13. Stanley Cavell, *This New Yet Unapproachable America: Lectures after Emerson and Wittgenstein* (Albuquerque, NM: Living Batch Press, 1989), pp. 4–6.
14. *KA* II, p. 182, *Athenäum* Nr.116, Firchow translation, pp. 31–32.
15. For a thorough dissection of this Fragment, see Eichner's Introduction to *KA* II, pp. LIX–LXIV.
16. Schlegel speaks of a "Sehnsucht nach dem Unendlichen" (*KA* XII, p. 7).
17. Schlegel claims that the infinite and our consciousness are the poles around which philosophy revolves (*KA* XII, p. 5).
18. *Philosophy and Literature*, p. 49.
19. *Six Memos for the Next Millennium. The Charles Eliot Norton Lectures 1985–86* (New York: Random House, 1988), p. 12. By September 1985, Calvino had finished writing five of six planned lectures that were to be read at Harvard University. Before leaving for the United States to deliver the lectures, he died of a stroke.
20. *Phaedrus*, pp. 274b–277a.
21. *KA* II, *Kritische Fragmente* Nr. 108, Firchow translation, p. 13.
22. "Die Überwindung der Metaphysik durch die logische Analyse der Sprache," *Erkenntnis*, 2 (1931), pp. 219–241. This has been translated by Arthur Pap as "The Elimination of Metaphysics through Logical Analysis" in *Logical Positivism*, ed. A. J. Ayer (New York: The Free Press, 1959), pp. 60–81.
23. Ibid., p. 240: "Metaphysiker sind Musiker ohne musikalishce Fähigkeit."
24. Ibid., p. 240, pp. 79–80, Papp translation.
25. "The Necessity of Inspired Reading," *The Chronicle of Higher Education* 42, no. 22 (February 9, 1996), p. A48.
26. Richard Rorty, "Philosophy as a Kind of Writing: An Essay on Derrida," in *Consequences of Pragmatism* (Minnesota: University of Minnesota Press, 1982), p. 92.
27. Arthur Danto and Jürgen Habermas have each responded quite critically to Derrida's views. See Danto, "Philosophy as/and/of Literature" and "Philosophizing Literature," in *The Philosophical Disenfranchisement of Art* (New York: Columbia University Press, 1986), pp. 135–161 and 163–186. See Habermas, "Excurs zur Einebnung des Gattungsunterschiedes zwischen Philosophie und Literatur," in *Der Philosophische Diskurs der Moderne* (Frankfurt: Suhrkamp, 1985), pp. 219–247 and "Philosophie und Wissenschaft als Literatur?" in *Nachmetaphysisches Denken* (Frankfurt: Suhrkamp, 1988), pp. 242–266.
28. See Habermas, "Excurs zur Einebnung des Gattungsunterschiedes zwischen Philosophie und Literatur," in *Der Philosophische Diskurs der Moderne* (Frankfurt:

Suhrkamp, 1985), pp. 219–247 and "Philosophie und Wissenschaft als Literatur?" in *Nachmetaphysisches Denken* (Frankfurt: Suhrkamp, 1988), pp. 242–266. For a response, see Hans Robert Jauß, "Italo Calvino: *Wenn ein Reisender in einer Winternacht* Pladöyer für eine postmoderne Ästhetik," in *Studien zum Epochenwandel der ästhetischen Moderne*" (Frankfurt: Suhrkamp, 1989), pp. 267–302. Jauß defends a theory of postmodern literature whereby it is not understood as a kind of narcissistic self-mirroring. He tries to show how Calvino's novel, in presenting life as a kind of reading, may even provide us with an instrument for a theory of communicative action.

29. Part One of Gadamer's *Truth and Method* provides a strong argument against such a view of aesthetic experience in general. He claims that our conception of aesthetic experience must not be limited to the subject, for then the being of the work of art becomes marginalized. Gadamer moves from the framework of aesthetic consciousness and the ensuing problem of aesthetic differentiation to the ontology of the work of art and aesthetic reconciliation. His move away from understanding aesthetics in terms of its subjectivization takes us in the right direction. See *Truth and Method*, trans. Joel Weinsheimer and Donald G. Marshall (New York: Crossroad, 1991).

30. Habermas writes: "Important critics and philosophers are also writers of rank. In their rhetorical achievements, literary critique and philosophy are related both to literature and to each other. But their relation is exhausted by this relation. For in each respective discipline, the rhetorical tools are subordinate to different forms of argumentation" (My translation of Habermas, 1988, pp. 245–246).

31. Habermas, 1988, p. 246.

32. *Six Memos*, p. 116.

33. In *The Transfiguration of the Commonplace. A Philosophy of Art* (Cambridge, MA: Harvard University Press, 1981), pp. 1–32.

34. Ibid., p. 9.

35. Recently, Colin McGinn, who notes that in light of the fact that "fiction fails to conform to any of the methodological paradigms that have dominated philosophy at large," the contributions of literary fiction to the realm of ethics have been neglected, has tried to remedy this situation. The result of his attempt to remedy this neglect is his book, *Ethics, Evil, and Fiction* (Oxford: Clarendon Press, 1997). In the course of the book, important connections between aesthetics and ethics are made.

36. *KA* II, p. 335, my translation.

37. Early in his career, Calvino compiled the most complete collection of Italian folktales; this would have taken him back to "that age of fairy-tales" where the "romantic" originated. Cf. *Fiabe Italiene* (Turin: Einaude, 1956).

38. *Philosophy and Literature*, p. 49.

39. *Six Memos*, p. 19.

40. *KA* II, *Über Tiecks Don Quixote*, pp. 281–283.

41. *KA* II, *Ideen* Nr. 69, Firchow translation, p. 100.

42. *KA* II, *Kritische Fragmente* Nr. 108, Firchow translation, p. 13.

43. Cited in Manfred Frank, *Unendliche Annäherung. Die Anfänge der philosophischen Frühromantik* (Frankfurt: Suhrkamp, 1997), p. 944.

44. *KA* II, 261, *Ideen* Nr. 48, Firchow translation, p. 98.

45. *Definitions of Territories: Comedies*, p. 62.

46. At the end of Chapter three of his book, *Leading a Human Life. Wittgenstein, Intentionality, and Romanticism*, Eldridge, after having given a brilliant account of Schlegel's use of irony, comes to a conclusion that is misleading. He claims that Schlegel's views empty the spontaneity of the human being of content, "reducing it to something more nearly resembling an animal function" and then goes on to talk of "Schlegelian nihilism." I cannot here show the problems with these claims,

but it is important to realize that just as Schlegel's irony does not make a mockery of the world, his acknowledgment of the openness of all philosophical inquiry and the incompleteness of our knowledge does not make him any sort of nihilist. Eldridge, *Leading a Human Life. Wittgenstein, Intentionality, and Romanticism* (Chicago: The University of Chicago Press, 1997), esp. pp. 83–85.

47. *KA* XII, p. 214.
48. *KA* XIII, pp. 55ff. and 173ff.
49. *KA* II, *Kritische Fragmente* Nr. 42, Firchow translation, p. 5.
50. See especially the essays in this volume by Henry Sussman and Ermanno Bencivenga. In particular, Bencivenga draws some conclusions that have great affinity with what I have presented here. He highlights the "agility of mind" that goes along with the liberation that comes as a result of both philosophy and literature disconnecting us from our ordinary context (p. 21). I have argued, following Calvino's insight, that a kind of agility that can be traced to irony forms the common root of philosophy's relation to literature.
51. *Six Memos*, p. 3.
52. *Six Memos*, p. 5.
53. *Six Memos*, p. 7.
54. *Six Memos*, p. 16.
55. *Six Memos*, p. 12.

8

HENRY SUSSMAN

The Writing of the System: Borges's Library and Calvino's Traffic

Systemic Parodists

In its most strident clarity, the rapport to philosophical systems maintained by the writing of Jorge Luis Borges and Italo Calvino, and we could mention with them Umberto Eco, Franz Kafka, and Maurice Blanchot, is at best murky and ambiguous. Any of us who have ever taken Borges's guided tour through the maniacally symmetrical hexagonal galleries of the Babel Library, bearing important similarities, by the way, to the monastery library in Eco's *The Name of the Rose*, or have ever negotiated the traffic patterns that Calvino elaborates with philosophical rigor in "The Chase," or have contemplated business with the bureaucracy of Kafka's Castle knows that systematic presumptions and processes are at the heart of these writers' fictive experiments and games. Their fictive productions, as cultural artifacts, almost plead to be written off as systematic parodies. The latest, still-influential nineteenth-century projects of philosophical system-making, so this narrative runs, generated an aesthetics of systematic parody. In different pretexts and under different guises, writers as diverse as Kafka, Bataille, Artaud, and Beckett, not to mention Borges and Calvino, rush in to give the lie to systems that, however meticulously they accounted for the torque and distortions exerted by their representational and nonrepresentational linguistic media, ultimately privilege determination and repetition over linguistic allegory and play.

This scenario—of Borges, Calvino, and their ilk as systemic parodists—is a compelling one, and I have already submitted to its full sway in my efforts to formulate the aesthetic contracts prevailing in modernism and postmodernism.[1] Certain aesthetic subcontracts to modernism,[2] such as futurist or dadaist manifestoes, the elaborate overdetermination in the structuration of the different segments comprising Joyce's *Ulysses*, or the fragmentations of cubism, import systematic dimensions, patterns, and pretensions wholesale, which they then joyfully demolish in explicit fashion. The aesthetic experiments of postmodernism, according to this scenario, elide the systems that may have been their occasion and deposit on the public docket of art the material residues of system-confounding strategems. These remains may well include Thomas Bernhard's endlessly self-referential and correcting sentences,[3] the musical minimalism of Glass or Reich, or closer to home, Calvino's image of the "soft moon,"[4] a lunar body whose vertical elevation and separation dissolve into the consistency of Cheese Whiz.

As philosophical discourse, in its circumspection and innovation, moves toward the consideration of writers such as Borges, Calvino, and Eco, language peels off of the scaffolding of conceptual systematization and metamorphoses itself into a radically different, more disruptive and intransigent sort of stuff. Borges, Calvino, and, closely allied to them, Blanchot, become philosophers of a writing, which, in the wake of deconstruction, allegorizes the freedom that systems delineate but cannot contain. The semantic, conceptual, and even physical play evidenced by Borges's and Calvino's systematic parodies may be interpreted as escapes, or at least interludes away from systematic control. I could launch, just at this point, a reasonable overview of parodic, self-questioning systems in Borges's and Calvino's fiction that would be more or less compelling, and that might convince a certain number of us that we had not egregiously misspent our time in hearing out the enumeration.

What Are Systems?

But this approach to Borges and Calvino, at a rare philosophical forum devoted to their importance, begs at least two pivotal questions: what, after all, are systems? And isn't the relation to conceptual systems by asystematic art and aesthetics more nuanced than one of simple one-upmanship or unmasking? If conceptual systems, by virtue of their architecture, or their perdurance, or their iterability, always exert some sort of repressive gravitational force, then the artifacts of structured language playing *off* of systems are *always* oppositional, extending the avant garde still current in Borges and Calvino far backward in the histories of literature and art.

We need furthermore consider the question of complicity. What if systematic parodies, such as reach a high degree of hilarity in Borges's image of *hrönir*,[5] units of mimesis and derivation on Tlön, or in Calvino's fifteen-page recapitulation and expansion of Dumas' *The Count of Monte-Cristo*,[6] evidence a higher degree of collaboration with the matrix of control than we, under the Western conventions of aesthetic disinterest and freeplay, are wont to allow? In terms of one of Borges's *Ficciones*, the hero, at least the thinking man's hero, or thinker, in a situation of war or other sociopolitical polarization, is the likeliest suspect to become a traitor,[7] for aesthetic creativity acknowledges a labyrinthine proliferation of viable avenues of action, among them the renunciation of "true" belief. The cultural audience that equated aesthetic play and systematic opposition with liberal political values was infuriated by his decoration, at the end of his career, by Chile's General Augusto Pinochet. At the same time, Borges's later *ficciones*, such as comprise *Doctor Brodie's Report*, abound with ethical images of the lamentable after-effects of extremism, in situations of professional competitiveness, sexual jealousy, and even nationalistic pride.[8]

What if the lesson we draw from Borges's and Calvino's fiction is as much of the complicity between parodies and the systems they play off of as of the opposition? This collaboration might complexify, in a salutary fashion, our notions of the language justifying the sense of Borges, Calvino, Blanchot, Benjamin, and Derrida as philosophers of language. In a world of collusion between repressive—because structured, repetitive, and ultimately deterministic—systems, even the language of parody is inflected by what might be called the style or tonality of a system, or its shadow, as in Wittgenstein's early turn of phrase, "the shadow of a fact."[9] As I hope to suggest below, in Borges and Calvino, and the demonstration may well extend to others, the parodic bad-boys of philosophical systematization may derive much in tone, style, and imagery from the conceptual machines from which they presumably part company.

The law of genre may also be germane to the complex rhythm of opposition and complexity most likely prevailing between conceptual systems and their parodic renderings. However brilliantly Borges and Calvino occasionally mock the dimensions, processes, and tonalities accruing from the systematic works of Kant and Hegel, there is no reason why asystematic discourse should rest solely in the hands of artists, literary or otherwise. The positionality of Borges and Calvino, as putative philosophers of writing, may be more akin to that of Fichte, who taught knowledge literally between the systematic lineaments of Kant and Hegel, and of Kierkegaard, who organized a literal shutdown of Hegelian dialectics, than that of literary system-makers, whether Dickens or Eliot, Mann or Pynchon.

Twelve Ways of Looking at a System

So what are systems? However diverse their forms and manifestations, they, along with their aspirations, have occupied a pivotal place in culture for a long time. And if we attempt to know them from their actions rather than their essence, what do systems do?

In a Borgesian Chinese encyclopedia, this is how conceptual systems might fare:

1. A system is an interactive language tool such that certain elements predicate others, whose value and function through this process become

predictable. The identity of the machine, which will surely belie its linguistic nuance and complexity, becomes conflated with its repetitive function, its ability to reproduce its own action.

2. A system is a linguistic artifact achieving certain organic properties, in which the whole predicates certain elements, which in turn stand for the system in entirety, although the linguistic medium is itself distinctly inorganic.

3. A system is a mechanism of sufficient perdurance and predictability to allow for the state of affairs in which "only that which happens every three hundredth night is true" (*F*, p. 26).

4. A system is a linguistic configuration of concepts better designed, more fully fitted out, than other units of discourse to consummate acts and perform functions. It is better geared to performatives, speech-acts, and writing-acts than a parallel composition of asystematic script. Asystematic writing opens up a dynamic whose operational function, on the other hand, is always already impaired, a medium that revels in this crippled function. This crippling becomes a motif in the asystematic fiction that performs its own status, whether Borges's Funes, whose memory, as resistant to logical and epistemological formats of organization as it is relentless, is a byproduct of his having been thrown by a horse (*F*, p. 109), or Beckett's Molloy, whose ambulatory dysfunctions make him reliant upon a bicycle, itself chainless and broken down.[10]

5. We say of a phenomenon or tendency that it is "systematic" when we refer to its comprehensiveness, the degree to which it is pervasive. The regularity and repetitiveness of systems endow them with the specific mode of expansiveness consisting in an extension, or iteration, to certain types of situations, always in the same way. The effects of a circumstance may be random, or even fanciful, but a system tends toward foregone conclusions in every situation in which it plays.

6. A system is interconnected. Other composite entities may incorporate diverse components and functions that, however, do not interrelate. Texts of the minimal degree of design rendering them beyond pure functionality, say the functionality of the telephone directory, are also interconnected. Hence, there are frequent and understandable conflations of texts and systems. But whereas textuality, an amalgam of linguistic features involving the semantic, semiotic, phonetic, grammatical, and syntactical registers of language, defines the linguistic cohesion of written artifacts, systems crystallize through relations of logic, succession, function, and operation. This is a critical difference between texts and systems, one worth noting.

7. A system deploys units. Its infrastructure is greater or on a higher level than the units over which it presides. These units may comprise entities, functions, acts, structures, or points of view, all of which play, for

example, in the system that Hegel designs and composes in *The Phenom-enology of Spirit*. Whatever the nature of its units, a system would purport to deploy them consistently at all levels of operation, in all arenas, that is, systematically.[11]

In the variety of components that he incorporated into his systematic substructure, and in the range of settings in which he deployed them, Hegel may be considered the first French structuralist, even though he was not French and died a 130 years before this attitude or set of studies coalesced. There is a strong affinity between the powerful iterability of Hegelian structures and tropes and the permutational aesthetics that Borges shared with, among other instances, Kafka's mythological exper-iments and Lévi-Strauss's "Structural Study of Myth."[12] Where struc-turalist approaches to linguistics, anthropology, history, and related disciplines attempted to finesse the question as to whether structures are above all formal or substantive in nature, structural fabulations in litera-ture, as in Borges's permutational fiction (e.g., "The Garden of Forking Paths," "The Library of Babel," "The Babylon Lottery," or "Death and the Compass"), aestheticized the play of structures, and in this sense sidestepped the issue.

8. Systems, in their distinction between infrastructure and units of opera-tion, implicitly differentiate between levels of operation, some higher, some lower. Yet they are designed to operate identically on each of the levels that they encompass. One clear strategy for asystematic writing is to offer the trappings of mechanical function with neither the vertical articulation nor the presumption of perfect repetition. Kafka, for one, exploits this systematic vulnerability as he stages the demolition of the execution machine in "In the Penal Colony."[13]

9. Because conceptual systems expand our possibilities of thinking, they, in reciprocal rapport to their "subjects," are figured as expanding their own dimensions. Conceptual systems gravitate toward outer limits that are, by definition, sublime, in the Kantian sense. The trajectory of systematic thought is outward bound. Kant sets this agenda for modern systematic thought in the overall approach to the Transcendental in *The Critique of Pure Reason*. As the treatise and its constructs circulate closer and closer to the Transcendental, the features of this register become more sublime, even though Kant has not yet postulated the formal aesthetics of sublimity.[14]

10. Systems, in keeping with their own implicit Enlightenment ideology, are self-regulating. Their internal mechanisms are both restrictive and stochastic. The mechanism by which systems expand and govern them-selves is one and the same. It is in this sense that Lönnrot, the ill-fated detective of "Death and the Compass," experiences the Kabbalistic web of clues that he must decipher in order to solve a spate of murders

as a progression along a sequence of integers with occasional, near-magical points of expansion. Among the examples that the narrative cites of this expansion that breaks out, occasionally and arbitrarily, along a progressive series are God's "ninth attribute, eternity" (*F*, p. 131), and "a hundredth name—the Absolute Name" of God (*F*, p. 132), which, according to the Hasidim, lifts His prior ninety names to a new level.[15]

11. The disclaimers or at least allowances that systems make for their claims, whether of comprehensiveness, consistency, self-reflexivity, or whatever, are as pervasive as their magnitude and seriousness of purpose. Systems are instruments of language guaranteeing their own malfunction as inevitably as new machinery comes fitted out with its own warranty. A work with systematic pretensions apologizes for itself even while it presses its claim. This foregone apology constitutes a rhetorical subgenre; affectively, this admission amounts to existentialist bad faith. Systematic work would hope that giving the lie, in advance, to the force and dimension of its design *excuses* it of its shortcomings and excesses. In an offhand manner, then, a philosophical system and its literary simulacrum, as opposed to the poem and the fragment, is an instrument of language distinguished by being always already equipped with its own bad-faith excuse. The systematic disclaimer disarms the aggression that might be directed toward the systematic claim.

12. Systematic writing therefore maintains a privileged rapport to its own destruction. The story, the poem, the argument, the critique as such make a certain offer. There is an inherent finitude to their claim. The espousal of their limit serves as an insurance policy to their design. Imperfections, anomaly, inconsistency, and parallel traits are all protected under the aesthetic contract prevailing over modernity in the West. Systematic writing aspires to much more. In its multifaceted claim is the violation of each one of its features. The thrill of the system is that each one of its pretensions hovers on the shoal of its own dismemberment. The Kantian drama of the sublime has anticipated this thriller. The science fiction scientist, who is a close relative to the speculator of sublimity in Kant, fully anticipates the vengeful attack by the monster, the figuration of the Transcendental, that only he has managed to predicate and track.

Borges: An Asystematic Writer

Page for page, "Tlön, Uqbar, Orbis Tertius" is the most intense, fully and successfully designed work of asystematic writing in a nonphilosophical mode that I have ever encountered. It is the first of Borges's *Ficciones*. Like the other *ficciones*, it is in part a miniaturized recapitulation and extension of preexisting literary genres. The text, in this case, draws on the conventions of science fiction and fantastic literature. What is so inventive and brilliant about this brief work is how systematically it sets out the conditions of an alternate universe whose features correspond to those of Western metaphysics, but in an a priori state of deconstruction (if one be permitted to coin this phrase). The traits of this imaginary world (or rather uncannily related subworlds) are not merely set in relief against the Western philosophical conventions that they challenge. They are products, as poetic constructions, of positive imaging. It is in this context that knowledge and thought on Tlön attain a systematic coherence. "The metaphysicians of Tlön seek not truth, or even plausibility—they seek to amaze, astound" (*CF*, p. 74). By the same token, mathematical values are relative rather than precise. "Visual geometry is based on the surface, not the point" (*CF*, p. 76). "Books are rarely signed, nor does the concept of plagiarism exist: It has been decided that all books are the work of a single author who is timeless and anonymous" (*CF*, pp. 76–77). "Their fiction has but a single plot, with every imaginable permutation" (*CF*, p. 77). "All nouns . . . have only metaphoric value" (*CF*, p. 75). The philosophy, mathematics, literature, and religion of this imaginary domain, like Borges's most significant literary and philosophical models, subjugate Being, essence, identity, truth, and rectitude to the dynamics of language itself. "Their language and those things derived from their language—religion, literature, metaphysics—presuppose idealism" (*CF*, p. 72). The extreme idealism that is perhaps Borges's ultimate caption for this world in a preexistent state of deconstruction is a condition in which figments of language influence reality and vice versa. There is no more fanciful talisman of this threshold at which textuality, as a modern-day monadology, reconfigures the protocols and expectations of established philosophical systems than the *hrönir*, units of originality, derivation, and duplication that operate in no knowable sequence or determinable pattern.

I shall not dwell on "Tlön, Uqbar, Orbis Tertius" on this occasion, having belabored its compression, expansiveness, and extreme idealism elsewhere.[16] But I mention it as I set out on a survey of Borges as an asystematic writer because it perfectly defines and dramatizes the relation between the Borgesian *ficcion* and that aspect of philosophical work purporting to systematic dimensions. "Tlön, Uqbar, Orbis Tertius" does not simply substitute whimsy or playfulness for the Western manias for directionality in time, precision in mathematical value, decisiveness in juridical procedure, linearity in literary plot, and uniqueness in questions of identity and creative originality. It verges on the limits of systematic aspirations and dimensions by imposing systematic protocols on itself. "Tlön, Uqbar, Orbis Tertius" must be accorded every seriousness as the blueprint for a nonexistent universe at the same time that its prevailing notions of time, space, quality, quantity, duration, and succession are foils to their counterparts as they could derive from the encyclopedias of Western philosophy.

The universe (which others call the Library) is composed of an indefinite, perhaps infinite number of hexagonal galleries. In the center of each gallery is a ventilation shaft, bounded by a low railing. From any hexagon one can see the floors above and below—one after another, endlessly. The arrangement of the galleries is always the same: Twenty bookshelves, five to each side, line four of the hexagon's six sides; the height of the bookshelves, floor to ceiling, is hardly greater than the height of a normal librarian. One of the hexagon's free sides opens onto a narrow sort of vestibule, which in turn opens onto another gallery, identical to the first—identical in fact to all. To the left and right of the vestibule are two tiny compartments. One is for sleeping, upright; the other, for satisfying one's physical necessities. (*CF*, p. 112)

This passage, which initiates "The Library of Babel," hangs suspended between the sublimely repetitive architecture of an imaginary library and "physical necessities." It is a synecdochical miniature both of the *ficcion* that it heads and Borges's appeal and approach to systematicity. The passage juxtaposes the obsessive but inhuman, because utterly indifferent repetitions that give the library its style, to the fundamental, because earthly and leveling, human needs. The *ficcion* absorbs any hypothetical character that might inhabit this landscape and place the reader in a labyrinthine and self-contained, but expanding system, whose features link it inextricably to the processes of reading, exegesis, and writing. As in the internal landscapes of Piranesi's prisons and Poe's tales of horror, a distinctive fascination, even allure, will accrue to the very indifference and inhumanity of the design. There are laws at work in this architecture. They have been issued with sublimity by the moral imperative. All galleries are hexagonal. Four sides of each are covered by five long shelves of books. Concessions to human scale and necessities are uniform throughout the architecture. An interminable display of identical galleries, giving the Library what Borges elsewhere calls "the numbered divisibility of a prison" (*F*, p. 129), lends the construction the aura of panoptical oversight.

Within this overdetermined landscape, "The Library is 'total' . . . its bookshelves contain all possible combinations of the twenty-two orthographic symbols (a number which, though unimaginably vast, is not infinite)—that is, all that is able to be expressed, in every language. *All*" (*CF*, p. 115). The arbitrariness and overdesign of the Library's architecture extend to the works on its shelves. These result not from the imagination or creativity of their authors, but from the combinatory potential of the orthographic symbols. As in Tlön, the literary activity culminating in the works of the Library is an impersonal operation along the functions and registers of a manifold of symbols, graphemes, phonemes, and marks. Any notion of authorship is collective, and of creativity automatic and accidental. The totality ascribed to the Library is not the unimaginable amalgam of human creativity, and its metaphysics, but a mathematical sum or reckoning of all the combinations in the signs. This of course introduces a chance factor of potentially hilarious anomalies and provides a tonal antidote to the dry arbitrariness of the architectural blueprint.

> One book, which my father once saw in a hexagon in circuit 15-94, consisted of the letters MCV perversely repeated from the first line to the last. Another (much consulted in this zone) is a mere labyrinth of letters whose penultimate page contains the phrase *O Time thy pyramids*. This much is known: For every rational line or forthright statement there are leagues of senseless cacophony, verbal nonsense, and incoherency. (I know of one semi-barbarous zone whose librarians repudiate the "vain and superstitious habit" of trying to find sense in books, equating such a quest with attempting to find meaning in dreams or in the chaotic lines of the palm of one's hand). (*CF*, pp. 113–114)

We are already gathering enough data from "The Library of Babel" to begin positing some surmises regarding Borges's theoretically aware approach to systems and systematicity. The ultimate system lending the *Ficciones* their sublime, spacy, labyrinthine quality is, of course, the system of language itself, understood, in keeping with surrealism as well as structuralism, as an impersonal combinatorial matrix at the level of Chomskyan deep structure, on a level that would have to be described as subpsychological. "The Library contains all verbal structures" (*CF*, p. 117), specifies the narrator of our *ficcion*, rendering explicit the link between the absurdities of our library building and the linguistic medium that its works, however tangentially, join. Throughout *Ficciones* and his other writings, Borges configures figurative simulacra of language, and these are characterized by systemic features. The aspect of language that Borges is highlighting in his involuted fabulations, whether the Library of Babel or the labyrinthine plot in which, in "The Garden of Forking Paths," a World War I Chinese spy for the Germans and a British sinologist are enmeshed, is the deep grammar, the impersonal features that belie the intimate roles in thinking and interpersonal communication to which language is put. Although Borges clearly belongs to those twentieth-century writers, among them Kafka, Proust, Beckett, Calvino, and Eco, most theoretically attuned to the linguistic ground, underpinnings, and dynamics making fiction, and indeed all representation possible, he is quite selective with regard to which linguistic gestures he installs into his fantastic landscapes or labyrinthine constructions. He gravitates to the impersonal, machine-like features, the extreme of *langue* on the continuum also extending to street-talk or *parole*. These inhuman dimensions of the linguistic medium in which even our most private, inadmissible, and intimate thoughts are couched he figures as expansive matrices or labyrinths in space, to wit,

"The Library of Babel" or the Paris/Buenos Aires of "Death and the Compass," but also in time. This utterly fantastic notion of a labyrinth in time is one of Borges's most striking and original syntheses:

> Unlike Newton and Schopenhauer, your ancestor did not believe in a uniform and absolute time; he believed in an infinite series of times, a growing, dizzying web of divergent, convergent, and parallel times. That fabric of times that approach one another, fork, are snipped off, or are simply unknown for centuries, contains *all* possibilities. In most of those times, we do not exist; in some, you exist but I do not; in others I do and you do not; in others still, we both do. (*CF*, p. 127)

Borges populates the landscape of his writing with inhuman and impersonal constructions whose features are a deliberate subset of linguistic functions in part so that he can trace out their absurdities or anomalies on a human scale. He introduces human considerations into his fictive settings in part as limiting cases of systematicity. He configures mock systems indistinguishable from their linguistic parameters so that he can lay them low with anomalies also corresponding to features of language, this time at the level of arbitrariness and singularity, the coordinate of the continuum verging on the parole. He traps his reader, and indeed his whole fictive world, in a feedback loop shuttling endlessly, but not infinitely, between the systematic parameters and the singularities within the linguistic medium. Toward the overdetermined and impersonal sweep of this trajectory, he lends efforts at system-making, whether on the part of Kant, Hegel, or Schopenhauer, more credence than we might initially allow. Yet he endlessly questions this gravitation toward systematization, one as inevitable as linguistic articulation itself, by staging the absurdities arising when system and intractable particular are set on a collision course. Asystematic writing, under Borges's stewardship, is a release of the repression or constraint demanded by an inevitable positing of the universe as an expansive rhetorical figure.

This double act of construction, this parry-and-thrust, does much to illuminate the brief sections of "The Library of Babel" that we have begun to approach. For it turns out that the breathtaking universe of the Library is as sensible as it is fantastic and impossible. I speak here not only of the architectural acknowledgment of the "physical necessities." Let us consider the unique volume that the narrator's father, an earlier librarian, opening up the issue of intellectual as well as genetic patrimony, discovered "in a hexagon in circuit number 15-94." The textual material out of which the book's single grammatically correct phrase emerges is not meaningless word-salad; it is a seme consisting of the letters MCV repeated innumerable times. MCV is also a Roman numeral amounting to 1105. (A dictionary of dates reveals that in 1105 C.E., Tancred defeated the Turks at Tizin; also, that Henry V of the Holy Roman Empire imprisoned his father, Henry IV. In 1594, Henry IV of

France was crowned at Chartres. Is this confusion of Henrys a historical correlative to the contingent generation of meaning in the Library?)

Even while the Library and the works comprising it push our standard notion of meaning to the extreme, they do not abolish it. There are epiphenomena of meaning everywhere, even in the constructed discourse designed to put this traditional notion to the extreme test. Borges's demonstration is clear. The world of *ficciones*, or of the "extreme idealism" pressing backward to the terrain at which, always mediated by language, ideas and things generate one another, retains the residue of the systematicity that fictive language might otherwise seem to negate. Fiction bears the trace of system to the same extent that system is already discombobulated by the inherent play and radicality of the medium—language—making it up. This observation of my own is borne out by the phrase that emerges, as if by magic, out of the cacophony of the MCVs. It is "O Time thy pyramids," a phrase presenting the enigma of time as the riddle of the sphynx. (The pyramids, of course, stand adjacent to the Egyptian Sphynx.) What interests me more about this phrase than its exotic (in an orientalist sense) provenance is the sublimity of its content and tone. The meaning that the absurd and inhuman system of the Library puts forth on a bad day, when mechanism gives way to sense, is sublime. Sublimity, of course, is the position that the Kantian speculations reach at the end of a long trajectory in which the Transcendental remains the bedrock and landmark of human culture and civilization, but only as deduced and evolved, in keeping with European emancipatory ideology, from human capability. The system eventuating in the Kantian sublime makes an accommodation for human traits and lineaments just as the interminable hexagons of the Babel library contain commodes for fecal necessities.

The sublime, and a long chain of systematic works struggling to effect a synthesis between the transcendental basis of Western metaphysics and the modern, in Foucault's sense, resuscitation of the human, not only Kant's, thus leave their imprint on Borges's fantastic, and I would add asystematic, counteruniverse.[17] The interaction between systematic thought and the twentieth-century writers who set it in an abyss or parodied it is, alas, not simple. It is not the joyous and invariably uplifting struggle between Tom and Jerry and their many analagons. The system marks asystematic writing, even as the latter measures the claims and efficacies of systems. This standoff, as suggested above, may belong more to the suspended ambiguity of collusion than to the edifying ethos of liberation.

Calvino's "The Chase"

Whereas it likely constitutes an oversimplification to assert that Italo Calvino's asystematic writing parts ways definitively from the modality of the sublime, I may not be entirely wrong in suggesting that Calvino, in comparison to Borges, leaves more room in his fiction for the everyday, and its particular register of humor. There are many instances that could be inserted at this point in the argument: the meditation on Zeno's paradox and matters of spatiality, as well as their application to the fatal leap of a lion in the title story of *t zero* and the synthesis of a biological rhetoric of mitosis, meiosis, and death in articulating the love-drama uniting Qfwfq and Priscilla in the segmented romance of the latter's name. But by its explicit invocation of systematic dimensions and dynamics, in exploration of time and movement in space, I am drawn to Calvino's miniaturized thriller, "The Chase." Calvino is no less a philosophically motivated writer than Borges. But in toning down his indebtedness to sublimity, above all as invoked by Kant and the Romantics—and this particular appropriation is evident throughout Borges's fiction, especially in the Library galleries and the ineluctable Babylon lottery—Calvino is free to explore other twists and plays of the philosophical concept.

The conceptual richness and profundity of the everyday is the compost out of which Calvino tills the turns of plot and humor in his fictive writing. We cannot be certain as to the existential conditions (criminal conspiracy, the Oedipal triangle, irrational mutual antipathy) that compel the narrator of "The Chase" in his traffic-driven fight to the death with a like-minded Other. But from the outset, Calvino's narrative places us in a dual and abruptly shifting perspective in which we vacillate between the experience of the situation, its phenomenological dimensions, and a systematic apprehension of it, which is Other. It is the abrasive juxtaposition, the always tenuous fusion, on the verge of collapse, between psychosocial experience and its phenomenological coordinates and a systematic reinscription of that experience, that comprises the true motive and object of "The Chase."

> That car that is chasing me is faster than mine; inside there is one man, alone, armed with a pistol, a good shot, as I have seen from the bullets that missed me by a fraction of an inch. In my escape I have headed for the center of the city; it was a healthy decision; the pursuer is constantly behind me but we are separated by several other cars; we have stopped at a traffic signal, in a long column.
>
> The signal is regulated in such a way that on our side the red light lasts a hundred and eighty seconds and the green light a hundred and twenty, no doubt based on the premise that the perpendicular traffic is heavier and slower. A mistaken premise: calculating the cars I see going by transversely when it is green for them, I would say that they are about twice the number of those that in an equally long period manage to break free of our column and pass the signal. (*tz*, pp. 112–113)

Enemy bullets are missing the narrator only by "a fraction of an inch." His existential status could not be more tenuous. But this does not stop him from calculating, in a somewhat dispassionate and philosophical manner, how the preprogrammed traffic lights favor the perpendicular stream of traffic at the corner where he is stalled. By the same token, Calvino situates his text at the corner where subjective metaphysics, with its life-and-death dramas, and systematic apprehensions merge. It is on this corner, between the cheesiness, say, of "The Soft Moon" and the romance that it serves as a talisman, and the cold calculations of astronomy that Calvino chooses to locate the constructions of his fiction.

> I realize that when, in this description, I oppose "us" and "them" I include in the term "us" both myself and the man who is chasing me in order to kill me, as if the boundary line of enmity passed not between me and him but rather between those in our column and those in the transverse one. But for all who are here immobilized and impatient, with their feet on the clutch, thoughts and feelings can follow no other course but the one imposed by the respective situations in the currents of traffic; it is therefore admissible to suppose that a community of intention is established between me, who cannot wait to dash away, and him who is waiting for a repetition of his previous opportunity. . . .
>
> It should be added that the community implied in the term "us" is only apparent, because in practice my enmity extends not only to the cars that cross our column but also those in it; and inside our column I feel definitely more hostile toward the cars that precede me and prevent me from advancing than those following me. . . .
>
> In short, the man who at this moment is my mortal enemy is now lost among many other solid bodies where my chafing aversion and fear are also perforce distributed. (tz, pp. 113–114)

The narrator of "The Chase" is quick to note his simultaneous membership in two collectivities: in the duel with his adversary, in which he has a tangible stake in dodging the bullets, in ultimately coming out on top, and in the flow of traffic, in which his shared interest with his adversary, for they are in the same lane of the same column of traffic, supersedes his rather pressing personal preoccupations in importance. If the narrator can be accused of achieving a philosophically rigorous position of indifference in the midst of his travail, and I believe this to be the case, this purview entails the precedence of systematicity over dialectical interest or self-interest.

Like Borges's protagonists, the surrogates in the world of Calvino's fiction, however pedestrian they may be, however much their clutch-feet may be jammed into the automotive carpet, also verge on a vast expansion of the everyday through the opening up of systems much broader than their limited concerns. Long before the narrator distinguishes between "the system that includes all the vehicles moving in the center of a city where the total surface of the automobiles equals and perhaps exceeds the total surface of the streets; on the other hand the system created between an armed pursuer and an unarmed pursued man" (tz, p. 122), thereby making the systematicity of the traffic flow and of the Master/Bondsman reversals in the duel explicit, the story's rhetoric has hinted at this broader dimension or register underlying the attention to the empirical data. The "calculations" in which both pursuer and pursued are engaged (*tz*, pp. 115–116), the narrator's exploration of "every hypothesis because the more details I can foresee the more probabilities I have of saving myself" (*tz*, p. 117), conceding that his driverly maneuvers "above all are not decided by us but dictated by the traffic's general pace" (*tz*, p. 120) are all considerations intimating a speculative, general, and systematic dimension to the situation, making it a philosophical diorama or cloud-chamber. Traffic is an annoying aspect of contemporary urban and suburban life that benights us. It is also an instance of what Bergson or Merleau-Ponty might have called "the systematicity of everyday life,"[18] the systematic analagon to Kant's deployment of consensus regarding beauty as an everyday instance of judgment, and the immanent conceptual operating system upon which it is based, in the ordinary lives of ordinary people.

"The Chase" bears witness to the birth of a philosophical subspecialization that I hope will become prevalent throughout the discipline, namely, to the philosophy of traffic.[19] Once the systematic scope of traffic and the urban plans that direct and control it opens up, there are no limits to the philosophical concepts and traditions falling under its sway.

> It is the bodies therefore that determine the surrounding space, and if this affirmation seems to contradict both my experience and my pursuer's . . . it is because we are dealing with a property not of single bodies but of the whole complex of bodies in their reciprocal relationships, in their moments of initiative and indecision, of starting the motor, in their flashing of lights and honking and biting nails and constant angry shifts of gear: neutral, first, second; neutral, first second, neutral . . .
>
> Now that we have abolished the concept of space (I think my pursuer in these periods of waiting must also have reached the same conclusions as I) and now that the concept of motion no longer implies the continuous passage of a body through a series of points but only disconnected and irregular displacements of bodies that occupy this point or that, perhaps I will succeed in accepting more patiently the slowness of the line, because what counts is the relative space that is defined and transformed around my car as around every other car in this traffic jam. In short, each car is the center of a system of relationships which in practice is the equivalent of another, that is, the cars are interchangeable, I mean the cars each with its driver inside; each driver could perfectly change places with another driver, I with my neighbors and my pursuer with his. (*tz*, pp. 122–123)

So fundamental are these speculations eventually attaining systematic proportions that they revert to an analytic of space and time, in which even the dimensions of the body, and the possibility of corporeality itself, are up for grabs. The gravitation away from the banalities of self-concern and petty rivalry is also a momentum toward increasingly fundamental categories of philosophical speculation, such as a body situated at the very coordinates of space and time. This is no longer a body that in conventional fiction insinuates itself into different sensual apotheoses; this is a body in the purest, in the Kantian sense, form: a body that is a unit of space and time, an element of movement, a shifter of identity and difference, sameness and reciprocity, a body both epitomizing and parodying Cartesian space.[20] So powerfully does the traffic situation in which the pursuers are enmeshed assert itself on a systematic level that one space is interchangeable with another; a body indistinguishable from another. The dimension of systematicity abolishes spatial and corporeal singularity just as it has mocked the melodrama of the life-and-death chase experienced on the existential level.

Calvino's systematic fiction, like that of Borges, expands in the sense that it uplifts beyond the constraints of circumstance and materiality. But where the Borgesian *ficción* luxuriates in the arabesques of complication, labyrinths, lotteries, and endlessly twisting plots, a modernist and postmodern embroidery on possibilities latent in the Hegelian dialectic, Calvino's systematic writing looks back over its shoulder at the pure elements of philosophical speculation. Perhaps in a more Kantian fashion, Calvino reverts backward toward the irreducible elements in the grammar of the intellectual operating system of the universe, obscure but objectifiable. Both Borges and Calvino adopt the features of their narrative to the point at which they articulate not only the writing of one system or another, but the writing of the system, the systematic parameters imprinted upon theoretically aware writing itself. It is at this point where they leave us, and we leave them.

Notes

1. See Henry Sussman, *Afterimages of Modernity: Structure and Indifference in Twentieth-Century Literature* (Baltimore: Johns Hopkins University Press, 1990), pp. 1–20, 161–205.
2. I develop my notion of the aesthetic contract in *The Aesthetic Contract: Statutes of Art and Intellectual Work in Modernity* (Stanford, CA: Stanford University Press, 1997), pp. 150–177.
3. See Thomas Bernhard, *Correction*, trans. Sophie Wilkins (Chicago: University of Chicago Press, 1979), pp. 8, 13, 46–47, 108, 156, 200, 242, 267.
4. Italo Calvino, "The Soft Moon," in *t zero*, trans. William Weaver (New York: Harcourt Brace Jovanovich, 1976), pp. 3–13. All citations of Calvino in this essay refer to this volume, henceforth abbreviated "*tz.*"
5. This is an image from Jorge Luis Borges's story "Tlön, Uqbar, Orbis Tertius," in *Ficciones* (New York: Grove Press, 1962) pp. 29–30, henceforth abbreviated "*F.*" Longer quotations from Borges in this essay refer to *Collected Fictions*, trans. Andrew Hurley (New York: Penguin Books, 1998), henceforth abbreviated "*CF.*"
6. See Italo Calvino, "The Count of Monte Cristo," in *t zero*, pp. 137–152.

7. See Jorge Luis Borges, "The Theme of the Traitor and Hero," in *Ficciones*, pp. 123–128.
8. Jorge Luis Borges, *Doctor Brodie's Report*, trans. Norman Thomas Di Giovanni (New York: E. P. Dutton, 1978), pp. 63–78, 89–96.
9. See Ludwig Wittgenstein, *The Blue and Brown Books* (Oxford: Basil Blackwell, 1964), p. 36.
10. Samuel Beckett, *Molloy* (New York: Grove Press, 1955), pp. 19–20.
11. See G. W. F. Hegel, *The Phenomenology of Spirit*, trans. A. V. Miller (New York: Oxford University Press, 1977), pp. 6–7, 11–12, 16–17, 20, 29–30.
12. See Claude Lévi-Strauss, "The Structural Study of Myth," in *Structural Anthropology*, trans. Claire Jacobson and Brooke Grundfest Schoepf (New York: Basic books, 1963), pp. 206–231.
13. See Franz Kafka, "In the Penal Colony," in *The Complete Stories* (New York: Schocken, 1977), pp. 163–166.
14. Immanuel Kant, *Critique of Pure Reason*, trans. Norman Kemp Smith (New York: St. Martin's, 1965), pp. 297–300.
15. I owe this insight regarding systematic self-regulation and stochastic expansion to Wladimir Kryzinski of the University of Montreal. This stochastic point of view enters the frameworks of critical theory and philosophy by way of fractal mathematics. For an excellent rereading of Proust from this perspective, see "Fractal Proust," in J. Hillis Miller and Manuel Asensi, *Black Holes; or Boustrephedontic Reading* (Stanford, CA: Stanford University Press, 1998), pp. 349–363.
16. See "Kafka in the Heart of the Twentieth Century: An Approach to Borges," in my *Afterimages of Modernity*.
17. I am referring to Foucault's reinscription, in *The Order of Things*, of a human impact upon socioeconomic, natural, and linguistic process elided by the logic prevailing during his "Classical" age of scientific discovery, the seventeenth and eighteenth centuries. See Michel Foucault, *The Order of Things*, trans. Richard Howard (New York: Vintage, 1973), pp. 307–312, 318–335, 346–355.
18. See Henri Bergson, *Matter and Memory*, trans. N. M. Paul and W. S. Palmer (New York: Zone Books, 1991), pp. 25–44, 218–223; Maurice Merleau-Ponty, *The Visible and the Invisible*, trans. Alphonso Lingis (Evanston, IL: Northwestern University Press, 1968), pp. 50–104.
19. My feeble attempt at facetiousness should not obscure the fact that traffic constitutes one manifestation of the general flow that Gilles Deleuze and Félix Guattari monitor in their "Capitalism and Schizophrenia" diptych. Their gravitation toward flow enables their discourse, at the cost of some specificity, to link textual and extratextual phenomena. Their readings of Spinoza, Kleist, Kafka, Artaud, Miller, and Burroughs, among others, go hand in hand with a sociology of outmoded sociopolitical formations (e.g., "nomadic despotism") nonetheless exerting a subliminal and persistent impact on contemporary "advanced" culture. The construct of flow goes a long way toward making their distinctive perspective, corresponding to the schizo's eye-view of the world, possible. See Gilles Deleuze and Félix Guattari, *A Thousand Plateaus*, trans. Brian Massumi (Minneapolis: University of Minnesota Press, 1987), pp. 48–57, 70, 112, 190–191, 202–207, 223–231.
20. This body bears some affinities to Deleuze and Guattari's "BwO," or "body without organs," the locus of an experience not organized by the tried and true formats of propriety and reason. For the body without organs, see Gilles Deleuze and Félix Guattari, *Anti-Oedipus*, trans. Robert Hurley, Mark Seem, and Helen R. Lane (Minnesota: University of Minnesota Press, 1983), pp. 1–5, 8–16, 281.

9

ROCCO CAPOZZI

Knowledge and Cognitive Practices in Eco's Labyrinths of Intertextuality

> A book is not an isolated being: it is a relationship, an axis of innumerable relationships.
>
> —J. L. Borges

This essay deals with Umberto Eco's use of libraries, encyclopedias, intertextuality, and rhizomes as open epistemological systems. Eco's possible worlds of fiction can be viewed primarily as cognitive experiences through which narrators and readers arrive not at truth(s), but at a better understanding of semiosic practices and philosophical notions concerning a variety of topics such as perception, interpretation of signs, language, meaning, the relativism of truths, the diffusion of knowledge, cultural history, and the omnipotence of God. My references to thinkers such as Aristotle, Roger Bacon, Kant, Wittgenstein, Derrida, Nelson Goodman, and Richard Rorty, just as my mentioning of several authors ranging from Dante to Galileo and to Thomas Pynchon, are meant to illustrate Eco's notion that through intertextuality we can contextualize texts, culture, events, works, and universal philosophical issues. Although he entertains his readers with witty intricate stories, Eco seems to reiterate that today, in our postmodern ways, we discuss basically the same rhetorical, epistemological, and metaphysical concerns that assailed our forefathers.

The debates surrounding Aristotle, realism versus nominalism and idealism, order, God, or philosophy of language, narrated in *The Name of the Rose*, the cabalistic, alchemistic, and hermetic doctrines illustrated in *Foucault's Pendulum*, and the search for a universal (Adamic) language, the nature of imagination and metaphors, and various practices of cognition that we witness in *The Island of the Day Before* are all examples of these concerns cleverly narrated within their proper historical and cultural frame and at the same time presented as universal issues that we recognize as being pertinent to our times.

I shall add immediately that I will be speaking mainly about literature and knowledge and I will not be examining the questions about "Literature as, or, and, in, through Philosophy" so well argued in Deborah Knight's opening essay in this volume, especially in references to A. Danto's and P. Jones' views on the relationships between philosophy, art, and literature. These views, like others proposed by several scholars, for example, those in the collected essays edited by Cascardi, or by Lamarque and Olsen, *Truth, Fiction and Literature* (1994), have certainly concerned Umberto Eco. I shall also point out a myriad of philosophical issues addressed by Eco. Nonetheless I feel that my colleagues from the philosophy department are much better qualified than I am to speak in depth about Eco's interpretation of philosophers such as Plato, Roger and Francis Bacon, Locke, Vico, Kant, or Wittgenstein.

Eco is well trained in philosophy and in his essays, as in his novels, he loves to recall his favorite thinkers whenever he theorizes on philosophy of language or when he emphasizes philosophical views about the ongoing debates on realism and idealism and on the relationships between language and reality, and concepts and the outside world. In his novels mimetic realism is used primarily for contextualizing the story and the intellectual debates. At times it may even appear to be subservient to the myriad of metaliterary and philosophical discussions. Indeed, three key features of Eco's fiction are intertextuality, epistemological discourses, and an argumentative style called for by the investigative nature of his stories, all extremely rich with numerous discussions on language, knowledge, and power.

The relationship between knowledge and power is one of the many lessons that Adso of Melk learns from the protectors of the library and from his mentor William of Baskerville in *The Name of the Rose*. Similar lessons are learned by the main protagonists in *Foucault's Pendulum* and *The Island of the Day Before* where power is associated with knowledge of secrets, codes, plans, plots, and even of oneself. And we would easily agree that learning processes and the quest for knowledge are unquestionably central themes in all three novels. However, although in *The Name of the Rose* critics have appreciated the presence of several philosophers such as Aristotle, Bacon, Occam, Kant, and Wittgenstein, and in *Foucault's Pendulum* critics have noticed the allusions to thinkers such as Wittgenstein, Foucault, Derrida, and Bloom, we are still waiting for analyses of *The Island of the Day Before* that examine the references to Locke, Hume, Wilkins, Kant, and Spinoza in relation to Eco's expositions on imagination, perception, categories, cognition, and God, as well as on the relationships between language and knowledge of the external world.

Eco's narrative is unquestionably populated by a variety of thinkers extending from Plato to our times. But does this make Eco's novels philosophical? And are they of philosophical importance? These are in fact some of the questions that come to mind when trying to define the genre within which Eco's fiction falls. The well-known Italian critic and semiotician Maria Corti, after the appearance of *Foucault's Pendulum*, affirmed that they are not really essay-novels and not quite detective or historical novels and that perhaps a new category must be found for Eco's fiction.

Throughout this essay I shall refer to Eco's intellectual narratives as encyclopedia superfictions. Also, keeping in mind Eco's fundamental belief that "a text is a machine for generating interpretations" (Eco, 1979, 1994) I shall treat Eco's cognitive value of literature, or better of his metafictional intertextual machines, as pretexts for accessing a myriad of other authors and texts used for generating more interpretations. Furthermore, my examples from Eco's work are meant to illustrate how our well-known semiotician, beginning with one of his major milestones, *The Open Work* (1984; trans. *Opera aperta*, 1962), has viewed libraries, encyclopedias, intertextuality, and the World Wide Web as cognitive tools that open up epistemological systems.

From the late 1960s to the present, and mainly in conjunction with the various debates on postmodernism, the issues surrounding the possibility or impossibility to exhaust literature have made John Barth one of the most frequently quoted authors of the last two decades. Barth, in his by now historical essays "The Literature of Exhaustion" (1967) and "The Literature of Replenishment" (1980),[1] pays homage to one of his favorite postmodern writers, Jorge Luis Borges, as he discusses encyclopedias, labyrinths, and one of Borges's most anthologized stories, "Tlön, Uqbar, Orbis Tertius." Perhaps a brief quotation from "A note on (toward) Bernard Shaw" can provide a good indication of why Barth was fascinated with the Argentinean writer:

> [A] book is more than a verbal structure or series of verbal structures; it is the dialogue it establishes with its reader and the intonation it imposes upon his voice and the changing and durable images it leaves in his memory. . . . Literature is not exhaustible, for the sufficient and simple reason that no single book is. A book is not an isolated being: it is a relationship, an axis of innumerable relationships. (Borges, *Labyrinths*, 1964, pp. 213–214)

This elucidating statement, as we shall see, is most pertinent to our discussions on Borges, Calvino, and Eco while it brings to mind Michael Bakhtin's notions of polyphony and intertextuality and Yuri Lotman's definition of a text: "A text is a mechanism constituting a system of heterogeneous semiotic spaces, in whose continuum the message . . . circulates [. . . .] When a text interacts with a heterogeneous consciousness, new meanings are generated" (Lotman, 1994, pp. 377, 378). Bakhtin and Lotman, I must add, are two central figures of influence in Eco's writings.

Paying Homage to J. L. Borges

Borges's *Ficciones* became an international best seller soon after the collection of short stories appeared in French and in Italian in 1955. Today it is difficult to speak of libraries and encyclopedias without thinking of Borges's "Library of Babel." In the past four decades the Argentinean master of fantastic fictions has inspired numerous authors who have dealt with literary motifs such as labyrinths, encyclopedias, libraries, mirrors, palimpsests, alephs, forked paths, and the dissolution of the barrier between reality and fiction (or dream).

In Calvino's distinction between library and literature, from a 1969 book review of Northrop Frye's *Anatomy of Criticism*, we recognize echoes of Borges:

> Literature is not composed simply of books but of libraries, systems in which the various epochs and traditions arrange their "canonical" texts and their "apocryphal" ones. A library can have a restricted catalogue, or it can tend to become a universal library.... Literature is a search for the book hidden in the distance that alters the value and meaning of the known books; it is the pull toward the new apocryphal text still to be rediscovered or invented. (Calvino, 1986, pp. 60–61)

Italo Calvino has recalled the remarkable imagination of Borges in his essays (1980)[2] and in his novels—especially in *Invisible Cities* (1972), *The Castle of Crossed Destinies* (1973), and *If on a Winter's Night a Traveler* (1979). Throughout *If on a Winter's Night a Traveler* Calvino has fun exploiting both the "Library of Babel"and the notion of *incipits* ("beginnings") of texts, convinced that "All books continue beyond" (p. 71). Books, especially those that are deliberately conceived as "open works," continue with readers as they take their favorite "inferential walks" (Eco, 1979) outside of the text that they are reading and into the world of numerous other texts and, possibly, into their own world. Moreover, without ever mentioning the names of Deleuze and Guattari nor the word "rhizome" (an "acentered" structure made up of "lines"; *A Thousand Plateaus*, p. 21), Calvino speaks of rhizomatic structures (see Chapters 7 and 8: "In a network of lines that enlace" and "In a network of lines that intersect"), which I will mention later on.

Within the parameters of the relationships between texts, interpretation, and intertextuality that I will be discussing, it is also relevant to mention that *If on a Winter's Night a Traveler*, among many other things, is a wonderful parody of reader reception theories proposed by W. Iser (*The Implied Reader*, 1974; *The Act of Reading*, 1978), R. Barthes (*Le plaisir du texte*, 1973), and U. Eco (*The Role of the Reader*, 1976). This is not the place to indulge in a discussion on "intentional fallacy," autonomy of a literary text, and "implied authors" (some of the much debated topics on the theories of interpretation in the 1970s and early 1980s), however, we should remember that as Eco himself has suggested (1992), his *The Open Work* (1962) may have actually started the whole process of encouraging interpretations that tend to dismiss completely the role of the author.[3]

Calvino and Eco have followed very closely the debates on reader reception theories but have not entirely embraced the notion of the death of the author. From the days of *The Open Work* in the 1960s, to those of *The Role of the Reader* in the 1970s, and more recently to those of *The Limits of Interpretation*, Eco has toyed with the idea of the death of the author (and to some extent the pessimistic endings of his novels may even support this view);[4] however, it is questionable that he has actually fully subscribed to such a notion. From his works it can be assumed that for Eco an author is made up of intertexts, and, thus, of other authors. His playful exploitations of palimpsests and pastiches are mainly a parodic demonstration of how today it is difficult to avoid the "anxiety of influence" and how often one writes novels/texts with the help/texts of many authors.

Entering a Library

> Often books speak of other books. Often a harmless book is like a seed that will blossom into a dangerous book.... Now I realized that not infrequently books speak of books: it is as if they spoke among themselves. In the light of this reflection, the library seemed all the more disturbing to me. (Eco, 1981, p. 285)

> The library is a great labyrinth, sign of the labyrinth of the world. You enter and you do not know whether you will come out. You must not transgress the pillars of Hercules. (Eco, 1981, p. 157)

These two quotations about libraries, intertextuality, labyrinths, and the thirst/quest for knowledge are quite familiar to Umberto Eco's readers who, with patience and curiosity, after coping with a great deal of historical, semiotic, and metaliterary references, have entered the medieval library that dominates the monastery in *The Name of the Rose* (1983). Eco's library is a place in which intertextuality abounds as the reader becomes both intrigued and frustrated by the presence of so many books. For the novice Adso, because of the perilous adventures that he experiences together with his talented master William of Baskerville, the mysterious library becomes a "disturbing" place. Actually, even without having to solve a mystery, entering Eco's library can be intimidating by the mere fact that it reminds us of how many books (in different languages) we have not read.

In his most clever ways Eco has often praised Borges, and in *Postscript to*

The Name of the Rose he openly admits that in his first novel he has paid some debts to the great master of "fictions." Many critics have followed Walter Stephens' example[5] from "Ec(h)o in fabula" and have examined the presence of Borges in *The Name of the Rose*[6] identifying interesting similarities (especially in reference to "Death and the compass") and at times even insisting a little too much on Borges's influence on Eco. My own theory is that perhaps even more so than the often quoted short stories, Eco is intrigued by Borges's essays.[7] Elsewhere I have argued that for Eco it is not a question of influences as much as a question of demonstrating the mechanisms of intertextuality and of constructing possible worlds (Capozzi, 1983, 1989, 1997). I think that a much more interesting study could be one that focuses on Borges's precursors examined in relation to how they also pertain to Eco. Such a study would reveal how Eco was attracted to Borges because they shared the same concerns about realism versus idealism, about philosophers such as Hume, Locke, Wilkins, Bradley, and Kant, and about narrative strategies involving *mise en abîmes*, universal language, and mirror and double motifs. Some of the essays in Borges's *Other Inquisitions* can confirm this (see, above all, the brief essays on Pascal and Coleridge, and the longer one, "The refutation of time," in which readers will also notice the repeated statement that Coleridge had observed that all men "are born Aristotelian or Platonist").

In his essay "Fantasia of the Library" Foucault examines Flaubert's *The Temptation of Saint Anthony*, which, in his estimation, is a "monument in meticulous erudition" (1977, p. 89). The author adds: "As a work, its form relies on its location within the domain of knowledge: it exists by virtue of its essential relationship to books" (p. 91). Michel Foucault seems intrigued by the writings of authors such as Flaubert, Cervantes, and Borges, who by means of intertextuality speak about many other books and authors:

> In writing *The Temptation*, Flaubert produced the first literary work whose exclusive domain is that of books; following Flaubert, Mallarmé is able to write *Le livre* and modern literature is activated—Joyce, Roussel, Kafka, Pound, Borges. The library is on fire. (p. 92)

In the above reference, as in Foucault's opening chapter in *The Order of Things* (1970), we find some of the key elements (such as Borges, Baroque aesthetics, cultural history, and intertextuality) that are narrated in Eco's colorful superfictions. Is this just an interesting coincidence? Or are these similarities part of Eco's intentional references to authors who send us back to issues about origins and to great encyclopedia works?

Eco's intellectual and highly imaginative fictional worlds reflect (parodically and ironically) the contemporary postmodern theoretical climate in which we live and at the same time allow us to discover innumerable connections between people, events, and ideas throughout history. However, when we examine his ludic illustrations of potentially unlimited intertextuality and endless semiosis it is important to keep in mind that for Eco literature is much more than a self-reflecting linguistic activity. It is true that Eco agrees with Roland Barthes' notion of endless chains of signifiers; however, he believes that ultimately a referent/truth can be found in experience, in history, in the visible and concrete world, and in our own personal encyclopedia of knowledge. As argued in *Interpretation and Overinterpretation*, contrary to a Derridean idea that there is nothing beyond the language of a text except more texts and more language (*Of Grammatology*, 1976 pp. 157–158), and following C. S. Peirce's pragmatic approach, Eco is confident that ultimately readers can move from signs and from the meaning(s) of language and texts to corresponding meanings found in the real world. (Naturally we are not speaking of signs such as the often quoted unicorn that Eco discusses in his novel as well as in his semiotic essays.) As we are reminded in *The Name of the Rose*: "A book is made up of signs that speak of other signs, which in their turn speak of things" (p. 393).

Staying mainly with Eco's fiction here I will deal very briefly with his most recent work *Kant and the Platypus* (1999). In this unusual complex text made of philosophical and semiotic observations illustrated through legends, history, and pop culture, the author reexamines some of the questions related to icons, codes, the interpretation of signs, and the "dynamic object" that he had developed in *A Theory of Semiotics* (1976) and *Semiotics and the Philosophy of Language* (1984).

Kant and the Platypus is of interest to our discussion because as the author examines various processes of perception, (re)cognition, naming, labeling, and categorizing, he brings together Kant and Peirce's pragmatics in the triangular relation of sign, "interpretant," and "dynamic object." Moreover, as a reviewer has justly pointed out, even as he disagrees with several of Eco's views, this difficult text tackles a variety of issues that in the past three decades have seen not only Hume, Kant, Heidegger, and Wittgenstein, but also Quine, Sellars, Carnap, Putnam, Goodman, and Rorty on center stage (Blackburn, 2000) debating the connections between concepts, language, and outside world.

How do we know something completely new? "What Kant would have done had he come across a platypus"? (p. 89). This, in a nutshell, is at the core of Eco's essay on the interrelationships between perception, language, naming, knowledge, and experience. In addition to the extensive discussions on the production and interpretation of signs, the text deals with fascinating topics such as being, icons, inferences, logic, schema, categories, taxonomy, mirrors, and the Peircean distinctions between Immediate and Dynamic Objects.

Here too, as we have seen in his other scientific studies, the author demonstrates that he has an outstanding talent for instructing and entertaining at the same time. His so-called postmodern technique of embedding theoretical and scholarly issues with samples from popular culture in *Kant and the Platypus* is displayed through several examples such as his references to the "smurfs" (4.7.2), to "files and directories" (4.2), to "e-mail," or to "Dr. Jekyll and Mr. Hyde." In the opening remarks in Chapter Three, "Cognitive Types," the author states that he has chosen to demonstrate certain theories with the help of fables, stories, anecdotes, history, science, possible worlds, and literary works. The author also adds: "Most of my stories are about something fairly similar to what Kant held to be empirical concepts" (pp. 124).

With *Kant and the Platypus* it becomes even more evident that from the early 1970s Kant and C. S. Peirce continue to play a major role in Umberto Eco's theoretical studies on the semiotic practices of perceiving, producing, and interpreting signs. Moreover, in a number of passages (see, for example, the discussions on "strong ontology") we realize how similar references to Kantian thought were dramatized in *The Island of the Day Before* for the debates between Roberto and Father Caspar on being, death, nothingness, void, infinity, and the power of God (see, above all, Chapter 34, "Monologue on the plurality of worlds"). We recognize that these are also some of the provocative ontological and epistemological questions that assail Adso in *The Name of the Rose*. As we recall, in the opening pages of the novel William amazes Adso with his skills in interpreting signs and with his abductions in guessing the name of the horse "Brunellus"; he then proceeds with several explanations about the differences between "particular" and "universal." Bacon, Occam, Kant, and Peirce come together as William professes to Adso notions such as the following: "So I found myself halfway between the perception of the concept 'horse' and the knowledge of an individual horse. And in any case, what I knew of the universal horse had been given to me by those traces, which were singular" (p. 28).

Throughout *Kant and the Platypus* Eco often refers to C. S. Peirce as reader of Kant—in particular where he examines the process of perceiving a new object/sign for the first time and assigning to it a verbal sign. In his enviable inventive and witty way Eco relates how an animal that had never been seen before is perceived and then named. This is illustrated by three fascinating examples: Marco Polo's first sight of a rhino—at first he had thought that the rhino was a unicorn (2.1); the first encounter of a horse by the Aztecs and then by their king Montezuma (3.3); and the first report from Australia, in the late 1700s, of the existence of a duckbilled platypus (2.7).

From Intertextuality to Hyperintertextuality

So far, my emphasis on "archaeology of knowledge," history of ideas, encyclopedias, rhizomes, and unlimited semiosis and intertextuality could suggest that I am recommending a reading of Eco's novels primarily in view of the works of M. Foucault, G. Deleuze, and F. Guattari. Likewise, my talking about Eco's fiction as if it were an "aleph" (or like a black hole) in which centuries of culture are concentrated may hint that his possible worlds should be read as crafty variations of narrative themes and structures of J. L. Borges's fiction. And in suggesting that Eco may have read quite closely Calvino's fiction from the days of *Cosmicomics* on I may be implying that Calvino has had a strong influence on Eco. This may all be true, but my goal is not to identify any specific "anxiety of influence" echoed, strongly or faintly, in Eco's novels. I am proposing, instead, that writers such as Peirce, M. Bakhtin, Y. Lotman, G. Deleuze, M. Foucault, J. Derrida, H. White, N. Goodman, or R. Rorty, philosophers such as Vico, Kant, and Wittgenstein, and narrators such as Poe, Joyce,[8] Borges, Barth, Calvino, or Pynchon[9] can help us to comprehend Umberto Eco's own treatment of "archaeology of knowledge" and "new historicism" in narrative form. The author never hides the fact that in his fiction he is parodically demonstrating Borges's view that every writer creates his own precursors.[10] By the same token, his theoretical and scientific works on semiotics, aesthetics, and narratology make up a large portion of the intertextual echoes in his highly learned postmodern encyclopedia novels (Capozzi, 1983). And I do not feel that I am exaggerating in stating that as we read his novels we often get the feeling that we are also revisiting some of his pages from *Semiotics and the Philosophy of Language*, *The Role of the Reader*, and *The Limits of Interpretation*.

At this point I find it helpful to take a quick look at Gilles Deleuze and Felix Guattari's closing pages of *Rhizome* (1976), in which the two authors explain why they quote from literary books[11] and hope to present a rhizome and to build machines that can easily be taken apart: "A book must serve as a machine for something. Not representation of the world, nor world as a signifying structure. The book is not a tree-root, it is part of a rhizome, a plan for a rhizome." Two of the last authors that they quote are Foucault, for whom a book is "a box of tools," and Proust, who considers his book a pair of eye glasses: "just try and see if you can see better with them." Furthermore, maintaining that there is no "death of the book" and that there is only a new way of reading, Deleuze and Guattari also make the following affirmation that is pertinent to Eco and to our discussion: "The combinations, permutations and utilizations are inside the text, but depend always on such or such a connection from the outside."[12]

One of the best demonstrations of the importance of *Rhizome*[13] in Eco's novels can be seen in the extremely intricate intertextual structure of *Foucault's Pendulum* (1989). In *Rhizome* we find the following statement about chapters versus "plateau": "We call a 'plateau' any multiplicity connected to another multiplicity by superficial underground stems in such a way as to form or extend a rhizome. We are writing this book as a rhizome. It is composed of plateaus.... Each plateau can be read starting anywhere and can be related to any other plateau" (p. 22). With this in mind if we look at the structure of *Foucault's Pendulum*, we see that each of the 120 sections or plateaus (the 120 sections of the novel can hardly be considered chapters in a traditional sense)—each starting with an epigraph, with a quotation from a book—constitutes a multiplicity of texts connected to other multiplicities of books in a labyrinth of possibly infinite intertextuality.

Eco's work shows that in the 1970s the author begins to abandon his interests in codes, dictionaries, binary systems, and Chomsky's models of syntagmatic chains, as he focuses more and more on C. S. Peirce, encyclopedias, open works/systems, rhizomes, mechanisms of interpretation, intertextuality, narratology, metaphors, paradigmatic structures, and R. Barthes' chains of signifiers. Some of Eco's most interesting remarks about encyclopedias and rhizomes are found in *Semiotics and the Philosophy of Language* (1984), in which we read: "The project of an encyclopedia competence is governed by an underlying metaphysics or by a metaphor (or an allegory): the idea of labyrinth" (p. 80). Eco defines three types of labyrinths: the classical (linear), the manneristic (a maze), and the net. The first two are not of great interest to him, but when it comes to the one structured as a net we find that he is in fact speaking of a web, or of a rhizome:

> In a labyrinth of the third type is a net (maybe the word *meander* characterizes it as different from the maze and from a *plain labyrinth*). The main feature of a net is that every point can be connected with every other point, and, where the connections are not yet designed.... A net is an unlimited territory. A net is not a tree.... On the contrary, the abstract model of a net has neither a center nor an outside. The best image of a net is provided by the vegetable metaphor of the rhizome suggested by Deleuze and Guattari. (p. 81)

Eco goes on to explain the relationship between encyclopedia and culture:

> The universe of semiosis, that is, the universe of human culture, must be conceived as structured like a labyrinth of the third type: (a) It is structured according to a network of interpretants. (b) It is virtually infinite because it takes into account multiple interpretations realized by different cultures.... (c) It does not register only 'truths' but, rather, what has been said about the truth or what has been believed to be true. (p. 83)

Recently Eco has edited four volumes of *Encyclomedia*: *Il Cinquecento, Il Seicento, Il Settecento*, and *L'Ottocento*—four multimedia CDs that readers will find particularly helpful as reference texts for a closer reading of Eco's novels.

Il Settecento is most useful for reading *The Island of the Day Before* because it provides us with a plethora of information on music, art, literature, and historical events of the seventeenth and eighteenth centuries that Eco himself must have consulted before writing his third novel. The type of interactivity and intertextuality illustrated in the *Encyclomedia* CDs also gives us an excellent indication of how Eco approaches his own research in preparation for the composition for his fiction.

Elsewhere I have treated Eco's interests in hyperintertextuality theorized by George P. Landow (Capozzi, 1997). Here I would just like to mention that the author's experience with "hyperlinks" has reinforced my theory that Eco's encyclopedic rhizomatic works have been constructed/generated like hyper/cybertexts, rich with "internet hyperlink" features that allow users to move from one topic to another by merely clicking on a word, image, title, or suggested link. Let me add that in his humorous weekly column that appears in the national magazine *L'Espresso* (under the tile "La bustina di Minerva"— literally "Minerva's little envelope") Eco has written about the World Wide Web search engine Yahoo. Speaking of Swift and Borges in "Internet between Swift e Borges" the author makes this affirmation: "It is no mystery that the so called WWW, the mother of all hypertexts, is that which resembles the most the Library of Babel of Borges, an infinite repository of universal knowledge, so rich and complete that one could pass many lives without ever visiting in its entirety the labyrinth in which is contained so much information to make one insane if he thought of controlling it."[14]

Eco's focus on libraries, encyclopedia, and rhizomes as open structures and as tools used to gain access to all sorts of information is part of his belief that our databases of knowledge are made up of bits and pieces of information, images, frames, and ideas that can be interconnected through a series of links and by our encyclopedia competence—a competence that we derive mostly from our reading of texts but also from other media such as movies, TV, and art. These pieces of texts, films, and images are in essence bits of preconstructed familiar frames that we associate with other stories, images, names, events, myths, etc., in the process of reading books, watching movies, looking at paintings, hearing a lecture, and so on. Eco has discussed frames on several occasions (see, for example, Eco, 1984, pp. 71–72) and in *The Role of the Reader* he has examined in depth how the paradigmatic associations of frames set in motion our "inferential walks" in and outside of whichever text, or movie, or painting we are analyzing.

Reading Eco's novels is in many ways like surfing on the Internet, or consulting the *Encyclomedia* CDs, or visiting a library. The intratextual and intertextual links in his narrative help us to move from Eco to Aristotle, to Dante, to Borges, to Foucault, to Deleuze, to Rorty, etc., and possibly back to Eco, forming an encyclopedia loop of links in a web, or network, that readers can expand according to their own competence. Of course one can begin with Eco's work and close with Eco in the same session; or one can look up other authors and, in the process, decide to temporarily set aside Eco's text. Either way we can see that this is the author's technique of explaining ideas, texts, and authors with other ideas, texts, and authors that in a final analysis also helps us to better understand culture, literary and philosophical theories, and Eco's own writings.

Postmodern Intertextuality: Pastiches and Parodies

On the inside of the book cover of the first edition of *Il nome della rosa* the author points out that his text is "a weaving of other texts, a mystery fiction of quotations, a book made of other books."[15] And, as already mentioned, although William and Adso illustrate quite well Bakhtinian concepts of polyphony and intertextuality (showing that indeed "books speak of other books"), the novel popularizes several other literary theories and narrative strategies that were at the center of literary criticism in the 1960s and 1970s. Thus, *The Name of the Rose* reminds us that today through Jacques Derrida, Richard Rorty, Hilary Putnam, Nelson Goodman, and Stanley Fish we are still debating Aristotelian and Platonic issues on realism versus nominalism and idealism reproposed by Roger Bacon and William of Occam in the Middle Ages. This is because Eco wishes to demonstrate that in the history of knowledge more than progress and originality we have mostly recapitulations and variations (repetition and difference) of the same basic knowledge of our predecessors. This is a view that fits in very well within Eco's definition of postmodernism that we see outlined in his *Postscript to The Name of the Rose.*

As we recall, William of Baskerville, as he teaches Adso about signs, logic, inferences, syllogisms (p. 261), universal laws (p. 207), and infinite semiosis (p. 316), often quotes his teacher Roger Bacon and at the same time does not neglect to recall opposite views expressed by his friend William of Occam (see, for example, pp. 63, 206–208, 263). Perhaps just as Adso becomes frustrated with William's unwillingness to take a final position on certain issues, such as on faith and heresy,[16] readers will be frustrated by Eco's lack of final commitment on realism and nominalism. However, this is exactly Eco's strategy: to contextualize and to bridge opposite theories without necessarily advocating one or the other as his own position. Thus, coherent with his theories on open works and on the cooperation of the reader in completing the meaning(s) of a text, he shifts the responsibility to the reader to act as critic and/or philosopher. Furthermore it is also the reader's responsibility to move from acquaintance (information and knowledge of) to understanding and interpretation of texts and ideas.

When it comes to fabricating his possible worlds Umberto Eco does not seem as concerned with originality as he is interested in finding analogies, in exploiting practices of found manuscripts, in constructing ingenious metaphorical relationships, and in having fun with parodic reconstructions of well- and not so well-known texts. He has stated in public lectures that in his novels he invents very little and that he is mainly recalling, quoting, or alluding to (both consciously or unconsciously) other texts. This is illustrated repeatedly throughout *The Name of the Rose* and is explicitly pointed out in *Foucault's Pendulum*. In short, Eco's theories on the importance of connections and analogies in the history of knowledge are put into practice (narrated, performed) in his novels fully confidently. By teasing their thought processes readers derive a special pleasure from recalling the *déjà vu*, from recognizing quotations (*déjà lu*), and from identifying as many pieces as possible in a collage.

For convenience or for lack of any other definition, Eco's intricate metafictions are frequently labeled as postmodern fictions. We may ask, is it because they defy any definition of a specific narrative genre? Or is it because postmodernism (like Bakhtinian carnivalizations; or like laughter and humor—think of the *coena cipriani*—in *The Name of the Rose*) is also associated with desecrating and contaminating subject-matter and with transgressing all boundaries? Of course, the author is partly responsible for encouraging critics to adopt the postmodern label for his fiction. In *Postscript to The Name of the Rose* he defines postmodernism in relation to modernism and the *avant garde* and speaks specifically about the role of history, stating: "The postmodern reply to the modern consists of recognizing that the past, since it cannot really be destroyed, because its destruction leads to silence, must be revisited: but with irony, not innocently" (1983, p. 67).

In my work I have also used the label postmodern as an all-englobing term (*bon à tout faire*, says Eco, 1983, p. 65) to refer to his novels. I have done so with increasing reluctance after critics began to list Umberto Eco among postmodern novelists without ever explaining what the label means for the author or how his definition of postmodernism fits culturally and philosophically within G. Vattimo's notion of "weak thought." Consequently, I prefer to refer to his fiction as essay-novels and encyclopedia superfictions in which erudite and popular culture meet in a harmonious fashion (and perhaps with equal status, taking Leslie Fiedler's suggestion from his essay on "Cross the Border-Close the Gap"). In Eco's narratives creative writing and literary theories combine to become integral parts of an enjoyable narrative discourse, and where the Middle Ages,[17] the age of Baroque, and our contemporary postmodern world—three eras characterized by major changes in all sectors of social and intellectual life—are all interlinked.

The deliberate saturation of intertextual and metaliterary references to found manuscripts, the art of writing best sellers, and books that speak about other books—including the Bible, which plays an important role in all three novels—has become a trademark of Eco's fiction. In *Foucault's Pendulum* we find numerous metafictional remarks about writing and publishing books that are also meant to mirror Eco's own practice. When Belbo, Casaubon, and Diotallevi talk about the Garamond Publishing House and "vanity presses" they make interesting observations on pulp fiction and on popular novels that point to Eco's art of writing popular superfictions. For example, in section 97, in the discussion about "Great Art" versus "dime novels," we can detect specific allusions to the author's clever way of playing with his own fiction:

> Great Art makes fun of us as it comforts us, because it shows us the world as the artist would like the world to be. The dime novel, however, pretends to joke, but then it shows us the world as it actually is—or at least the world as it will become. . . . History is closer to what Sue narrates than to what Hegel projects. . . . The fact is, it's easier for reality to imitate the dime novel than to imitate art. (pp. 495–496)

In this same section we are introduced to Belbo's files, secretly hidden in his computer Abulafia:

> Afterwards, I found this file, in which Belbo translated our discussion into fictional form, amusing himself by reconstructing the story of Saint-Germain without adding anything of his own, only a few sentences here and there to provide transitions, in a furious collage of quotes, plagiarism, borrowing, clichés. Once again, to escape the discomfort of History, Belbo wrote and re-examined life through a literary stand-in. (p. 496)

These are just two of the many ironic authorial winks that are directed at the reader in order to bring to his attention not only poststructuralist and post-modern theories, but also the author's assertion that in his novels he does not invent very much and that, instead, he is mainly (re)constructing stories (texts) with pieces (frames) from a variety of sources.

Self-referential allusions to the art of writing novels are even more obvious in *The Island of the Day Before* in which in addition to found manu-scripts and palimpsests that send us back to the novels of A. Dumas, R. L. Stevenson, and J. Verne, or to the baroque and metaphysical poets G. Marino and J. Donne, or to the illusionist paintings of G. Arcimboldo (1527–1593), we find an actual novel within the novel. As we recall, the psychological war between Roberto and his imaginary twin brother Ferrante is developed mostly through a diary-like metanarrative that Roberto writes in the second part of the story. The metafictional *mise en abîme* gives us some interesting insights about Roberto's youth, education, fears, and desires. In these pages we can also detect how Roberto is essentially echoing the author's views on narrative strategies and on the art of creating possible worlds (see, above all, Chapter 28, "On the Origin of Novels").

Eco's narrators and main protagonists are constantly searching for truth and order, a metaphorical grail, "fixed points," and certainties, but, more often than not, they end up dealing with alchemy, irrationality, disorder, chaos, and doubts. From *The Name of the Rose* to *The Island of the Day Before* Eco depicts events and characters that illustrate how logical, scientific, and rational thinking are not always clearly distinguishable from paranoid and irrational reasoning. But I must reiterate that we must also take into consideration Eco's use of irony because the author does not accept disorder or hermetic drift as a normal condition. The author's ironic vision is important in understanding why at the end of *The Name of the Rose* William claims that there is no order (divine or apocalyptic) even though he discovers the truth about Jorge de Burgos and the library. Eco's irony is also central for a deeper appreciation of *Foucault's Pendulum*, in which the three protagonists find out that there is no "secret cosmic plot" and that their own invented story of the Templar's Plan was not much more than a deadly cabalistic game. In other words, the author's parodic and ironic vision allows us to go beyond the surface detective story about Sefirot, cabala, Abulafia, and secret sects, which shows how Diotallevi, Belbo, and Casaubon create a "golem" that will turn against them.

Eco's possible answer to the hermetic drift and postmodern manifestations of irrationality that surround us is hinted at in *Foucault's Pendulum* when Lia explains how the mysterious (coded?) message is nothing more than a laundry list (see section 106). Through the motherly figure of Lia, Eco proposes a return to common sense as a way to avoid the dangers of paranoid criticism and hermetic semiosis whereby "tout se tient." Common sense, it must be added, is something that Eco reminds us of quite often throughout his works. The author certainly shares Gadamer's praises (*Truth and Method*, 1960) of G. B. Vico's stand that *sensus communis* is extremely important. In an essay on theories and practices of translation, *Experiences in Translation* (2001), we see Eco advocating various approaches to translation and ultimately suggesting that common sense must be taken into consideration so that excessive or far fetched interpretations can be avoided.

The danger of hermetic drift in *Foucault's Pendulum* is summarized in section 118, which opens, in a most *à propos* fashion, with an epigraph from Karl Popper's *Conjectures and Refutations*, "The conspiracy theory of society . . . comes from abandoning God and then asking: Who is in his place?" (p. 617). Immediately we are tempted to ask if this is yet another of Eco's ironic allusions to the "death of the author" and to the Nietzschean death of God. Casaubon's explanation of the rules of their associations (of their *ars combinatoria* gone mad) certainly seems to allude to excessive (deconstructive?) approaches of interpretation:

In our game we crossed not words but concepts, events, so the rules were different. Basically there were three rules:

Rule One: Concepts are connected by analogy. There is no way to decide at once whether an analogy is good or bad, because to some degree everything is connected to everything else. . . .

Rule Two says that if tout se tient in the end, the connecting works. . . .

Rule Three: the connections must not be original. They must have been made before . . . by others. Only then do the crossings seem true, because they are obvious. (p. 618)

Of Eco's narrative trilogy *Foucault's Pendulum* is the most difficult work and the one most intertextually loaded with literary theories and philosophical issues. As we get deeper and deeper in the story of the alleged secret plan of the Templars and other secret sects, we witness many examples of illogical conjectures that emphasize a predominance of irrational thinking (overinterpretations?) throughout our history. The controversial views about Eco's second novel have been the subject of several articles and full length works.[18] In general, the novel has been received quite favorably in France and especially in North America, in which critics[19] have examined *Foucault's Pendulum* in relation to theories of interpretation, poststructuralism and deconstructionism, hermetic drift, and postmodernism, to the writings of M. Foucault and J. Derrida, and to the studies on cabala by Moise Idel and Harold Bloom.

This is hardly the type of material for the making of a popular novel we may say. Perhaps, but I would be inclined to believe that Eco gives us a clue of his own art of *docere et delectare* when he has his protagonist say that comic books can also "educate the reader in an entertaining way" (p. 49). This same notion that in *The Name of the Rose* was first proposed in reference to puns, irony, wit, and humor in general (82), in *The Island of the Day Before* is reiterated even more explicitly in the middle of the pedantic debates between Roberto and Father Caspar on void, infinity, and the omnipotence of God, where we are reminded: "you could be learned in a playful fashion" (p. 431). And this leads us to ask if indeed Umberto Eco, through his novels, is not telling us that it is possible to incorporate metaphysical and philosophical issues in fiction, comic books, or a Woody Allen[20] movie. Supporters of postmodern poetics would certainly subscribe to this point.

On a light note, Umberto Eco's novels are ludic intellectual collages saturated with philosophical ideas, literary theories, and historical events that are debated or illustrated by some rather unusual characters. On a more serious note we can say that they are witty epistemological lessons on a variety of subjects such as semiotics, philosophy, and narratology. The main protagonists William, Adso, Belbo, Casaubon, and Roberto are fascinating *raisonneurs* and skilled logicians who can get most readers involved in different debates on a myriad of issues. And it is not a coincidence that in his novels we have several demonstrations of the ancient maieutic system of teaching through which learning takes place as teacher and student engage in lively exchanges of questions and debates. The frequent discussions between William and Adso in *The Name of the Rose* illustrate this notion extremely well. In a similar fashion, in *The Island of the Day Before*, we notice how Roberto, throughout his entire life, is constantly debating with his teachers, such as Saint-Savin, Father Emanuele, and Father Caspar (Capozzi, 1996). Eco's model reader should have very little difficulty in recognizing which teacher is Aristotelian, Platonic, Cartesian, Kantian, or Wittgensteinian— especially as the author frequently quotes or alludes to his favorite thinkers.

Eco's encyclopedic novels provide us with new forms of the *grand récits* that allegedly, as Jean-François Lyotard laments, have disappeared with post-modernism. And although this is a topic for a larger discussion it is worth mentioning that critics who see postmodernism in terms of fragmented knowledge consider Eco's novels as proof of this problem. However, Eco's fiction, as it *collages* bits and pieces of various works, actually combines inter-textually (and rhizomatically) a plethora of fragments of knowledge in order to provide as much as possible a sense of continuity to our cultural history. Granted, the type and degree of dynamic synthesis that can be drawn from his analogies are left to the reader who decides how and how many inferential walks he or she will take in the labyrinth of the library.

Umberto Eco's novels are complex possible worlds intended for general entertainment, even though they have been written by a semiotician and narratologist who perhaps pays particular attention to "model readers" (Eco, 1976) with encyclopedic competence and who are well aware of theoretical and literary issues. But in a final analysis what are Umberto Eco's thought-provoking "literature machines" (to recall Calvino's term) all about? In my estimation Umberto Eco's fiction is at once entertaining and didactic and, most of all, it offers plenty of research material for acquiring additional knowledge on numerous topics in different fields of knowledge. His hybrid metafictions, as critics have argued, are indeed excellent examples of *Bildungsroman*, adventure stories, detective fiction, historical novels, and of postmodernism at its best. However, they are primarily possible worlds that function like interactive epistemological metaphors (to say it with Max Black, 1978) that bring together in an interactive way different texts and different fields of knowledge (Capozzi, 1996). Just as important, they are also witty testimonials of our postmodern way of writing, thinking, and communicating.

In the essays in this volume we have tried to come to terms with the complex and even ambivalent relationships between philosophy and litera-ture. But, in my estimation, this is not a problem for Umberto Eco who has often praised Galileo's prose, in which rhetoric, science, and literature are not in conflict but complement one another. The abundance of philosophical and semiotic discussions in Eco novels indicates that for the author these disciplines can complement each other as they elucidate complicated thoughts and at the same time contextualize cultural issues. More important, whether it comes from fantastic fiction (like Borges's or Calvino's), literary discourse (such as Derrida's or Rorty's), philosophical texts, or allegorical and metaphysical literature (like Dante's or Donne's), and so on, ultimately it is the knowledge and understanding of certain universal issues about our being, our perceptions, our interpretations of all form of signs all around us, and our communicating of our ideas that really matter for Eco.

The narrators and main protagonists of *The Name of the Rose*, *Foucault's Pendulum*, and *The Island of the Day Before*, in their knowledge-seeking adventures, make no truth claims. This is mainly because Eco's novels have been constructed as cognitive tools with a great potential for stimulating literary and philosophical discussions through a myriad of analogies and intertextual echoes. Like libraries and encyclopedias Eco's novels are both archives of accumulated knowledge and instruments for working in the realm of knowledge. Our semiotician narrator has structured his encyclopedic superfictions pretty much in line with William of Baskerville's belief that "to know what one book says you must read others" (p. 285). In conclusion, recalling the Peircean notion of signs, we could say that Eco's novels are something by which we (may?) know something else. What and how much of something else? It depends completely on the reader's curiosity, access to libraries, and encyclopedic competence[21] in being able to navigate through the labyrinths of our archives of knowledge.

Notes

1. Barth's articles, published thirteen years apart in *The Atlantic* (August 1967, pp. 29–34; January 1980, pp. 69–71), now appear with several other interesting essays on literature in *The Friday Book. Essays and Other Nonfiction* (1994).
2. Several of Calvino's essays on literature, from *Una pietra sopra* (1980), now appear in *The Uses of Literature*. For an excellent collection of articles on the Borges-Calvino connections see the two volumes from the international congress held at Poitiers in 1995: *Borges, Calvino, La Literatura. Coloquio internacional*.
3. In "Interpretation and Overinterpretation: The Rights of Texts, Readers and Implied Authors," I have examined several reasons why I do not believe that Eco could embrace a theory of interpretation that overlooks, entirely, the role and competence of an author who during the act of writing has his readers already in mind. One of these reasons is linked to Eco's first lessons on aesthetics and interpretation (from his much admired teacher and philosopher Luigi Pareyson) that he has never forgotten. See *Reading Eco. An Anthology* (1997), pp. 217–238.
4. At the end of his novels Eco seems to intentionally kill the authors of his narratives and thus we are left only with the manuscripts of Adso, Casaubon, and Roberto. Casaubon summarizes this notion very well when at the end of *Foucault's Pendulum* he states: "truth is brief . . . the author has to die in order for the reader to become aware of this truth" (p. 633).

5. W. E. Stephens' "Ec(h)o in fabula" is among the first, and perhaps one of the best, treatments of the analogies between Borges and Eco.

6. For some more recent work on the Eco–Borges relationships see Nilda Guglielmi's *El Eco de la rosa y Borges* (Buenos Aires: Editorial Universitaria, 1988); Christine de Lailhacar's "The Mirror and the Encyclopaedia: Borgesian Codes in U. Eco's *The Name of the Rose*," in Aizenberg's *Borges and His Successors*; and Leo Corry's "Jorge Borges Author of *The Name of the Rose*," *Poetics Today* 3 (1992), pp. 425–446.

7. See the collected essays in *Relaciones literarias entre J.L. Borges y U. Eco* (Calvo and Capozzi, 1999).

8. Eco's bibliography shows that from the late 1950s the author has been analyzing the works of James Joyce—an encyclopedic author in his own right—and explaining a variety of linguistic and narrative strategies. Here I do not discuss this extremely important anxiety of influence that would require a separate study, but I will mention that Joyce (and especially his *Finnegans Wake*) is one of the first key narrators to whom Eco is indebted for his own experiments with fictions. This is one anxiety of influence that critics have yet to deal with in great depth in reference to Eco's narrative strategies. It is sufficient to mention that one of Eco's earliest publications was *Le poetiche di Joyce* (Milano: Bompiani, 1966). See *The Aesthetics of Chaosmos. The Middle Ages of James Joyce*. Trans. Ellen Esrock (Cambridge, MA: Harvard University Press, 1989). It contains a superb introduction by David Robey.

9. I am speaking primarily of Pynchon's *V, The Crying of Lot 49*, and *Gravity's Rainbow*—three novels with which Eco seems to be familiar. Moreover, my guess is that Eco is also familiar with some of the North American criticism on Pynchon and especially the collection of essays edited by Harold Bloom on *Gravity's Rainbow*. I am speaking specifically of Pynchon's fiction because, as masterfully examined by Edward Mendelson, "Gravity's Encyclopedia" (1986, pp. 29–52), his novels, just like Eco's, can best illustrate what constitutes an encyclopedic narrative in which we find works ranging from Dante to James Joyce and samples from other media such as TV and movies.

10. See Borges's essay "Kafka and His Precursors," in *Labyrinths* (New York: A New Direction Book, 1964, p. 201).

11. I am translating rather freely from the French original (1976) because the English translation in *A Thousand Plateaus. Capitalism and Schizophrenia* (pp. 3–25), does not contain the passages with the references to Foucault and Proust (pp. 72–73): "Quand on demande à Michel Foucault ce qu'un livre est pour lui, il répond: c'est une boîte à outils. Proust. . . disait que son livre était comme des lunettes: voyez si elles vous conviennent, si vous percevez grâce à elles ce que vous n'auriez pas pu saisir autrement; sinon laissez mon livre" (p. 73).

12. "Nous ne prétendons pas constituer une Somme ou recostituer une Mémoire . . . faire ainsi un rhizome, faire des machines avant tout démontables. . . . Le livre n'est pas une image du monde, encore moins un signifiant. Ce n'est pas une belle totalité organique, ce n'est pas non plus une unité de sens. . . . Le livre doit faire machine avec quelque chose, il doit être un petit outil sur un dehors. Les combinations, les permutation, les utilisations ne sont jamais intérieures au livre, mais dépendent des connexions avec tel ou tel dehors" (*Rhizome*, 71–73).

13. The importance of rhizome in Eco's work cannot be minimized. Before *Rhizome* became popular and was translated in other languages, Eco was one of the first supporters of the applications of rhizomes, especially in relation to intertextuality and unlimited semiosis. In the late 1970s Eco wrote "Dall'albero al labirinto," which later appeared in a text on labyrinths edited by Achille Bonito Oliva (1981). Soon after he outlined "L'antiporfirio"—a study of rhizomes and encyclopedia versus trees, binary systems, codes, and dictionaries that we find elaborated in

Semiotics and the Philosophy of Language. Gianni Vattimo and Pier Aldo Rovatti included this essay in their anthology on "weak thought," *Il pensiero debole* (1983)—in which several writers discuss postmodernism, semiotics, and philosophy (mostly in reference to Nietzsche and Heidegger) within poststructural and deconstructive methodologies.

14. My translation of a passage from "Internet tra Swift e Borges. Da dove vengono gli Yahoo?" "Non è un mistero che il cosiddetto WWW, la gran madre di tutti gli ipertesti, è la cosa che assomiglia di più alla Biblioteca di Babele di Borges, repositorio infinito di tutta la sapienza dell'universo, così ricco e completo che si può passare molte vite senza averlo visitato tutto, labirinto in cui è contenuta tanta informazione da condurre alla follia chi credesse di poterla padroneggiare tutta" (p. 234). In the article Eco also discusses how Swift's Yahoos are also present in one of Borges's writings.

15. The paratextual reference on the Italian first edition of *The Name of the Rose* has been translated in its entirety by Walter E. Stephens (1983).

16. "And you," I cried, in an access almost of rebellion, "why don't you take a position, why won't you tell me where the truth is?" (*The Name of the Rose*, p. 204).

17. Teresa Coletti's *Naming the Rose. Eco, Medieval Signs and Modern Theory* (Ithaca, NY: Cornell University Press, 1988) is one of the most documented studies on Eco's fusion of creative writing and scientific research dealing with the Middle Ages.

18. In the late summer of 1988 I was in Italy when the publication of *Foucault's Pendulum* was first announced. For nearly two months I followed the polemics that surrounded Eco's second novel and later documented the reaction of several critics who participated in this debate in "Troppi movimenti intorno al Pendolo di Foucault" and "*Il Pendolo di Foucault*: Kitsch o neo/post-moderno?," *Quaderni d'italianistica*: IX (1988), pp. 301–313, and XI (1990), pp. 225–237. See also F. Pansa and A. Vinci's *Effetto Eco* (Roma: Nuova Edizione del Gallo, 1990) and M. Ganeri's *Il caso Eco* (Palermo: Palumbo, 1991).

19. See, for example, Margherita Degli-Esposti's "The Poetics of Hermeticism in U. Eco's *Il pendolo di Foucault*," *Forum Italicum* 25 (1991), pp. 185–204; JoAnn Cannon's "The Imaginary Universe of Eco. A Reading of *Foucault's Pendulum*," *Modern Fiction Studies* 38 (1992), pp. 895–909; Linda Hutcheon's "Eco's Echoes: Ironizing the (Post)Modern,"*Diacritics* 22 (1992), pp. 2–16; and "Irony-clad Foucault" (in Capozzi, 1997); Norma Bouchard's "Critfictional Epistemes in Contemporary Literature. The Case of *Foucault's Pendulum*," *Comparative Literature Studies* 32, no. 4 (1989), pp. 50–67; and the articles of Rubino, Vernon, Artigiani, Coletti, and Juarrero in "Swinging *Foucault's Pendulum*," in the Comparative Literature Issue of *Modern Language Notes* (December 1992). For an example of how North American critics are examining literary and critical theories in *The Island of the Day Before*, see Norma Bouchard's "U. Eco *L'isola del giorno prima*: Postmodern Theory and Fictional Praxis," *Italica* 72, no. 2 (1995), pp. 193–208; and Capozzi (1996).

20. Woody Allen is quoted in the epigraph of section 106.

21. As Calvino maintains: "Literature can work in a critical vein or to confirm things as they are and as we know them to be. The boundary is not always clearly marked, and I would say that on this score the spirit in which one reads is decisive: it is up to the reader to see to it that literature exerts its critical force, and this can occur independently of the author's intentions" (1986, p. 26).

10

WLADIMIR KRYSINSKI

Borges, Calvino, Eco:
The Philosophies of Metafiction

Introduction

To understand the transformations of literature, particularly in the 1960s, 1970s, and 1980s, requires accounting for the metadimensionality of literary texts. The term "metadimension" means that some literary texts problematize the relationship between the narrative process and its internal self-reflection or its dialogical external interpretation. Examining these relationships reveals the extent of their variation in formal modalities, discursive emphasis, semantic finalities, and intertextual games.

The prefixion of fiction by "meta" rests on the assumption that in some of its discourses, literature has developed operational ways of questioning itself and dealing with its unlimited semiosis, that is to say with the meaning-making process. Although the Greek prefix "meta" (*after*) has a predecessor in Aristotle's *Metaphysics* (which came after his natural science works, *after* "physics"—"metaphysica"), the Greek borrowing does not have the same denotation in reference to "metafiction." Paradoxically, what is metafictional (with its adjectival suffix) may deal with the metaphysical, but this is not necessarily one of its prerequisites. Metafiction pertains to a critically exposed attitude toward the representational process and the autonomous language of metafiction. Hence an obvious semantic displacement produces itself with respect to the prefix "meta," which means "above" or "about" rather than just "after." Thus a novel about a novel writing (e.g., Gide's *The Counterfeiters*) is a metanovel.

Because a surprisingly broad terminological extension has been conferred on the meaning of metafiction, particularly in postmodern criticism, I propose to explore the following aspects of its very rich problematics in the following areas: in the diversity of its forms and discourses and their relationship to the logical concept of formal languages and of metalanguage; in the manner in which it determines the metamorphosis of literature; and in the diverse philosophies of metafiction reflected in the works of Borges, Calvino and Eco.

What Is Metafiction?

Throughout the twentieth century, the relationship between narrative form and metafictional distance or the self-reflexive has been systematically explored, enhanced, and put to the test by writers such as André Gide, Samuel Beckett, Arno Schmidt, Giorgio Manganelli, Donald Barthelme, Philippe Sollers, Julian Rios, John Fowles, John Barth, Oswald Wiener, Walter Abish, Thomas Pynchon, Giuseppe Pontiggia, Claude Simon, and Julio Cortazar. What emerges from their metafictions is the idea that metafiction is not a homogeneous monoreferential discourse arising out of a limited series of problems linked to the narrative or novelistic process. Metafiction is rather a polyvalent problematization of the critical, reflexive, analytical, or playful perspective of that which is narrated reflected upon itself. Three examples illustrate this process: *The Counterfeiters* by André Gide, *Mercier et Camier* by Samuel Beckett, and *Pourquoi. Une voix de fin silence II* by Roger Laporte.

In Gide's well-known novel, the narrative conveyed in the plot is discursively paralleled and problematized in Edouard's *Diary*. This parallel structure clearly constitutes the metafictional level of the novel's narrative (the Profitandieu, Molinier, and Veda Azaïs families). What Gide refers to as "mise-en-abîme" is tantamount to "metafiction," the reduplication and transformation of the narrative into a "para" or beyond narrative. Edouard's *Diary* mirrors the *Counterfeiters*. It is a novel within the novel that deconstructs the naturalistic novel that Gide considered impure and that he sought to replace with the pure novel. At the same time, metafiction in *The Counterfeiters* is a critique of the novel as a record of the slices of life and a proposal for a musically oriented pure verbal construction.

In Beckett's *Mercier et Camier*, the author plays with the narrative by inserting summaries, which follow each chapter. The summaries briefly restate the narrative of each preceding chapter. In problematizing the reflexive relationship between the affirmative discourse of each chapter's narrative and its quasitautological paraphrase in the summaries, the author creates an ironic distance. Thus, Beckett appears to interrogate the problem of how to write about writing in order to understand what the narrative process means.

In Laporte's *Pourquoi. Une voix de fin silence II (Why. A voice of cunning silence II)*, metafiction is inscribed into the discourse of the narrator who is at the same time a self-narrator of his own writing. Metafiction becomes indistinguishable from the fiction *tout court*. It is paradoxical that Laporte wrote about writing, metafictionally inasmuch as his subject is writing itself. Thus the constant interrogation of writing, such as it is, is expressed in its very immediacy. Laporte's fiction and his autosubjective narrative, the referents of which are metafiction and the narrator's self, are therefore good examples of an interiorized, self-reductive, and self-theorized metafiction. Systematically submitted here to the mirroring commentary is the very impulse of writing. To ask "Why?" does not lead to any conclusive outcome. Instead, the metafiction repeats the pace of instinctual creative energy, and in so doing, reveals textures with mystical undertones. The book is dedicated to "All my Jews" and concludes, "My progression, constantly broken, is it the remote trace, never completely exact, of the cruel migration of the pole in the heart studded with stars?"[1]

These three examples illustrate different metafictional strategies. Their radicality ranges from Gide's pure novel to Laporte's internalization of almost mystical scriptural passion. Beckett's game of tautological summarizing of the identical draws the reader's attention to the possibility of the summary's replacement of narration or imposes upon it a purposely reductive transformation. The tautologically oriented commentary is a Beckettian demonstration of a deadlock of literary discourse. Metafiction is here a tool of self-revelation for fiction.

Definition of Metafiction

Clear-cut definitions of metafiction are difficult to find. Even in critical works dedicated to metafiction, we stumble over numerous affirmations, statements, and quasidefinitions that circumscribe the concept from various points of view without providing an all-encompassing, descriptive, and functionally operational definition. Hence the recognition of the fact that metafiction may be or should be contextualized and only then deeply scrutinized.

In quoting some affirmations on metafiction, I draw attention here to some aspects of the complex problem of theorizing and historicizing. My observations on Borges, Calvino, and Eco, from the perspective of metafiction, are intended as a commentary on and as a critique of those theorizations of metafiction the main purpose of which seems to be to inscribe it into the area of postmodern literature. Metafiction and postmodernism at the intersection of history and ideology constitute a broad range of enigmas. Postmodern literary criticism tends to overcome and to classify modernism and/or modernity, the one-sidedness of its critical vision and polyvalence of literary writings, the many-sidedness of its critical analysis, and some specific critical codes at the origin of its critical extrapolations.

Inger Christensen defines metafiction as

> fiction whose primary concern is to express the novelist's vision of experience by exploring the process of its own making. This definition indicates that only those works are considered metafiction where the novelist has a message to convey and is not merely displaying his technical brilliance.[2]

In a work specifically devoted to metafiction, Patricia Waugh observes

> Metafiction may concern itself, then, with particular conventions of the
> novel, to display the process of their construction.
>   Metafictional novels tend to be constructed on the principle of a funda-
> mental and sustained opposition: the construction of a fictional illusion (as in
> traditional realism) and the laying bare of that illusion.
>   Metafiction explicitly lays bare the conventions of realism; it does not
> ignore or abandon them. Very often realistic conventions supply the 'control'
> in metafictional texts, the norm or background against which the experi-
> mental strategies can foreground themselves.[3]

Polyfunctionality and different definitional aspects of metafiction emerge
from many of Waugh's observations. Yet, the major difficulty in grasping the
relevance of metafiction in terms of form, thematization, and messages lies in
the fact that its language is not univocal, as in the language of the novel.
Therefore, as Waugh remarks, metafiction is "an elastic term which covers a
wide range of fictions."[4] Although I agree with this observation, I would like
to stress that metafiction, like literature, relies on specific notions, concepts,
and discourses. It cannot escape complexity and the mixture of signs. Nor
can it rely on a clear definition of its metalanguage. It appears that a plurality
of meanings may emerge from any textually or discursively marked metafictional operation.

With respect to the problem of the metalanguage of metafiction, I draw
upon Alfred Tarski's definition of metalanguage from his 1933 study on "The
Semantic Conception of Truth."

> It is desirable for the metalanguage not to contain any undefined terms
> except such as are involved explicitly or implicitly in the remarks above, i.e.:
> terms of the object-language; terms referring to the form of expressions of
> the object-language, and used in building names these expressions and terms
> of logic. In particular, we derive *semantic terms* (referring to the object-
> language) to be introduced into the metalanguage only by definition.[5]

Metafiction remains in a relationship to the language of literature in terms
of a presupposed analogy where it remains metalanguage. And the language
of literature equals "object-language." This analogical equation is practically
impossible to pursue because what we call the language of literature involves
a considerable number of terms, which cannot be unequivocally defined.
Narrative, novel, character, point of view, realism, postmodernism, modernity do not belong to a unitary conceptual space. Object-language and metalanguage seen in terms of literature and metafiction cannot refer to a
consensual body of notions and understandings.

Because it is our intention to understand the evolution of narrative forms through metafiction and to understand metafiction through fiction in the context of Borges's, Calvino's, and Eco's metafictional and fictional texts, we will therefore consider metafiction a heuristic tool to facilitate discovery of complex systems of signs. Metafiction should be taken as both manifestations of deconstruction and of a cognitive process.

Epistemology of Metafiction

The salient question engages an epistemology of metafiction. The bases for our reflection and scrutiny are a series of open-ended entities constituted by narrative, fiction, the novel, event, plot, time, and character. These entities are set apart through the metafictional process and serve as conceptual unities to be metafictionalized as they undergo a critical, analytical, or playful treatment. The storyteller of fiction is transformed into the metafiction's teller (narrator?) and commentator. Goethe's celebrated formula from *Dichtung und Wahrheit* "Lust zu fabulieren" (Joy of telling the story) becomes "Lust zu um-fabulieren" (Joy to undo the act of telling the story). With respect to open-ended totalities, I recall Calvino's timely and correct observation in his essay on "The Novel as Spectacle."

> Nowadays one may have the impression that narrative reached at the same time a climax of its eclipse with the creators and the zenith of its favor with the critics-theorists.

> (Si direbbe che raccontare stia toccando contemporaneamente il culmine della sua eclisse dai testi creativi e il culmine dell'interesse critico-analitico.)[6]

This proliferation of commentaries leads to a situation in which we are confronted with different philosophies of metafiction instead of with a unique metafictional vision of the narrative discourse. Metafiction represents a specific worldview, thereby defining the writer's epistemological position vis-à-vis narration and representation as well as toward the general or particular meanings of a given literary work. Any metafiction involves an interpretative bias and may be viewed in terms of philosophy, that is, as a coherent interrogation about truth understood in Heideggerian terms, as *Ent-deckung* or unveiling.

It is my premise that Borges, Calvino, and Eco embody different types of metafictional processes. Their philosophies of metafiction variously reflect the finalities of literature and the diversity of metafictional meanings, the infinitude of narrative modalities, and the dialectics of metafictional distances.

Borges

Among many definitions and descriptions of Borges's way of writing and deciphering the meaning of the world, I cite Calvino's reference to the author of *Ficciones*. Borges epitomizes for Calvino the intellectual writer. At the same time, the very intellectual quality and method of Borges's writing entail the process of "plurireadability of the real" (plurileggibilità della realità). The world is therefore subject to interpretation in terms of constantly varying perspectives. Calvino's considerations of Borges are to be found in the chapters on "Quickness" and "Multiplicity" in *Six Memos for the Next Millenium*. In referring to Borges's idea that no book is ever written as an original literary work, Calvino captures the essence of Borges's writing.

> The idea that came to Borges was to pretend that the book he wanted to write had already been written by someone else, some unknown hypothetical author—an author in a different language, of a different culture—and that his task was to describe and review this invented book.[7]

Calvino expresses admiration for Borges's style, rhythm, and narration, and for his quickness and multiplicity. More particularly, he notes:

> Borges has created a literature raised to the second power and, at the same time, a literature that is like the extraction of the square root of itself. It is a "potential literature" to use a term applied later on in France.[8]

In the chapter on "Multiplicity," Calvino describes Paul Valéry's original and unique pursuit of the "Total Phenomenon, that is, the Totality of conscience, relations, conditions, possibilities, and impossibilities."[9] For Calvino, Borges is the author who has

> perfectly achieved Valéry's aesthetic ideal of exactitude in imagination and in language, creating works that match the rigorous geometry of the crystal and the abstraction of deductive reasoning.[10]

Calvino's observations enable us to capture the sense of the metafictional operations achieved by Borges throughout his work. In Borges, the relationship between fiction and metafiction reduces itself to what I describe as the principle of cognitively cooperative interrelational telescoping of fiction into metafiction and of metafiction into fiction.

At the core of Borges's writing lies the postulate of an unfinished condition of interpretativeness of the world. This postulate is based on the idea and the intricate practice of the interencompassing of a countless variety of worlds, temporalities, facts, texts, statements, histories, and narratives. He achieves a constant virtuality of literary discourse. What is literary is endlessly potential in its multiciplicity of forms. Borges's story tactically telescopes philosophical, interpretative, and argumentative discourse and can at any moment effectuate a detour through philosophy. It is the vehicle or enigmatic medium of virtually all phenomena. The very hybridity of Borges's text imparts that the reading process becomes a wandering through the labyrinth. Any path is a forking path. Any temporal perspective, objectively grasped, is a series of temporal bifurcations. Hence, the vertiginous idea of the infinite multiplicity of times. As the narrator of "The Garden of Forking Paths" puts it in the excerpt quoted by Calvino,

> Una red creciente y vertiginosa de tiempos divergentes, convergentes y paralelos (a growing and bewildering network of divergent, convergent and parallel forms of time).[11]

In Borges's vision of time, the Aristotelian definition of time as "the cipher of movement" transforms itself into an understanding of time as the absolute parallelism of the concomitant and yet not interrelated subjective temporalities. The ciphers of movement of these subjective temporalities are not palpable. From the point of view of literary criticism, this conception of time relativizes the Bakhtinian idea of chronotope. The necessary chronotopical coming together of space and time, according to Bakhtin's concept, is subject to considerable modification since divergence, convergence, and parallelism of times do not entail a precise identification in each time of its respective adjacent space. The subjective position of each time does not presuppose the precise occupation of a point in space. Temporal subjectivities can project themselves into an indeterminate place of the boundless universe.

The mental experience of time seems to negate its objective calculus. Consequently, time is neither the cipher of movement nor a permanent and fatal partner of space, as a polyvalent and subjectively experienced movement presupposes a "displacement" of time. In the following commentary on Borges's "Tlön," Solange Fricaud provides relevant confirmation of the inadequacy of time and space conceived in terms of chronotope.

> On Tlön, time is a pure flowing of thought, without any parallelism with Space. The Leibnizian idealism or the Kantian one is further reduced from dualism to monism. If, in the tradition of philosophical idealism, Time and Space function as two forms of the human mind, measurable in terms of the Newtonian physics—one can calculate the speed and the place of a mobile object—on Tlön there is no correspondence to assign between Time and Space. Borges imagines a sort of pure Time without any spatial signification, but instead of discovering the internal duration of consciousness (as Saint Augustine, Pascal, Bergson), the author emphasizes the succession of the instants not related by the memory since there is no conservation of the same object in Space.[12]

Literary discourse à la Borges is the brilliant confirmation of its infinite imaginary potentialities. It confirms, within the realm of metafiction, the idea of playful manipulation of such open-ended entities as literature, story, plot, history, character, meaning, point of view, and interpretation. Within this unique configuration of the serious and playful, of an infinite gallery of mirrors and the centrality of the narrator's voice, the reader may find some principles that serve to fulfill the objectives of Borgesian discourse. I identify them as (1) the principle of the hermeneutical infinite, (2) the principle of the cosmological infinite, and (3) the principle of metaknowledge.

"Tlön, Uqbar, Orbis Tertius," "The Garden of Forking Paths," "The Circular Ruins," and "The Library of Babel" (just to mention a few well-known stories) constitute, like mirrors and labyrinths, both fixed and stochastic universes. They facilitate the play of the interpretative game involving semiotics, philosophy, myths, theology, literature, and history. But all the possible meanings that may be established with the help of the above-mentioned disciplines and approaches remain working hypotheses, enigmas, and conjectures.

The world created by the Borgesian imagination is an aleatory structure based on the vertiginous expansion of the reflexive, the inventive, and the paraphysical and metametaphysical. In its deepest impulse, it is a decon-structive gesture that concerns the problem of sign. Nicolas Rosa observes that in Borges

> Sign ceases to represent and to express in order to signify by itself: that is to say in order to put into relief the work of writing (para poner en evidencia el trabajo de la escritura). It reminds us of Joyce. In this problematics, a text does not stay in any relation of manifestation or of reflection. It is possible to read it as social production, as a particular language where an individual subject does not speak *as an individual subject*, but as the combinatory struc-ture of a subject who utters himself or herself through the laws of a system (que se enuncia en las leyes de un sistema). We have to ask ourselves on all levels how Borges instrumentally uses the codes which he receives from the semiotic reality, that is to say language, economy, science, culture, etc., which are the dominant elements of his structuration in order to investigate his ideology.[13]

These observations provide a useful basis for a discussion of the principle of the hermeneutical infinite. Because the sign becomes a convergence of different codes, it is above all a formal structure. It is polysemic, opaque, and not representative. The signs of short stories underlaid by narration and by narrative, by the active participation of the characters in the action, and above all by the voice of the narrator do not provide the necessary clues to reach a clear configuration of meaning. Borges's short stories render everything complex. In the final analysis, they are the conjectural discourse of presuppositions, ambiguities, and polysemic constructions. The hermeneutical infinite signifies that any interpretation of Borges's texts opens up a labyrinth. Unlike Heidegger's conceptions, the universes constructed by Borges are not visions of a represented world. They are musical scores in which the composer-narrator, either by narrating or quoting, conveys various hypotheses, points of view, sentential formulas, maxims, and different philosophical opinions. In this intergalactic configuration of signs proliferating in various directions, the narrative is not a discursive paradigm for the intelligibility of the world. It is rather a tool of complexification. Stories such as "Tlön, Uqbar, Orbis Tertius" give us sufficient information to perceive the hermeneutical infinite. On the one hand, they present the impossibility of capturing the complex entanglement of facts, judgments, evoked affirmations, and quoted opinions, and on the other hand, the impossibility of logical interpretation. What the narrator is saying exceeds the reader's competence:

> Every mental state is irreducible: the simple act of giving it a name—i.e. of classifying it—introduces a distortion, a "slant" or "bias." One might well deduce, therefore, that on Tlön there are no sciences—or even any "systems of thought." The paradoxical truth is that systems of thought do exist, almost countless numbers of them. Philosophies are much like the nouns of the northern hemisphere; the fact that every philosophy is by definition a dialectical game, a *Philosophie des Als Ob*, has allowed them to proliferate. There are systems upon systems that are incredible but possessed of a pleasing architecture or a certain agreeable sensationalism. The metaphysicians of Tlön seek not truth, or even plausibility—they seek to amaze, astound. In their view, metaphysics is a branch of the literature of fantasy. They know that a system is naught but the subordination of all the aspects of the universe to one of those aspects—*any* one of them. Even the phrase "all the aspects" should be avoided, because it implies the impossible addition of the present instant and all those instants that went before. Nor is the plural "those instants that went before" legitimate, for it implies another impossible operation.[14]

Metafictional Basis of Borges's *Ficciones*

Once more I would like to emphasize the metafictional basis and framing of Borges *ficciones*. To paraphrase Cervantes' claim, "Soy el primero que he novelado en lengua de Castilla," we can attribute the following affirmation to Borges. "Soy el primero que he ficcionado asi en español." ("I am the first one who has fictionalized like this in Spanish.") Though Borges's literary discourse is unique, it is undeniable that it has roots in literature. Writers such as Robert Browning, Leopoldo Lugones, Macedonio Fernández, Kafka, Horacio Quiroga, Edgar Allen Poe, Mallarmé, Paul Valéry, and Alfonso Reyes are among his precursors. But Borges's synthesis is based on a metafictional discourse that retells literature as an already scrutinized body of institutional, stylistic, semiotic, and fictional possibilities. As an open-ended entity of potentialities, literature becomes for Borges a laboratory of cognitive experimental maneuvers. A new vision and dynamics of literature result from the experiment. Before I summarize this process with some synthetic and problematizing formulas, I must recall that together with the principle of the hermeneutical infinite, two other principles determine the Borgesian metafictional rewriting of literary discourse. I refer to the principles of the cosmological infinite and of metaknowledge.

The principle of the cosmological infinite presupposes that Borges invents numerous imaginary and possible worlds. Their boundaries are unverifiable. Those worlds fulfill themselves in time rather than in space. Borges continuously plays with verisimilitude in the context of a conjectural or purely a-referential narrative reality. These narratively dreamed worlds acquire the ambiguous status of the absolute labyrinth-boundedness. In *The Garden of Forking Paths*, the narrator comments on the labyrinth to be constructed and described by the Chinese writer Ts'ui Pên. The narrator recalls that Ts'ui Pên devoted thirteen years to "these heterogeneous tasks, but the hand of a stranger murdered him—and his novel was left incoherent and no-one found the labyrinth." The narrator concludes in an imaginary manner:

> I pictured it as infinite—a labyrinth not of octagonal pavillions and paths that turn back upon themselves, but of rivers and provinces and kingdoms.... I imagined a labyrinth of labyrinths, a maze of mazes, a twisting, turning, ever-widening labyrinth that contained both past and future and somehow implied the stars. Absorbed in those illusory imaginings, I forgot that I was a pursued man; I felt myself, for an indefinite while, the abstract perceiver of the world.[15]

Labyrinth epitomizes the principle of the cosmological infinite. It encompasses the idea of complex spatiality and of an "abstract perceiver of the world."

The principle of metaknowledge functions as an intense textual circulation of various knowledges and information. Such knowledges are factual, doxological, conjectural, provocative, and occasional without any subordination of one to the other. These configurations of knowledge refer to "Borges" as a central subject of utterance and as a semiotic coordinator of all references conveyed by his stories. He detains the metaknowledge, that is to say a place of petition and of reorganization of the information circulating in his work. As a subject of this metaknowledge, Borges reveals new cognitive perspectives of the world's understanding. His discourse is by no means unilateral. Nor is his vision fixed on the narration alone. It is altogether a mixed and hybrid narrative, paranarrative, and metanarrative vision, and a constantly expanding epistemological quest for knowledges either potentialized or subordinated to another knowledge.

Through a way of writing, which constantly implicates the idealism of time, spatial uncertainty, the hermeneutical infinite, and metaknowledge, Borges interrogates the institutional rules of literature. Borges's fiction challenges and annuls the rule of representation, the rule of the author's hegemonic position, the rule of sufficient meaning, and the rule of the privileged passionate capacity of being a literary creator. Thus, in Borges, the romantic conception of literature is overcome by the idealistic vision of Time. In "The Examination of Herbert Quain's Work," a story with a metafictional title, Borges summarizes four metaphorical texts by Quain: in "God of the Labyrinth," "April March," "The Secret Mirror," and "Statements." Borges concludes that literature, in its putative kinship to the idea of labyrinthine time, is not a privileged human activity. Nor is it the original gesture of the author as genius. In "Pierre Menard, Author of *Quixote*," the narrator synthesizes his idea of literature through the paradoxical rewriting of *Don Quixote* by the fictive Pierre Menard.

> "Thinking, meditating, imagining," he also wrote me, "are not anomalous acts—they are the normal respiration of the intelligence. To glorify the occasional exercise of that function, to treasure beyond price ancient and foreign thoughts, to recall with incredulous awe what some *doctor universalis* thought, is to confess our own languor, or our own *barbarie*. Every man should be capable of all ideas, and I believe that in the future he shall be."[16]

Various conceptions of modernity converged in the recognition of the transgressive and dialectical as crucial elements of the repetitive gesture of transformation and of innovation. Modernity was similarly based on the recognition of its telos. Borges, for whom a teleology of literature has lost all relevance, discards it. In Borges emerges the a-temporal, the a-modern, the antitransgressive, and also the a-representational. The "why" of literature is no longer linked to representation and to subjectivity. The narrator in Borges is a cybernetic machine absorbing and spewing quotations, knowledges, and paradoxes. The world is no longer an alterity of text or its beginning. Situated beyond any classificatory intention, Borges's discourse has the right not to say something and not to affirm it ultimately. It has the right to invent anything and to doubt everything. By his discourse he overcomes representational ambition, and by the strength of his writing, literature transforms itself into this utterable but indeterminate "something." No theory, neither the most modern nor postmodern, could discipline this eternal return of the different.

Borges's fictions of fiction establish a boundary and a fascinating imitation of the extraterritorial. In terms of transgressive modernity, this extraterritorial imitation is a limit that cannot be transgressed. Borges's metafictional reflexivity eradicates both the mimetic and intentional fallacy. Those who follow Borges will and must, consenting or not, depend on the Borgesian intertextuality understood as an open-ended multiplicity of textual universes and metafictional operations. To conduct a story is no longer an innocent enterprise.

Calvino

Such are precisely the cases of Italo Calvino and Umberto Eco, who in their distinctive ways venture into the same complex territory of new critical parameters. Borges's lesson could be interpreted in the following way: he displaced and disintegrated some the most important literary dogmas (such as those grounded in the secular tradition of literary discourse from Aristotle until the twentieth century). His idealistic theory of Time opened the way to countless inventive (a)fabulations. Under the impact of Borges's philosophy of metafiction, the system of traditional narrative criteria became obsolete.

Calvino's achievement is his remarkable inventiveness in the realm of the imaginary leading to the creation of forms and signs encompassing both narrative and novel, literary criticism, and philosophical thinking about literature. Calvino's philosophy of metafiction may be characterized thus: he is above all a writer of semiotic consciousness; his interdisciplinary command of literature enables him to inventively use such literary structures as fable, story, plot, novel, and narration; and his literary discourse is always at least second-degree, dynamically conceived and practiced metafiction. For Calvino, writing fiction as a metafiction means reusing preexisting literary or discursive patterns in order to reach a new meaning and to convey a new message. But this reutilization does not prevent Calvino from achieving his own *ars combinatoria*.

> We could recycle used images in a new context and that changes their meaning. Postmodernism may be seen as the tendency to make ironic use of the stock images of the mass media, or to inject the taste for the marvelous inherited from literary tradition into mechanisms that accentuate its alienation.[17]

As a writer of semiotic consciousness, Calvino is committed to literary process in terms of semiosis, that is, the process of meaning making through the interaction of signs as referred objects and their *interpretans* in a constant discursive movement. Literature for Calvino is moreover a communicative process. In Calvino's writing the sign, in a way understood as a referential and as an indicative social interrelational force, is a protagonist. The source of his contribution to the renewal of the literary landscape (thanks to Borges) is a literary and discursive inventiveness that enabled him to establish certain maximal paradigms of varying types of literary discourse. In a certain sense, he put Borges's intuitions into practice. For Calvino, literature is a machine of cognition. I identify and characterize a few of his most significant texts.

Il castello dei destini incrociati (The Castle of Cross Destinies)

In this text shaped by a ludic paradigm, the principle of the overwhelming game acts as a tool to utter and to narrativize an *ars combinatoria*. This gives way to a vision of the world in which, between life-world-literature-fiction and game, the vision establishes itself as a pleasure principle. In this work, Calvino proceeds by narratively using what he calls "fantastic iconology."

> What I was trying to do in *The Castle of Crossed Destinies (Il castello dei destini incrociati)* is a kind of "fantastic iconology," not only with the tarot but also with great paintings. In fact I attempted to interpret the paintings of Carpaccio in San Giorgio degli Schiavoni in Venice, following the cycles of St. George and St. Jerome as if they were one story, the life of a single person, and to identify my own life with that of this George-Jerome. This fantastic iconology has become my habitual way of expressing my love of painting. I have adopted the method of telling my own stories, starting from famous pictures or at any rate pictures that have made an impact on me.[18]

Se una notte d'inverno un viagiatore (If on a Winter's Night a Traveler)

Calvino calls this a hypernovel; there is a metanarrative structuring of the novel along with a metacommunicative process of reading the novel. In fact, the couple of readers committed to the reading of *If on a Winter's Night a Traveler* symbolize both the process of understanding and the mechanical process of identification through reading.

Se una notte d'inverno un viagiatore is a self-reflexive and metafictional novel *in statu nascendi*. Calvino himself defines it in the following terms:

> My aim was to give the essence of what a novel is by providing it in a concentrated form, in ten beginnings; each beginning develops in very different ways from a common nucleus, and each acts within a framework that both determines and is determined.[19]

Lezioni americane

This last text written before he died, an unfinished book, is Calvino's last will and testament. The English edition is entitled *Six Memos for the Next Millennium*. The work is about literature and the world and is a metafictionally understood fiction. Surprisingly, to characterize literature, Calvino uses scientific notions from physics such as lightness and quickness, and other epistemological notions such as exactitude and multiplicity. Calvino's rich reflections weave an ideal, almost utopian text, an absolute text of literature that he defines as follows:

> Over-ambitious projects may be objectionable in many fields, but not in literature. Literature remains alive only if we set ourselves immeasurable goals, far beyond all hope of achievement. Only if poets and writers set themselves tasks that no one else dares imagine will literature continue to have a function. Since science has begun to distrust general explanations and solutions that are not sectorial and specialized, the grand challenge for literature is to be capable of weaving together the various branches of knowledge, the various "codes," into a manifold and multifaceted vision of the world.[20]

Calvino's philosophy of metafiction presupposes achieving a complete practical knowledge of literature in order to practice it as a synthesis of rhetoric, narrative models, and a mosaic of styles. In terms of philosophy understood as reflexive grasping of the conditions of knowledge, Calvino's philosophy of metafiction may be described as a synthesis of *logos* and *techné*, that is to say as a reflexive and problematized thinking of literature and as an aesthetic praxis of literary discourse. Calvino points out that the relationship between literature and philosophy is the one between a rigorous literary representation of the world and Man (as in Dostoievsky, Kafka, Beckett, Camus, and Genet), and an interpretive mode that characterizes philosophy. Thus Calvino remarks:

> It is only when the writer writes before the philosopher who interprets him, that the literary rigour can serve as a model for the philosophical rigour— even though writer and philosopher live together in the same person.[21]

By naming *Robinson Crusoe*, *Don Quijote*, and *Hamlet* philosophical works, Calvino emphasizes the fact that they "announced a new relationship between the phantasmatic lightness of the ideas and the weight of the world."[22]

Eco

To understand Umberto Eco's novels in terms of his philosophy of metafiction requires a grasp of the basic cognitive operation, which is both semiotic and literary. This operation is at the heart of Eco's novelistic creation. Language for Eco, in semiotic terms, is technique above all. Language is given as a differentiated totality of signs, syntagms, and narrative. It should be used technically, as a form of practically adopted knowledge. Adopted and applied to a specific sphere of actions and functions, Eco's novels constitute a practical recycling of such literary and semiotic models as the thriller, the gothic novel, the medieval romance, the labyrinthine or daedalic narrative, the psychological novel, and the social-popular novel. These genres and subgenres coincide and function in his novelistic texts. In a paradoxical sense, Eco's novels are almost totally metafictional. We can consider Eco's literary production as the outcome, or inheritance, of Borges's lesson of the labyrinth. Calvino, for whom the labyrinth is also a necessary narrative model, is similarly Borges's heir.

We can, therefore, establish the following succession of labyrinthine perspectives in the literary genealogy encompassing Borges, Calvino, and Eco: (1) Borges: a fascination with the labyrinth and constant multiplication of various labyrinthine structures leading to a permanent narrative and the hermeneutical "growth" of the structures; (2) Calvino: the labyrinth as an epistemological model for understanding and challenging the world; and (3) Eco: the labyrinth as a dynamic and heuristic model for interpreting the world.

Interpreting the world is a complex process, and this very fact of complexity constitutes the subject of *Foucault's Pendulum*. In this novel, we witness a growing complexity of the plot and of interpretive presuppositions, and a kind of constant widening of the interpretative matrix.

The metafictional relationship between story and commentary establishes itself in a series of discourses entitled "Filename." In *Foucault's Pendulum* "Filename" functions as a quasiparallel novel. It may even be named "metanovel" if we assume with Mario Perniola that what characterizes a metanovel is first an autoreferential relationship toward itself.[23] It is highly intertextual and self-referential. For instance, in the first "Filename" the narrator says:

> *Where were you last night, L*
> There, indiscreet reader: you will never know it, but that half-line hanging in space was actually the beginning of a long sentence that I wrote but then wished I hadn't even though let alone written it, wished that it had never happened. So I pressed a key, and a milky film spread over the fatal and inopportune lines, and I pressed DELETE and, whoosh, all gone.[24]

In the numerous "Filename" passages, the reader will find more and more self-referential and intertextual allusions. For example:

> Could a story like this be made into a novel? Perhaps I should write, instead about the women I avoid because I can have them. Or could have had them. Some story. If you can't even decide what the story is, better stick to editing books on philosophy.[25]

You're an author, not yet aware of your powers.[26]

Begin the story in a bar. The need to fall in love.
Some things you can feel coming. You don't fall in love because you fall in love; you fall in love because of the need, desperate, to fall in love. When you feel that need, you have to watch your step: like having drunk a philter, the kind that makes you fall with the first thing you meet. It could be a duck-billed platypus. . . .[27]

There comes the dinner with Dr. Wagner. At the lecture he had just given a heckler a definition of psychoanalysis. La psychanalyse? C'est qu'entre l'homme et la femme chers amis ça ne colle pas.
     There was discussion: the couple, divorce as a legal fiction. Taken up by my own problem. I participated. We allowed ourselves to be drawn into dialectic exchanges, speaking while Wagner was silent, forgetting there was an oracle in our presence. . . .[28]

The reading process of *Foucault's Pendulum* is a polyreferential one. It involves deciphering the story itself as well as the proliferating interpretive commentary that goes in different directions. A multiplicity of stories and of metastories, of intertextual signals, as well as of intellectual allusions makes of *Foucault's Pendulum* a sort of *compendium* of encyclopedic narrativity (including myths and archetypes, popular novels, thrillers, etc.) and narration understood as a process of utterance producing diverse narratives, various philosophical worldviews, as well as information on the mystical and occult.
     Philosophically speaking, and with Wittgenstein as a point of reference, Eco explores the boundaries of the novelistic language to show that it has no limits in practice. Metafictional use of the narrative language presupposes a dialectical relationship toward another language and another universe. For instance, one of the perspectives of *Foucault's Pendulum* is the following triple relation: novel vs. fiction vs. psychoanalysis.
     Thus, within the polycontextual narrative universe of *Foucault's Pendulum*, Wittgenstein's affirmation: "*The boundaries of my language* mean the boundaries of my world" (*Die Grenzen meiner Sprache* bedeuten die Grenzen meiner Welt)[29] can be interpreted as follows: who sets the boundaries of my language? The narrator, so enthusiastically disposed toward unfinished worlds of information, does not see any limits for his fiction. As an open-ended novel, and also as a world-mirroring and a world-explaining novel, *Foucault's Pendulum* is an endlessly self-mirroring text whose commentary and interpretation do not stop. On the contrary, they open into new nodes, stories, and presuppositions. Intertextually interwoven, *Foucault's Pendulum* is a sort of indestructible infernal machine. It constantly displays its infinite perspectives.

Interpretations of Eco

Beyond their enormous international successes, Eco's novels have given rise to scores of critiques and studies with innumerable interpretations. It is quite significant that almost at the same time as the publication of *Foucault's Pendulum*, Eco dealt with the problem of interpretation and of overinterpretation. What strikes me in the numerous interpretations of this novel is the fact that some interpretations do not grasp all the subtle and refined prescriptions put forward by Eco in his theoretical writings. Quite often, instead of interpretation, we find violent attacks known as "stroncature" in Italian. Some critical readers blast the author instead of attempting to understand the meaning of Eco's semiotic and metafictional operation. Salmon Rushdie's reading of *Foucault's Pendulum* is a case in point. Stemming from an obvious misinterpretation of Eco's novel, it is in every respect unjust.

A more general problem may be formulated concerning whether it is possible to acceptably interpret a complex novel of such unbounded and limitless dimensions. The novel is a postfactum utilization of cabalistic, magic, scientific, philosophical, religious, and literary sources. What sort of *intentio operae* and *intentio auctoris* can we fruitfully attribute to such metafictional writing? It remains an open question.

Indeed, the planetary setting, intention and themes, writing and reading processes of *Foucault's Pendulum* are quite evident. This mammoth project can thus either be accepted in all its complexity or rejected as a pretentious and confusing enterprise. Here, anthropos, logos, and cosmos meet somewhere in a secret, fictitious place. To achieve an optimal thematic understanding of this novel, we must realize that it is a multilayered text with each layer constituting an enigmatic actual or possible world.

Let us consider what Rushdie faults in *Foucault's Pendulum*. I cite some passages of this above-referenced intemperate critical outburst.

About twenty years ago the bookshops seemed to be full of volumes with titles like *Illuminatus*, in which it was suggested that the world was run by this or that occult conspiracy. In the aftermath of the Kennedy assassination, the notion that "visible" history was a fiction created by the powerful, and that this "invisible" or subterranean histories contained the "real" truths of the age, had become fairly generally plausible.

Pynchon once wrote a short story called "Under the Rose," its title an Englishing of the Latin *sub rosa*. *Foucault's Pendulum*, the obese new volume from Umberto Eco, is an illuminatus-novel for the end of the eighties, a post-modernist conspiracy fiction about, I suppose, the world under the name of the rose. It is, I regret to report, a very faint Eco indeed of those old Pynchonian high jinks. It is humourless, devoid of characterization, entirely free of anything resembling a credible world, and mind-numbingly full of gobbledygook of all sorts. Reader: I hated it.

Foucault's Pendulum is not a novel. It is a computer game.

And at the very end, in Casaubon's conclusion ("I have understood. And the certain(ty?) that there is nothing to understand should be my peace, my triumph"), there's more than touch of the ancient Japanese poet Basho who travelled to the seat of wisdom, the Deep North, to learn that there was nothing to learn in the Deep North.

Unfortunately, the journey to this truth is so turgid that it is impossible to care about reaching the goal. This is Spielbergery without the action or bull-whips, and if, as Anthony Burgess threatens on the jacket, "this is the way the European novel is going," we should all catch a bus in the opposite direction as soon as possible.[30]

It is evident that Rushdie misses the metafictional dimension of Eco's novel. In *Foucault's Pendulum*, Eco achieves a literary construction that consists of a dialogical mixture of the popular novel (*Illuminatus* in Rushdie's term) and uncharacterized characters, as they are the intellectual actans of the invented Plot. It is postmodern because it recycles old, popular, and contemporary literary structures and stereotypes. Like the world it is full of sound and fury. Like the contemporary world, it is full of stereotypes, vulgar literature (Trivialliteratur), scientific and specialized discourses. Viewed philosophically, it may be compared to Montaigne's essayistic and yet narra-tive prose. Like Burton's *Anatomy of Melancholy*—an anatomic novel—it is prose about knowledge of the world, an all-encompassing mélange, a Mischung, a digressive, open-ended, strongly self-referential, and provoca-tively extrareferential text.

Philosophies of metafiction are not as philosophical as Cartesian, Husser-lian, or Adornian discourses. However, they engender visions of the world as well as a critical discourse on representation. At stake here is the problem of mimesis. Metafictional novels confirm that mimesis is both wishful thinking and a vicious circle necessarily entering the discourse as semiotic process, the sign about signs about signs.

The objects of philosophical discourse are not the private property of philosophers. And the objects of literary discourse are not the private prop-erty of the literati. Metafiction is a state of affairs comparable to some extent to the proverbial "Spanish tavern," l'auberge espagnole, where philosophers and writers convivially lodge together, although each of them brings hetero-geneous subjects to the tavern.

They enjoy seeing horse and not horseness. When Joyce joyfully plays with the concept of "allhorse" by saying: "Horseness is the whatness of allhorse,"[31] he alludes to the opposition between Plato's idealism and Aristotle's rationalism. By the same token, he opposes the abstract to the concrete. In terms of metafiction, he opposes two conflictual languages.

In the play of stories, narrations, and abyssal discourses, philosophies of metafiction demonstrate that the interpretation of the world cannot escape fiction. Fiction is therefore the first condition of unveiling the world. Metafiction means that in potentializing the insufficiency of the fictional story, the commentary has a double role to play: it has to assess philosophically the efficacy of the story and relativize its absolutizing pretension.

Notes

I wish to thank Mr. Antoine Polgar for scrupulously editing my text.
1. R. Laporte, *Pourquoi? Une voix de fin silence II.* (Paris: Gallimard, 1967), p. 179.
2. I. Christensen, *The Meaning of Metafiction* (Bergen, Oslo, Tromso: Unversitetsforlaget, 1981), p. 11
3. P. Waugh, *Metafiction, The Theory and Practice of Self-Conscious Fiction* (London and New York, Methuen, 1984), pp. 4, 6, 18.
4. Waugh, p. 18.
5. A. Tarski, "The Semantic Conception of Truth," in *Semantics and the Philosophy of Language*, ed. L. Linsky (Urbana: The University of Illinois Press, 1952), pp. 22–23.
6. I. Calvino, "Il romanzo come spettacolo," in *Saggi 1945–1985* (Milano: Mondadori, 1995), p. 272.
7. I. Calvino, *Six Memos for the Next Millenium* (Cambridge, MA: Harvard University Press, 1988), p. 50.
8. Calvino, *Six Memos for the Next Millenium*, p. 51.
9. Calvino, *Six Memos for the Next Millenium*, p. 118.
10. Calvino, *Six Memos for the Next Millenium*, p. 119.
11. Calvino, *Six Memos for the Next Millenium*, pp. 119–120.
12. S. Fricaud, "Les figures du temps dans *Fictions* ou Comment la fiction d'un Temps idéal ébranle le mythe de la littérature," in *Borges, "Fictions" mythe et récit*, ouvrage collectif (Paris: Ellipses, 1988), p. 37.
13. N. Rosa, *Los fulgores del simulacro* (Santa Fe: Cuadernos de Extensión Universitaria, 1987), pp. 278–279.
14. J. L. Borges, "Tlön, Uqbar, Orbis Tertius," in *Collected Fictions*, trans. Andrew Hurley (New York: Penguin, 1998) p. 74. (Hereafter *CF.*)
15. Borges, *CF* 122.
16. Borges, *CF* p. 95.
17. Calvino, *Six Memos for the Next Millenium*, p. 95.
18. Calvino, *Six Memos for the Next Millenium*, p. 94.
19. Calvino, *Six Memos for the Next Millenium*, p. 120.
20. Calvino, *Six Memos for the Next Millenium*, p. 112.
21. I. Calvino, *La machine littéraire*, tr. M. Orcel and F. Wahl (Paris: du Seuil, 1984), p. 38.
22. Calvino, *La machine littéraire*, p. 44.
23. M. Perniola, *Il Metaromanzo* (Milano: Silva Editore, 1966), p. 22.

24. U. Eco, *Foucault's Pendulum*, tr. W. Weaver (New York: Ballantine Books, 1990), p. 23.
25. Eco, *Foucault's Pendulum*, p. 50.
26. Eco, *Foucault's Pendulum*, p. 60.
27. Eco, *Foucault's Pendulum*, pp. 195–196.
28. Eco, *Foucault's Pendulum*, pp. 196–197.
29. Ludwig Wittgenstein, *Tractatus logico-philosophicus* (London, 1922) sect. 5.6.
30. S. Rushdie, "Umberto Eco," in *Imaginary Homelands, Essays and Criticism 1981–1991* (London: Penguin Books, 1992), pp. 269, 270, 271, 272.
31. J. Joyce, *Ulysses* (New York: Penguin Books, 1988), p. 186.

11

ERMANNO BENCIVENGA

Philosophy and Literature in Calvino's Tales

The Watcher has a special place in Calvino's production.* Coming after four years of virtual narrative silence,[1] and the outcome of long, agonizing work stretching over a decade, it is difficult to classify (long short story? novella? extended meditation?) and signals a break in the style of that production. To be sure, even earlier Calvino felt (and expressed) the fascination of highly stylized, rarefied, "light" situations, and even later he continued to turn compassionate, somewhat startled, somewhat amused attention to everyday life; but there is no question that before *The Watcher* his fiction has a more standard structure (more of a conventional plot, more traditionally conceived characters), whereas after it experimental moves take over and dominate the page.

In *The Watcher* we read the following:

> For a long time he had been trying to avoid pure literature, as if ashamed of his youthful vanity, his ambition to be a writer. He had been quick to under-stand the error concealed in it: the claim to individual survival, having done nothing to deserve it beyond preserving an image, true or false, of oneself. Personal literature now seemed to him a row of tombstones in a cemetery: the literature of the living as well as of the dead. Now he sought something else from books: the wisdom of the ages or simply something that helped to understand something. But as he was accustomed to reason in images he went on picking from thinkers' books the image-filled kernel, mistaking them for poets. (II 49; 44)

The "he" in this passage is a thinly disguised version of Calvino: he had twice been involved with elections at the polls he describes (once, deliberately, as an election watcher), and the first name that immediately matched that "he" ("Amerigo") bears an obvious resonance with "Italo" (the last name went through a more tortuous route).[2] So suppose we take this disdain of "pure literature" to be somewhere in the background of Calvino's own mind, and suppose we borrow from him a name for the "something else"—the wisdom or understanding—he might himself have been looking for in books. Another obvious double of his, the (non)photographer Antonino Paraggi who, at the end of his adventure, having come full circle, "realized that photographing photographs was the only course that he had left" (II 1109; *Loves* 52),[3] at the beginning of the same adventure was described as follows: "his real passion was commenting to his friends on current events large and small, unraveling the thread of general reasons from the tangle of details; in short, by mental attitude, he was a philosopher, and he devoted all his thoroughness to grasping the significance of even the events most remote from his own experience" (II 1096–1097; 40–41). By applying this term, then ("philosopher"), to his own work, we can say that Calvino was increasingly tempted by philosophy, that literature per se he found less and less satisfying; and consequently that his work may constitute a precious case study for illuminating the tenuous, fuzzy relations between these two "disciplines." This is what I intend to do here, by telling a tale that goes through Calvino's tales—and eventually, because I am a philosopher, by spelling out what I take its moral to be.

At the beginning, there is nothing, and it is frightening: "Corsica vanished, engulfed by the light, but the border between sea and sky did not become firm: it remained that ambiguous, confused zone frightening to look at because it does not exist" (I 187; *Man* 55–56). What is frightening in nothing is its appeal: the enticing threat—the threatening enticement—to be swallowed in it, to *become* nothing. "[H]is wanting to avenge his father's death, his ardor to fight, to enroll himself among Charlemagne's warriors—wasn't that also a ritual to prevent plunging into the void, like this raising and setting of pine cones by Sir Agilulf?" (I 969; *Knight* 21).[4] But there is a more benevolent aspect to nothing, a reverse side to the scare it offers: it also works wonderfully as a backdrop for inventions, "the invisible line of the horizon . . . [can] part like an oyster revealing all of a sudden a different planet or a new world" (II 1167; *Loves* 104). And pleasure will accompany that experience. "At that moment he realized he was happy: the fog, erasing the world around him, allowed him to hold in his eyes the visions of the wide screen. . . . Bundled up in his overcoat, Marcovaldo felt protected from every external sensation, suspended in the void; and he could color this void with the images of India, the Ganges, the jungle, Calcutta. . . . [T]hings existed just to the slight extent that sufficed. . . . [A]s he stared beyond the panes at the empty night traversed only by undefined luminous presences . . . , [he found that to be] the perfect situation for daydreaming, for projecting in front of himself, wherever he went, a never-ending film on a boundless screen" (I 1123–1124; *Marcovaldo* 61).[5]

In fact, it is not necessary to stare into absolute void for this mythopoetic potential to be activated. All that is needed is to cancel the ordinary context of things, the ways we are used to dealing with them, the expectations we have formed as a result; and in the temporary, local emptiness thus created stories will begin to flow. "What fun! A shoe, such an ordinary object, particularly for a cobbler's apprentice like him, and a pistol, such a mysterious, almost unreal thing; by putting them up against each other one can do wonders, make them tell marvellous tales" (I 19; *Path* 15). "Even pistols, when talked about like this as one studies how they work, no longer seem instruments for killing people, but strange enchanted toys" (I 90; *Path* 86–87). And this change—or loss—of context issues from a different, strange way of looking at things: from a gaze that challenges them, that violates them, or that just looks at what no one else is looking at—or from a point of view no one else is taking. "[H]e realized that the pleasure didn't come so much from doing these unaccustomed things as from seeing everything in a different way: streets like the floors of valleys, or dry river-beds, houses like blocks of steep mountains, or the walls of a cliff" (I 1159; *Marcovaldo* 98). "[O]nce, a flight of autumn woodcock appeared in a street's slice of sky. And the only person to notice was Marcovaldo, who always walked with his nose in the air" (I 1079; *Marcovaldo* 13). "[T]he alien perspectives made every image alien" (II 92; *Cosmicomics* 13).[6]

The attitude involved in such straining and perverting activities could be described as playful,[7] but make no mistake about it: "playful" here is no antonym of "serious," nor is there anything funny about these activities—they are intently, passionately undertaken, with total, unrestrained commitment. "Grown-ups . . . don't take their games in the serious wholehearted way children do" (I 22; *Path* 17). "This is another of the games which only Red Wolf knows how to play; they are very complicated and absorbing games, but they don't make one laugh" (I 49; *Path* 45).[8] And, if performed with the appropriate seriousness, such games are highly instructive: without venturing into the unknown one will learn nothing. "In these cases (k)yK would snigger and chuckle as if his victories were something to be proud of, whereas he simply benefited from overbold moves on my part. Conversely, the more I went ahead, the better I understood the mechanism, and in the face of every new phenomenon, after a few rather groping bets, I could calculate my previsions rationally" (II 157–158; *Cosmicomics* 88).[9]

The practical implications of these views seem obvious: a writer of stories is to deny things and people their ordinary surroundings, their familiar, comfortable associations, and follow them patiently as they develop adequate responses to unheard-of solicitations, to never-even-conceived-before problems. He is to explore landscapes and forms of behavior alternative to what habit makes us think of as unquestionably "real";[10] to tell the structure of other possible worlds. *Baron* is Calvino's most sustained early effort in this direction:[11] the conditions of the problem are set early (never touch the ground again), and then the novel is a painstaking, resourceful following up of that absurd premise, as stubbornly faithful to it as Cosimo himself is. Appropriately, he begins by trial and error: "In those days Cosimo often challenged men on the ground to compete in aiming or skill, partly to try out his own capacities and discover just what he could manage to do up there on the treetops" (I 608; 58). And, as the apprenticeship proceeds, he realizes that he is living in "a whole different world, made up of narrow curved bridges in the emptiness, of knots or peel or scores roughening the trunks, of lights varying their green according to the veils of thicker or scarcer leaves, trembling at the first quiver of the air on the shoots or moving like sails with the bend of the tree in the wind" (I 620; 70). But this separation from the world of others does not imply asceticism: "in truth he had never rejected comfort; though on trees, he had always tried to live the best he could" (I 774; 215). It is rather a question of handling ordinary matters in his own, extraordinary context, and for that the experience of others may be a precious resource: "Cosimo was never tired of finding out how they had resolved problems that he had had to deal with too" (I 681; 128). Although certain things are going to remain doubtful, in the new, uncertain atmosphere created by his unconventional choice: "the question whether he had not already deviated from his unspoken inner laws by jumping from a tree with roots to the mast of a boat was too complicated to think out at that moment" (I 669; 116).[12]

The microphysics of this operation of estrangement deserves more careful attention. On the one hand, what is at issue here is a dividing up of oneself: an isolating of some strain that is typically overwhelmed by a mass of other detail and a pursuing of it in total purity, at the expense of everything else one also is. Once again, there is a classic text of Calvino in which this tactic is played out in full, where indeed we are told: "If only I could halve every whole thing like this . . . so that everyone could escape from his obtuse and ignorant wholeness. I was whole and all things were natural and confused to me, stupid as the air" (I 403; 191). That text is *Viscount*, in which not only is a man halved, but "man moved against himself, both hands armed with swords" (I 442; 243). And a similar antagonism with oneself recurs then frequently in other works: in *Plunge*, where it is customary for Quinto to be in conflict with himself—indeed to go against himself (metaphorically) sword in hand (I 846); in *Smog*, where the main character "had only to turn . . . [his] mood inside out (which wasn't hard for . . . [him] because it was like attacking [him]self")" (I 908; 92); in *Knight*, where Gurduloo is a graphic display of all sorts of physical and behavioral contradictions; and in *The Watcher*, where Amerigo has a "habit of looking at things from the adversary's point of view" (II 52; 47).

The flip side to such coming apart from oneself is that all that is available in carrying out this bold feat is, again, part of oneself. The voice that is let speak is not an entirely foreign one; the place one arrives at was already prefigured back home. It is a distilling of a particular flavor from a mixture, *not* the introduction of a whole new ingredient. As Kim wisely puts it in *Path*, this is what we do all the time, even when we are not telling stories: "This is what I believe our political work is, to use even our own human misery, to use it against itself, for our redemption, as the Fascists use misery to perpetuate misery" (I 107; 104). And it is even more true when we are telling stories: the only way to talk about a fantastic world is by transfiguring the very world we live in. "Yesterday, when I was writing of the battle, I seemed to hear in the sink's din the clash of lance against shield and armor plate, and the clang of heavy swords on helmets. From beyond the courtyard came the thudding of looms as nuns wove, and to me it seemed like the pounding of galloping horses' hooves. Thus, what reached my ears was transformed by my half-closed eyes into visions and by my silent lips into words and words and words" (I 992; *Knight* 49). "Marco smiled. 'What else do you believe I have been talking to you about? . . . Every time I describe a city I am saying something about Venice'" (II 432; *Cities* 86). In sum, what it takes to be successful here is not at all the ability (or the desire) to run to the farthest corners, to cut all ties connecting to one's (other) selves; but rather the capacity to remain in the presence of those selves as one chooses among them and takes charge of the consequences of one's choice. "The hermit's strength is measured not by how far away he has gone to live, but by the scant distance he requires to detach himself from the city, without ever losing sight of it" (II 598; *Castle* 106).

A frustrating aspect of this enterprise is its open-endedness. It is true both of real life and of written stories that the moment one starts playing with what is there, subjecting it to even minimal twists and turns, suddenly nothing is safe any more and no final outcome of one's playful action is in sight. "Once you begin rejecting your present state, there is no knowing where you can arrive" (I 1075; *Marcovaldo* 10). "You know how it is when you write. You begin by changing a comma, and then you have to change a word, then the word order of a sentence, and then it all collapses" (I 912; *Smog* 96). This uncertainty brings anxiety with it: "once you begin to suspect that everything concerning you is purely casual, subject to transformation, and that you could be completely different and it wouldn't matter at all, then, following this line of reasoning, you come to think it's all the same whether you exist or don't exist, and from this notion to despair is only a brief step" (II 1145; *Loves* 85).[13] The most natural way of fighting the anxiety is by convincing oneself that one has in fact gotten to the bottom of the search, not because one has told all the possible stories (playfully lived all the possible lives)—which is going to be implausible—but because perhaps one has found the basic principle(s) from which all stories (all lives) derive. "What a relief it would be if he could manage to cancel his partial and doubting ego in the certitude of a principle from which everything is derived! A single, absolute principle from which actions and forms are derived? Or else a certain number of distinct principles, lines of force that intersect, giving a form to the world as it appears, instant by instant?" (II 885; *Mr. Palomar* 16) "How to explain that, with his consuming thirst, neither this well nor that would suffice? What he wants is the cistern where the waters of all wells and all rivers are poured and mingled" (II 556; *Castle* 60).

If one were able to reach these final (or initial) principles, and they were limited in number, one might be able to set an upper bound on the number of possibilities and thus achieve completeness—the next best guarantee of security once you take the perilous path of denying ordinary reality. For such a goal to be attainable, the "principles" would have to be of a special character: not axioms from which indefinitely many theorems can be proved but rather atoms from which a finite number of (types of) molecules can be generated. The mathematics involved here, in other words, would have to be not set theory, and not even arithmetic, but rather combinatorics: a discipline that may well deal with very large aggregates, but never with infinite ones.[14] Consider for example the following passage from *Cities*: "The catalogue of forms is endless: until every shape has found its city, new cities will continue to be born. When the forms exhaust their variety and come apart, the end of cities begins. In the last pages of the atlas there is an outpouring of networks without beginning or end, cities in the shape of Los Angeles, in the shape of Kyoto-Osaka, without shape" (II 476; 139). Note an important contradiction in the passage: if the situation is as described, then the catalogue of forms is *not* endless (if not in the sense of "so long as to *appear* to have no end") because indeed an end for it eventually comes.[15] This contradiction is indicative of what the writer/thinker is now invoking: an enormous richness that is, however, compatible with a *total* reconnaissance operation.

The first time this theme emerges in Calvino's fiction, it is as a tongue-in-cheek comment on the nature of destructive occupations: "On the whole it is always the same stuff that passes from camp to camp and regiment to regiment in the same camp; what is war, after all, but this passing of more and more dented objects from hand to hand?" (I 983; *Knight* 38). But the theme receives its celebration in *Castle*, a combinatorial orgy which, interestingly, Calvino was never wholly satisfied with and kept tinkering with endlessly (!) in the search for a perfect scheme.[16] "[T]he task of deciphering the stories one by one has made me neglect until now the most salient peculiarity of our way of narrating, which is that each story runs into another story, and as one guest is advancing his strip, another, from the other end, advances in the opposite direction, because the stories told from left to right or from bottom to top can also be read from right to left or from top to bottom" (II 539; 41). "The tavern's customers jostle one another around the table, which has become covered with cards, as they labor to extract their stories from the melee of the tarots, and the more the stories become confused and disjointed, the more the scattered cards find their place in an orderly mosaic" (II 582; 89).

Let us stop for a moment to note that this combinatorial obsession is common to a number of those "thinkers" by whom the election watcher was fascinated. Whether it be a triadic scheme or a twelve-part table of judgments, philosophers have constantly been looking for "a guide for the discovery of all" something or other, which once discovered would leave the reader with only the auxiliary, and ultimately inessential, task of "providing the consideration and support of an *assistant*" in figuring out how to fill all the cases of the resulting system.[17] Even one of the most irreverent and unsystematic among them toyed with the idea that time would have to repeat itself endlessly (!) because the number of things that could happen in time was not endless. And, after this brief stop meant to generate a sense of familiarity and comradeship, let us hasten to note that in the course of Calvino's very celebration of combinatorics, we can sense a fundamental problem with it.

"The forest, the castle, the tarots have brought me to this point, where I have lost my story, confused it in the dust of the tales, become freed of it," says someone who has been telling *this* tale, and then he adds: "What is left of me is only the manic determination to complete, to conclude, to make the sums work out" (II 543; 46). But how is one to do that? How is one in fact to find the guide to the whole? If the effective limits of one's imagination are the traits (the lives, the selves) one has inside, if in the destinations of one's travels one can only ever discover one's native city, how is one to ever capture what one is not—those possibilities that fall without one's scope? And if one can never reach there, is it worth it even to get started? "[I]f . . . [the chariot] is moving, it might as well remain still, as happens to many people before whom the ramps of the most smooth and speedy roads open, flying on high pylons over valleys, piercing granite mountains, and they are free to go everywhere, and everywhere is always the same" (II 552; 56–57). What, then, "[i]f the only thing . . . [one] wished was to escape from individual limitation, from categories, roles, to hear the thunder that rumbles in molecules, the mingling of prime and ultimate substances?" (II 558; 62).

There are important analogies for these questions in the history of philosophy, concerning what we can possibly say of God in view of the fact that His being is entirely transcendent for us. And one approach to the latter line of inquiry is negative theology: you cannot say what God is, you can only say what He is not. Two of the very few philosophers mentioned by name in Calvino's fiction, Plotinus and Porphyry,[18] are among the most influential originators of this approach, and indeed Calvino's references are reminiscent of it: "According to Plotinus, the soul is a mirror that creates material things by reflecting the ideas of the higher reason" (II 769; *Traveler* 161). "'God himself, who cannot be seen either by the body or by the soul,' Porphyry writes, 'allows Himself to be contemplated in a mirror'" (II 774; *Traveler* 166). So suppose we apply the same tactic to the questions we can now see Calvino's various narrators to be in trouble with; what kinds of stories will we (they) end up writing then?

Stories that go in exactly the opposite direction from *Baron*. Whereas the latter patiently developed the detailed consequences of its unconventional premise, and in the process made us familiar with a specific possible world, one that is not actual but whose blueprint may have been already present in its inventor's individual repertory, if we now want to overcome that repertory and supersede all individuality, even individuality as such, if we want to "communicat[e] the indispensable, skipping all the superfluous, reducing ourselves to essential communication, to a luminous signal that moves in a given direction, abolishing the complexity of our personalities and situations and facial expressions" (II 340; *Ti Zero* 133), then we will have to say as little as possible, give as few details as we can get away with.

Near the end of *Ti Zero*, we are told that "[t]o plan a book—or an escape—the first thing to know is what to exclude" (II 356; 151). And a related comment occurs in *Castle*: "every choice has an obverse, that is to say a renunciation, and so there is no difference between the act of choosing and the act of renouncing" (II 552; 56). The point, as it applies to stories, is that there are all sorts of choices one has to make in building a tale's concrete fabric—what color hair its main character has, say, or what city he lives in—and they are all (one feels) somewhat extrinsic to the tale's *essence*: to the way in which the tale reflects the structure of a higher, universal reason.[19] It is in such choices that one's individuality is most likely to surface: one will give a character hair of a certain color, say, because that is the color hair one's fifth-grade teacher had. And then this individual quality will come back to haunt us: to rule out what does not belong to our personal, casual path through life ("The thing that most exasperates you is to find yourself at the mercy of the fortuitous, the aleatory, the random," II 636; *Traveler* 27) and, most important, to block perception of those principles a tale can only reflect but must also do its best, it seems now, to reflect well. So we will have to limit the number of choices/exclusions to a minimum—which means: limit to a minimum our concrete description of characters and plots.

Beginning with *Ti Zero*, Calvino makes a number of disparaging remarks about details. "There, I'm concentrating again on the details, a more suggestive method of description apparently, though in reality of only limited efficiency, because . . . it is only within the whole . . . that the single details must be considered" (II 229–230; *Ti Zero* 6–7). "Now it's not that I want to describe to you the forms of life over there; imagine them any way you can, more or less strange, it doesn't much matter" (II 240; *Ti Zero* 19). "There's no use my telling you in detail the cunning I used to succeed in returning to the Continent of the Birds. . . . If you don't like this story you can think up another one: the important thing is to have me arrive there" (II 244–245; *Ti Zero* 24). "The interpretation of this passage in the tale was not easy. It could simply mean 'it was a fine sunny day,' and in this case our narrator was wasting his cards telling us inessential details" (II 510; *Castle* 11). "The world is so complicated, tangled, and overloaded that to see into it with any clarity you must prune and prune" (II 854; *Traveler* 244). The elusive ideal aimed at by thus pruning and pruning is that of a crystalline purity: "a world of crystal," indeed, "an indestructible frozen springtime of quartz . . . , a topaz world that would leave out nothing" (II 251–252; *Ti Zero* 32–33). Not surprisingly, the stories told in that world would be as concise as they are pure, as simple as they are universal—which is just as well because the time of long stories is (or should be?) forever gone. "Long novels written today are perhaps a contradiction: the dimension of time has been shattered. . . . We can rediscover the continuity of time only in the novels of that period when time no longer seemed stopped and did not yet seem to have exploded, a period that lasted no more than a hundred years" (II 618; *Traveler* 8).[20] But the stories of the new period cannot limit themselves to being short: they must also be noncommittal, in a way in which only the beginnings of (ordinary) stories are, when the story has not yet settled and it is not yet clear where it is going. It is in *The Watcher* that this theme first surfaces: "So is what matters, in everything, only the beginning, the moment when all energy is tensed, when only the future exists?" (II 17; 14). And then it not only recurs constantly in, but even organizes the narrative structure of, *Traveler*, which *is* the book the writer in it dreams of: "a book that is only an *incipit*, that maintains for its whole duration the potentiality of the beginning, the expectation still not focused on an object" (II 785; 177).[21]

But now we find ourselves facing an even more formidable problem than the one this general approach was supposed to address. Maybe as long as we stayed within the confines of the possibilities we had within us we could never get rid of our intrusive individuality, never catch a glimpse of higher reason; but in the negative theology of the nonstory how do we know that we see anything at all? Those choices/exclusions that we were so unhappy with are also what provides any substance our vision can have—at least such a vision as is accessible to a writer. "It is only through the confining act of writing that the immensity of the nonwritten becomes legible, that is, through the uncertainties of spelling, the occasional lapses, oversights, unchecked leaps of the word and the pen. Otherwise what is outside of us should not insist on communicating through the word, spoken or written: let it send its messages by other paths" (II 791; *Traveler* 183). Even more generally, "what is the use of an eye, only an eye, detached from everything? It does not even see" (I 195). Even assuming that our detachment from all contexts we are familiar with left us with a visual organ of sorts, that organ can no longer exercise its function, because seeing is always seeing in a context—and one that we have at least minimal control of.

Nor is it just a matter of perception. Because I have been going neoplatonic here, it might be worth noting that the main engine of the neoplatonic world—love, that is—is also under pressure. Loves are difficult, indeed (as reads the title of the Calvino collection devoted to this theme), because what one loves in another is that person's specificity, who specifically he or she is, and it is hard to pay attention to specific matters—let alone be impressed by them—when one is concentrating on the abstract scheme of the whole. So, appropriately, a woman is reduced to a silent, available but also curiously manipulative presence, or to an embarrassingly naked body, or to an occasion for feeling better about oneself, or to the irrelevant objective of a night-long (lonely) train trip that is itself a "perfect night of love," or to a not entirely unwelcome disturbance from one's reading habits. Or, to sum it all up (and to bring out the connection with vision), she gets confused with the landscape in a nearsighted man's fuzzy world: mistaken for someone else, and then finally lost.[22] Because she was never there in the first place—and also, perhaps, because the "love" involved here is the same as the one "the hunter has for living things, and which he can only express by aiming his gun at them" (I 598; *Baron* 49). It is a destructive love, sterile and dumb, like the one typified in Calvino's fiction by the poet Usnelli, who "in all his poems . . . had never written a verse of love: not one" (II 1168; *Loves* 286).

This tale began with nothing, and is about to return there. As abstraction rules and "[t]he world is reduced to a sheet of paper on which nothing can be written except abstract words, as if all concrete nouns were finished" (II 861; *Traveler* 251), the nothing out of which stories originate is brought back into full view. "From this arid sphere every discourse and every poem sets forth; and every journey through forests, battles, treasures, banquets, bedchambers, brings us back here, to the center of an empty horizon" (II 537; *Castle* 39). So, as was the case with Raimbaut, we find that "the most solid presence . . . [we have] yet met . . . [is] the nonexistent knight's" (I 968; *Knight* 19).[23] "[N]othingness is stronger and has occupied the whole earth" (II 861; *Traveler* 251).

As it happens, this is not quite the end of Calvino's story. Two moves are still to be made. First, in the emptiness of words no longer attached to anything there surfaces one last concrete reference—to words themselves. Literature turns indeed into an analogue of Antonino Paraggi's final fate: that of a photographer who could only photograph photographs. It turns into a writing that can only be about writing (and reading), and as it does so it also brings out the limitations of writing and phantasizes of turning into something else—a map,[24] strip drawings,[25] even direct mimicry: "Only the expanse of snow could be seen, white as this page" (I 1182; *Marcovaldo* 121). Which outcome of course is supremely ironical because, with the pretense of reaching out to everything through words' universal referring power, it simply consigns the writer to the most trivial of his contexts—that indeed of being a writer. For, after all, writing (or speaking) is one of the many things—the many *concrete* things—one does and, "when you can do nothing because of the lack of an outside world, the only doing you can allow yourself with the scant means at your disposal is that special kind of doing that is saying"

(II 281; *Ti Zero* 67–68). So, as Calvino's archetypal reader, the one who seems to transpire through each and every act of reading (Ludmilla, that is), complains about the increasing professionalization of reading ("it would seem that those who use books to produce other books are increasing more than those who just like to read books and nothing else," II 700; *Traveler* 93), what emerges here is the sad destiny of the professional writer: that he may be left with no other subject matter for his writing than his own professional occupation.[26]

The second move consists of trying to reverse the inflexible logic that took you all the way here: to go back to valuing and practicing fine-grained description, with lots of details. This is what happens in *Mr. Palomar*; in an unpublished presentation of it preserved in his house and dated 1983, Calvino talks about "attempt[ing] to revalue a literary exercise fallen into disuse and regarded as useless: description" (II 1404).[27] And indeed it is true of Mr. Palomar that "certain things—a stone wall, a seashell, a leaf, a teapot—present themselves to him as if asking him for minute and prolonged attention: he starts observing them almost unawares, and his gaze begins to run over all the details and is then unable to detach itself" (II 968; 113). But the outcome of this attempt is no real description: it is rather an account of how hard description is—the description of a wave, say, which would involve identifying it and distinguishing it from all other waves[28]—and ends up providing in essence a demonstration of the impossibility of description. "He decides that he will set himself to describing every instant of his life, and until he has described them all he will no longer think of being dead. At that moment he dies" (II 979; *Mr. Palomar* 126). These are the very last words of Calvino's last sustained narrative effort, and they do indeed express the desire to reverse the course of his development as a writer in the most radical way: by going back to an infinitely minute telling of his own life. Mr. Palomar's desire is frustrated, of course; as for Calvino's (if indeed he shared such desire), he died two years later, having published virtually no other fiction after those two fateful sentences.[29]

I promised a moral for this tale, and one that could shed some light on the tortured relations between philosophy and literature. So here it is. Both philosophy and literature aim at disconnecting us from our ordinary context; the end of both is liberation, and the agility of mind that goes with it, and the more extensive knowledge and greater adaptiveness that issue from that agility.[30] Within this general liberating task, they play distinct but complementary roles, and Calvino himself suggests what they are: "For the writer who wants to annul himself in order to give voice to what is outside him, two paths open: either write a book that could be the unique book, that exhausts the whole in its pages; or write all books, to pursue the whole through its partial images. The unique book, which contains the whole, could only be the sacred text, the total word revealed" (II 789; *Traveler* 181). This suggestion, however, is not acceptable as it stands, because if one could really write all books one would also have automatically written the unique and sacred book, which would simply amount to the collection of all books. So we have to revise it: the writer who wants to give voice to what is outside him can either write a sacred book or nonsacred books—as many as he can get to, but never all of them, never enough.

What is characteristic of sacred books is that they tell the truth—something Calvino definitely found appealing. " 'Tis towards the truth we hurry, my pen and I," says the nun/narrator in *Knight* (I 1022; 87). And one can attempt to tell the truth by, indeed, trying to say everything or instead, more likely, by saying very little and claiming it to be all that matters—all that is relevant. The latter tends to happen in those heirs of sacred books that go under the appellation of "philosophical," where little is said and most of the time is spent *arguing* for the final, exhaustive relevance of that little. As becomes painfully clear in following Calvino's tale, what we find in the end, when we fall in with the temptation represented by this extreme economy of expression and extreme hypertrophy of justification is not liberating at all: the more abstract you become, the more you lock life in the shackles of triviality. "The ultimate meaning to which all stories refer has two faces: the continuity of life, the inevitability of death" (II 869; *Traveler* 259). But there is no need to get to that end; and, if you do not, the demand for truth can play an important role in the business of liberation.

We cannot take seriously, and play with all due concentrated attention, a game that is just silly, that has no consistency at all. More important, we would learn nothing from such a game—it would be just a way of killing time, a cheap evasion from which we would return even more firmly stuck in ordinary reality.[31] So any new game we play, any new story we tell, any new world we conjure up, at the same time as it throws us off with its diversity, must also carry with it, however implicitly, an argument in favor of its tenability, of its being *really* possible. And although it may be the case that real possibility can be established, finally, only for those things that are actual,[32] it is also the case that the closer we stay to the actual, the more we will trust the plausibility of what is going on. So a delicate balance must be struck between cutting loose and not cutting loose too much: severing some of the connections that tie us up and yet maintaining enough connections with ordinary practices so that what we say can be thought of as making sense. Just as in the first of the *Cosmicomics*, "The Distance of the Moon": where the influences of the Earth and the Moon are perfectly balanced, one does not fall into either, one floats in space.

The demand for truth, therefore, is not *external* to imagination: it structures it from the inside. An imagination that is truly liberating must combine novelty and routine: one can playfully join things that do not belong with one another, say, a shoe and a pistol, and tell the story of their strange encounter—and yet in that story the shoe and the pistol must continue to be recognizable as such.[33] For reasons partly articulated above, I like to think of the invention component of this operation as belonging to the literature side of it, and of the demand for truth that structures that invention as belonging to the philosophy side; and I like to think that when both work together well, liberation does ensue—one does indeed find oneself floating through space, free for once of some of one's chains. One way of looking at Calvino's work is as organized around this tension, this difficult balancing act, this tightrope walking; when that point of view is taken, one can appreciate the light touch with which he is often able to skate over the most ordinary occurrences as well as understand the weaknesses to which at other times he succumbs. One can see why he would be dissatisfied with a writing that provided no wisdom or understanding, and yet how it would have to be the case that for him—for the best in him—such wisdom could not be totally detached from its "image-filled kernel," and philosophers could not avoid being poets.[34]

Notes

*All Calvino references in the text are to his *Romanzi e racconti* (Milano: Mondadori, 1991–94; the Roman numeral indicates the volume and the Arabic numeral the page). In most cases they are accompanied by references to English translations of the various individual works, which however are often modified without further notice; a list of these translations is given in the bibliography. Calvino also produced a large number of essays, in which he sometimes directly addressed the issues dealt with here. But I have decided to focus on his practice as a writer rather than on his programmatic statements about it; and some of Calvino's own remarks in the essays reinforce my sense that that is the right choice. See, for example, the following: "The recurrent inclination to formulate general programs, of which these writings give evidence, was always counterbalanced by the tendency to forget them immediately and never return to them" (S 7). "[L]iterature is refractory to all projects, it does not let itself be contained by any discourse" (S 401). "We would never want to interrupt . . . [Pavese's] search by asking him for a work which, having clarified the reasons of its narration, was no longer an experiment but only a result" (S 1208). "Let it be clear . . . that I am very far from claiming that I can practice what I preach. Every time I write, I do what I can" (S 2711). Still, when a particular comment in his essays has seemed relevant to a point made in the text, I mentioned it in the notes; in these quotes, my references are always to the *Saggi* (Milano: Mondadori, 1995. Abbreviated S, as indeed already in the last few quotes). When applicable, these too are accompanied by references to English translations of individual works (for which, again, see the bibliography).

1. In a 1963 interview of Calvino, Alberto Arbasino salutes his return to literary productivity with *The Watcher*: "Calvino used to say that, at a time when people write too much, . . . silence acquires for a writer a particular value. . . . Then . . . here is a new story of his coming out, here is Calvino getting back into our century" (S 2760).

2. "I believe that the names of the characters are very important. When, in writing, I have to introduce a new character, and I am already very clear in my mind what this character will be like, I stop and look for a name even for half an hour or so, and until I find one that is that character's true, sole name, I cannot go on" (S 1746). "I believe that anodyne names are abstract ones: in reality we can always find a subtle, intangible, sometimes contradictory relation between name and

person, so that one always is what one is plus the name one has, a name that without him would mean nothing, but that once connected with him acquires a whole special significance, and it is this relation that the writer must be able to bring out for his characters" (S 1747).

3. The history of this piece is revealing. In 1955 Calvino published an essay in the weekly *Il Contemporaneo* entitled "La follia del mirino" ("The viewfinder's madness"), in which he voiced serious concerns about the growing photographic obsession of many Italians and sharply distanced himself from it: "I have never taken photographs since reaching the age of reason, and I refrain from taking any, and do my best to alert my friends to the dangers of this practice of theirs" (S 2217). "[A]s in the keeping of diaries and in general in autobiographical literature, so in photography—that is, in all these things that look like the culmination of reality, of sincerity, of clarifying rationality—there always lies in wait a tentacle of insanity. True human reason is choice, organization, invention" (S 2219). In March 1970 he wrote "The Adventure of a Photographer" (to be published in the same year in *Gli amori difficili*) on the basis of that essay. In the story, the original critical remarks appear as early thoughts and statements by the protagonist Antonino Paraggi, who eventually (and despite those thoughts and statements) comes to manifest the common obsession in an extreme form. It is natural to see in this development an implicit commentary by Calvino on his own earlier self-assurance.

4. See also I 1003; *Knight* 64: "A young man hurries, falls in love, uncertain of himself, happy, desperate, and for him his woman is the person who certainly exists, of which only she can give the proof. But the woman too both exists and doesn't. There she is before him, also trembling, and uncertain. . . . But the young man does not know, because he does not want to. What he yearns for is a woman who exists, a woman who is definite." And S 2298: "Desire has a meaning, as one of the names of Nothing, and I have a great deal of respect for Nothing as Nothing, but as Desire it seems to me a big swindle."

5. In preparation for things to come, notice that this daydreaming is not constituted by entirely new images, but rather preys on the movie Marcovaldo has just been watching.

6. See also II 436; *Cities* 91: "Many are the cities like Phyllis, which elude the gaze of all, except the man who catches them by surprise."

7. The aggressive connotations of the verbs used here are intended, as an element of violence and evil is involved in playfulness and in the intellectual vitality it expresses. "Pin has always been embarrassed by good people; one never knows how to treat them and always likes to bother them to see how they react" (I 56; *Path* 52). "This Belluomo . . . did not have enough memory or lively feelings to be vindictive" (I 533–534). Later we will see that unless this element is balanced out, the result can be very destructive indeed.

8. To appreciate the point better, it might be useful to note that the Italian words "gioco" and "giocare" translate both "(to) play" and "game." Also, contrast this sympathetic account of children's serious playfulness with Foffo's idiotic laughter in "Và così che vai bene" (II 1018–1034, where a sadder variant of Pin and Red Wolf, little Adelchi, is heard saying, "Are you stupid? One never plays in jest," 1032). And consider the following: "[Pinball machines manifest] a frivolousness and childishness which prevent . . . [them] from reaching the internal seriousness that is proper of games" (S 2215).

9. See also I 886; *Plunge* 246, where we are told that "[i]t's impossible to corner [Caisotti]" because "[y]ou can't ever tell what he's going to do next"; and the following statements from the essays: "Play has always been the great engine of culture" (S 535). "[W]e must not forget that games, whether of children or

grown-ups, always have a serious basis. First and foremost they are techniques for training the faculties and attitudes that will be required in life" (S 767; *Uses* 173).

10. See II 243; *Ti Zero* 23: "What everyone had thought he understood before, the simple and regular way in which things were as they were, was no longer valid; in other words: this was nothing but one of the countless possibilities; nobody excluded the possibility that things could proceed in other, entirely different ways."

11. There are, of course, later efforts as well: at least *Cosmicomics* and *Ti Zero* come to mind. But they run into complications I bring out below.

12. Cosimo's predicament is clearer in the original, as both "tree" and "mast" here translate the same Italian word: "albero."

13. "This is what the path is: a device for multiplying the garden, to be sure, but also for saving it from the vertigo of infinity" (S 585). "Sometimes I try to concentrate on the story I would like to write, and I realize that what interests me is something else entirely or, rather, not anything precise but everything that does not fit in with what I ought to write—the relationship between a given argument and all its possible variants and alternatives, everything that can happen in time and space. This is a devouring and destructive obsession, which is enough to render writing impossible. In order to combat it, I try to limit the field of what I have to say, divide it into still more limited fields, then subdivide these again, and so on and on. Then another kind of vertigo seizes me, that of the detail of the detail of the detail, and I am drawn into the infinitesimal, the infinitely small, just as I was previously lost in the infinitely vast" (686–687; *Memos* 68–69).

14. "Primitive oral narrative . . . is modeled on fixed structures, on, we might almost say, prefabricated elements—elements, however, that allow of an enormous number of combinations" (S 207; *Uses* 5). "Just as no chess player will ever live long enough to exhaust all the combinations of possible moves for the thirty-two pieces on the chessboard, so we know (given the fact that our minds are chess-boards with hundreds of billions of pieces) that not even in a lifetime lasting as long as the universe would one ever manage to make all possible plays. But we also know that all these are implicit in the overall code of mental plays" (S 210; *Uses* 8–9). "If we now know the rules of the 'romanesque' game . . . we can play at novels like playing at chess" (S 272–273; *Uses* 194).

15. The contradiction is not an artifice of translation, but is not as blatant in the original: the Italian word "sterminato" (translated here as "endless") does mean "without end," but the original then uses a different root ("fine") for the two subsequent words translated (correctly) as "end." See also the following: "since the human mind cannot conceive the infinite, and in fact falls back aghast at the very idea of it, it has to make do with what is indefinite, with sensations as they mingle together and create an impression of infinite space, illusory but pleasurable all the same" (S 682; *Memos* 63).

16. See II 1367, where we are told that the last revision to be found among Calvino's notes was dated as late as October 18, 1984 (in its entirety, *Castle* was published in October 1973; but the first part of it appeared in 1969).

17. The last two references are to Kant's *Critique of Pure Reason*, A70 B95ff and Axxi, respectively.

18. *The Watcher* contains references to Giannone (II 9; 8), Voltaire (II 40; 36), Kierkegaard (II 40; 36), Hegel (II 55; 50–51), and even a substantial quote from Marx (II 49–50; 45). In addition to them, I have noticed only a brief appearance as a character by Voltaire (I 697–698; *Baron* 143–144), and a reference to Lucretius (II 543; *Castle* 46). (Philosophers are, of course, much more present in the essays.)

19. "Every time the beginning is this moment of separation from the multiplicity of possibles: for the narrator it is the distancing from oneself of the multiplicity of

possible stories, so as to be able to isolate and tell the single story he has decided to tell tonight" (S 735).

20. "My temperament prompts me to 'keep it short,' and such structures as . . . [those of *Traveler* and *Castle*] enable me to unite density of invention and expression with a sense of infinite possibilities" (S 730; *Memos* 120). "[T]he true vocation of Italian literature . . . is more recognizable in brevity than in prolixity" (S 1294; *Classics* 239). "[After World War II I claimed] that the novel could not die; but I was not able to make one stand on its feet" (S 1512).

21. "The beginning is the literary locus par excellence" (S 735).

22. The references here are to a number of tales in *Loves*: "The Adventure of a Soldier," "The Adventure of a Bather," "The Adventure of a Clerk," "The Adventure of a Traveler," "The Adventure of a Reader," and "The Adventure of a Nearsighted Man." The one literal quote is from II 1125; *Loves* 66.

23. See also I 912; *Mr. Palomar* 46: "What can be more stable than nothingness?"

24. See I 1036ff; *Knight* 106ff.

25. See II 236ff; *Ti Zero* 15ff. See also S 1535: "If there has been an influence of cinema on some of my works, it was that of cartoons" (in French in the original). And S 478: "How not to feel here the eternal, unsuppressible envy of the writer for the painter?"

26. In 1946, at the age of twenty-two, Calvino wrote: "The occurrence of an unknown, who, remote from any literary environment, during the pauses of his humble job writes a masterpiece, is looked upon with skepticism in Italy, where literature has become more and more a matter for specialists, localized in well-defined milieus, a career like a station master's or a surgeon's, which allows for no dilettantism. There is a lack in Italy of that osmosis of men between life and literature which enriches the biography of American writers with all the multiplicity of their experiences and their encounters; stevedores, newsvendors, salesmen become writers, not only people sitting at a desk, shut off from every experience in the routine of an editorial office—not just experience made of paper, hence second-hand, not a literature monopolized by the middle class, weighed down by all of the latter's impotence and hysteria" (S 1170–1171). Then, of course, Calvino went on to spend his entire life either as an editor or as an independent writer—no stevedore experience was forthcoming. And he quickly lost his admiration for the sociology of American writers: "[T]he risk literature runs today is that of reducing itself to a subject matter for university studies; the phenomenon already notable in the United States of a literature produced and consumed almost exclusively within the campuses, does not open any pleasant prospects" (S 1461). "The American writer—in contrast with what happens, or used to happen, in Italy— . . . is someone who works at a university, who writes novels on the campus life, on the gossip of adulteries among professors, which is not a great world, is not a truly exciting thing" (S 2907–2908). Is this personal (and social) development a case of what happens to everyone as "the day comes when we bring our gaze down along the drainpipes and we can no longer detach it from the cobblestones" (II 412; *Cities* 66)?

27. Which was not easy for him: "The problem is that I am not what is called a good observer: I am very absentminded, absorbed in my own thoughts, incapable of concentrating my attention on what I see" (S 1853). So, once again, this is a case of struggling to bring out some other self, as indeed Calvino claims he is always doing: "Exaggerating a little, I could give this definition of my work: as soon as I convince myself that a certain genre of literature is beyond my possibilities, I can find no rest until I have tried [it]" (S 1855).

28. See II 875–879; *Mr. Palomar* 3–8.

29. The only volume of fiction Calvino published after *Mr. Palomar* was *Cosmicomiche vecchie e nuove*, an extensive collection of material that, however, contained very

little that was new: the two stories "Il niente e il poco" and "L'implosione," totaling (in *Romanzi e racconti*) fourteen pages. The posthumous collection *Sotto il sole giaguaro* contained an additional story written after 1983: "Un re in ascolto."

30. "[H]uman hands . . . are said to have become skilled after they no longer had to cling to boughs or press on the ground" (II 922; *Mr. Palomar* 57).

31. "[P]retending they lived in a world of great movement and adventure was a way of insulating themselves from petty annoyances" (I 468; *Ant* 165). Note also the vacuity of Amerigo's "agile play with possibilities" in *The Watcher* (II 29; 26), whose only effect is to let him avoid any action.

32. This is, I argue in my *Kant's Copernican Revolution*, Kant's view of the matter.

33. So the person telling such a story would have to combine the innocent creativity of a child with the real-world experience of an adult, as in Pin's wish: "Pin would like to be grown-up now, or rather not grown-up, but as he is yet admired and feared, a child and yet a leader of grown-ups on some marvellous enterprise" (I 139; *Path* 136). When, on the other hand, the innocence of childhood persists unchanged in adult life, the outcome is once again far from liberating. "These girls with their hair in braids, orphans perhaps or foundlings brought up in the institution and destined to remain there all their lives: at thirty they still had a slightly infantile look. . . . You would have said they went straight from childhood to old age" (II 24; *The Watcher* 20).

34. "Philosophy and literature are embattled adversaries. The eyes of philosophers see through the opaqueness of the world, eliminate the flesh of it, reduce the variety of existing things to a spider's web of relationships between general ideas, and fix the rules according to which a finite number of pawns moving on a chessboard exhaust a number of combinations that may even be infinite. Along come the writers and replace the abstract chessmen with kings and queens, knights and castles, all with a name, a particular shape, and a series of attributes royal, equine, or ecclesiastical; instead of a chessboard they roll out great dusty battlefields or stormy seas. So at this point the rules of the game are turned topsy-turvy, revealing an order of things quite different from that of the philosophers. Or, rather, the people who discover these new rules are once again the philosophers, who dash back to demonstrate that this operation wrought by the writers can be reduced to the terms of one of their own operations, and that the particular castles and bishops were nothing but general ideas in disguise. . . . The clash between philosophy and literature does not need to be resolved. On the contrary, only if we think of it as permanent but ever new does it guarantee us that the sclerosis of words will not close over us like a sheet of ice" (S 188–189; *Uses* 39–40). "Above all . . . [Cyrano] is a *writer* through and through, less interested in expounding a theory or defending a thesis than in setting in motion a merry-go-round of inventions equivalent on the level of imagination and language to what the 'new philosophy' and the new science were doing on the level of thought" (S 824; *Uses* 336).

Bibliography

Adorno, Theodor W. *Aesthetic Theory*. Trans. Robert Hullot-Kentor. Minneapolis: University of Minnesota Press, 1977.

Aizenberg, Edna, ed. *Borges and His Successors*. Columbia: University of Missouri Press, 1990.

Alazraki, Jaime. *Borges and the Kabbalah: And Other Essays on His Fiction and Poetry*. Cambridge: Cambridge University Press, 1988.

Anderson, Susan L. "Philosophy and Fiction." *Metaphilosophy* 23, 3 (1992): 203–213.

Bahm, Archie. "What Is Philosophy?" *The Scientific Monthly* 52 (1941): 553–560.

Balderston, Daniel. *Out of Context: Historical Reference and the Representation of Reality in Borges*. Durham, NC: Duke University Press, 1993.

Bambrough, Renford. "Literature and Philosophy." In *Wisdom: Twelve Essays*. Ed. Renford Bambrough. Oxford: Blackwell, 1974: 274–292.

Barone, Orlando, ed. *Diálogos: Borges Sábato*. Buenos Aires: Emecé Editores, 1996.

Barth, John. "The Literature of Exhaustion." *The Atlantic* 220, 2 (August 1967): 29–34.

———. "The Literature of Replenishment: Postmodernist Fiction." *The Atlantic* 233, 1 (January 1980): 65–71.

———. *The Friday Book. Essays and Other Nonfiction*. New York: G. P. Putnam's & Sons, 1994.

Barthes, Roland. *The Rustle of Language*. Trans. Richard Howard. New York: Hill and Wang, 1986.

Beardsley, Monroe C. *Aesthetics*. New York: Harcourt, Brace & World, 1958.

———. "Aesthetic Intentions and Fictive Illocutions." In *What Is Literature?* Ed. Paul Hernadi. Bloomington: Indiana University Press, 1978: 168–177.

Beckett, Samuel. *Molloy*. New York: Grove Press, 1955.

Behler, Ernst. *German Romantic Literary Theory*. Cambridge: Cambridge University Press, 1993.

Beiser, Frederick. *The Fate of Reason: German Philosophy from Kant to Niezstche*. Cambridge, MA: Harvard University Press, 1987.

———. *The Early Political Writings of the German Romantics*. Cambridge: Cambridge University Press, 1996.

Bencivenga, Ermanno. *Kant's Copernican Revolution*. New York: Oxford University Press, 1987.

Bergson, Henri. *Matter and Memory*. Trans. N. M. Paul and W. S. Palmer. New York: Zone Books, 1991.

Bernhard, Thomas. *Correction*. Trans. Sophie Wilkins. Chicago, IL: University of Chicago Press, 1979.

Black, Max. "More on Metaphors." In *Metaphor and Thought*. Ed. A. Ortony. Cambridge: Cambridge University Press, 1978.

Blackburn, Simon. "Professor Whatever. Kant and the Platypus." *The New Republic* (February 2000): 34–40.

Bloom, Harold. *The Anxiety of Influence*. New York: Oxford University Press, 1973.

———. *Kabbalah and Criticism*. New York: The Seabury Press, 1975.

———, ed. *Thomas Pynchon's 'Gravity's Rainbow.'* New York: Chelsea House Publishers, 1986.

Booth, Wayne. *The Company We Keep: "An Ethics of Fiction*. Berkeley: University of California Press, 1988.

———. "Why Banning Ethical Criticism Is a Serious Mistake." *Philosophy and Literature* 22, 2 (October 1998): 366–393.

Borges, Jorge Luis. *Obras completas*. Buenos Aires: Emecé Editores, 1974 (1932): 2 volumes.

———. *Borges: A Reader*. Ed. Emir Rodríguez Monegal and Alastair Reid. New York: E.P. Dutton, 1981.

———. *The Aleph and Other Stories 1933–1969*. Trans. Norman Thomas di Giovanni. New York: E. P. Dutton, 1970.

———. *The Book of Imaginary Beings*, with Margarita Guerrero. Rev. enlarged and trans. Norman Thomas di Giovanni in collaboration with the author. London: Penguin Books, 1969.

———. *Borges: Obras reseñas y traducciones inéditas, colaboraciones de Jorge Luis Borges en la Revista multicolor de los sábados del diario Crítica 1933–1934*. Ed. Irma Zangara. Buenos Aires: Editorial Atlántida, 1995.

———. *Borges oral: Conferencias* (1979). Buenos Aires: Emecé/Editorial de Belgrano, 1997.

———. *Collected Fictions*. Trans. Andrew Hurley. New York: Penguin Books, 1999.

———. *Doctor Brodie's Report*. Trans. Norman Thomas Di Giovanni. New York: E. P. Dutton, 1978.

———. *Ficciones*. Buenos Aires: Amici Editors 1956. Ed. Anthony Kerrigan. New York: Grove Press, 1962.

———. *El idioma de los argentinos* (1928) Madrid: Alianza Editores, 1998.

———. *Inquisiciones* (1925). Madrid: Alianza Editorial, 1998.

———. *Manual de zoología fantástica*, with Margarita Guerrero (1957). Mexico City: Fondo de Cultura Económica, 1984.

———. "La metáfora." In *Historia de la eternidad*. (1936)

———. *Labyrinths. Selected Stories and Other Writings*. Ed. D. A. Yates and J. E. Irby. New York: A New Direction Book, 1964.

————. *Other Inquisitions: 1937–1952*. Trans. Ruth L. C. Sims. Austin, TX: University of Texas Press, 1964.

————. *Para las seis cuerdas*. Illustrated by H. Basaldúa. Buenos Aires: Emecé Editores 1996.

————. *El tamaño de mi esperanza* (1926). Barcelona: Seix Barral, 1994.

————. *A Universal History of Infamy*. Trans. Norman Thomas di Giovanni. London: Penguin Books, 1970.

Bouchard, Norma, and Veronica Pravadelli. *Umberto Eco's Alternatives*. New York: Peter Lang, 1998.

Calvino, Italo. *The Baron in the Trees*. Trans. A. Colquhoun. New York: Harcourt, Brace, Jovanovich, 1977. (Abbreviated *Baron* in Bencivenga.)

————. *The Castle of Crossed Destinies*. Trans. W. Weaver. New York: Harcourt, Brace, Jovanovich, 1977. (Abbreviated *Castle* in Bencivenga.)

————. *"The Chase."* In *t zero*. Trans. William Weaver. New York: Harcourt Brace, Jovanovich, 1976, pp. 112–127.

————. *Cosmicomics*. Trans. W. Weaver. New York: Harcourt, Brace, Jovanovich, 1968.

————. "The Count of Monte Cristo." In *t zero*. Trans. William Weaver. New York: Harcourt, Brace, Jovanovich, 1976: 137–152.

————. *Difficult Loves*. Trans. W. Weaver et al. New York: Harcourt Brace, 1984. (Abbreviated *Loves* in Bencivenga.) The same volume also contains *A Plunge Into Real Estate*, a partial translation of *La speculazione edilizia* by D. Carne-Ross (Abbreviated *Plunge* in Bencivenga).

————. *If on a Winter's Night a Traveler*. Trans. W. Weaver. New York: Harcourt, Brace, Jovanovich, 1981. (Abbreviated *Traveler* in Bencivenga.)

————. "Il romanzo come spettacolo." In *Saggi 1945–1985*. Milano: Mondadori 1995.

————. *Invisible Cities*. Trans. W. Weaver. New York: Harcourt, Brace, 1974. (Abbreviated *Cities* in Bencivenga.)

————. *La machine litteraire*. Trans. M. Orcel and F. Wahl. Paris: Edicions du Seuil, 1984.

————. "Man in the Wasteland." Trans. W. Weaver. In *Difficult Loves*. New York: Harcourt, Brace, Jovanovich, 1984: 54–60. (Abbreviated *Man* in Bencivenga.)

————. *Marcovaldo*. Trans. W. Weaver. London: Secker & Warburg, 1983.

————. *Mr. Palomar*. Trans. W. Weaver. New York: Harcourt, Brace, Jovanovich, 1985.

————. *The Nonexistent Knight & The Cloven Viscount*. Trans. A. Colquhoun. New York: Random House, 1962. (The two novels are abbreviated *Knight* and *Viscount*, respectively, in Bencivenga.)

————. *The Path to the Nest of Spiders*. Trans A. Colquhoun. New York: The Ecco Press, 1976. (Abbreviated *Path* in Bencivenga.)

————. *Una pietra sopra*. Torino: Einaudi, 1980.

————. "Philosophy and Literature." In *The Uses of Literature*. Trans. Patrick Creagh. New York: Harcourt, Brace, Jovanovich, 1982.

————. *Six Memos for the Next Millennium*. Trans. P. Creagh. Cambridge, MA: Harvard University Press, 1988. (Abbreviated *Memos* in Bencivenga.)

————. *Six Memos for the Next Millennium*. Trans. P. Creagh. New York: Random House, 1988.

————. "The Soft Moon." In *t zero*. Trans. William Weaver. New York: Harcourt, Brace, Jovanovich, 1976: 3–13.

————. "The Chase." In *t zero*. Trans. William Weaver. New York: Harcourt, Brace, Jovanovich, 1976.

————. *The Uses of Literature*. Trans. and ed. P. Creagh. New York: Harcourt, Brace, Jovanovich, 1986. (Abbreviated *Uses* in Bencivenga.)

————. *The Uses of Literature*. Trans. and ed. P. Creagh. New York: Harcourt, Brace, Jovanovich, 1982.

————. *The Watcher & Other Stories*. Trans. W. Weaver and A. Colquhoun. New York: Harcourt, Brace, Jovanovich, 1971. (It includes *Smog and The Argentine Ant*, abbreviated *Ant* in Bencivenga.)

————. *Why Read the Classics?* Trans. M. McLaughlin. New York: Pantheon Books, 1999. (Abbreviated *Classics* in Bencivenga.)

Calvo, María Montoro, and Rocco Capozzi, eds. *Relaciones literarias entre J. L. Borges y U. Eco*. Castilla La Mancha: Ediciones de la Universidad, 1999.

Capozzi, Rocco. "Intertextuality and Semiosis: Eco's éducation sémiotique." *Recherche sémiotique/Semiotic Inquiry* 3, 3 (1983): 284–296.

————. "Palimpsests and Laughter. The Dialogical Pleasure of Unlimited Intertextuality in *The Name of the Rose*." *Italica* 66, 4 (1989): 412–428.

————. "Metaphors and Intertextuality in Eco's Neo-Baroque Narrative Machine." *Rivista di Studi Italiani* 14, 1 (1996): 165–189.

————. "Intertextuality and Hypermedia: Towards Electronic Hyper Intertextual Analyses." *VS* (Versus) 77/78 (May–December 1997): 162–174.

————, ed. *Reading Eco. An Anthology*. Bloomington: Indiana University Press, 1997.

Carnap, Rudolph. "Die Überwindung der Metaphysik durch die logische Analyse der Sprache." *Erkenntnis* 2 (1931): 219–241. Trans. Arthur Pap as "The Elimination of Metaphysics Through Logical Analysis of Language." In *Logical Positivism*, Ed. A. J. Ayer. New York: Free Press 1959: 60–81.

Cascardi, Anthony, ed. *Literature and the Question of Philosophy*. Baltimore: The Johns Hopkins University Press, 1987.

Cavell, Stanley. *This New Yet Unapproachable America: Lectures after Emerson and Wittgenstein*. Albuquerque, NM: Living Batch Press, 1989.

Christensen, I. *The Meaning of Metafiction*. Bergen: Universitetsforlaget, 1981.

Coletti, Teresa. *Naming the Rose. Eco, Medieval Signs, and Modern Theory*. Ithaca, NY: Cornell University Press, 1988.

Conley, Tom. "A Trace of Style." In *Displacement: Derrida and After*. Ed. Mark Krupnick. Bloomington: Indiana University Press, 1983: 74–92.

Currie, Gregory. "Work and Text." *Mind* 100 (1991): 325–339.

Danto, Arthur C. *Nietzsche as Philosopher*. New York: Columbia University Press, 1980.

———. *The Transfiguration of the Commonplace: A Philosophy of Art*. Cambridge, MA: Harvard University Press, 1981.

———. "Works of Art and Mere Real Things." In *The Transfiguration of the Commonplace: A Philosophy of Art*. Cambridge, MA: Harvard University Press, 1981, 1–32.

———. "Philosophizing Literature." In *The Philosophical Disenfrachisement of Art*. New York: Columbia University Press, 1986: 161–186.

———. "Philosophy as/and/of Literature." In *Disenfrachisement of Art*. New York: Columbia University Press, 1986, 135–161.

———. "Philosophy as/and/of Literature." In *Literature and the Question of Philosophy*. Ed. Anthony Cascardi. Baltimore, MD: The Johns Hopkins University Press, 1987.

Deleuze, Gilles. "The Conditions of the Question: What Is Philosophy?" Trans. Daniel W. Smith and Arnold I. Davidson. *Critical Inquiry* 17 (1981): 471–478.

———. *Rhizone*. Paris: Les Editions de Minuit 1976. Trans. Brian Massumi as A *Thousand Plateaus. Capitalism and Schizophrenia*. Minneapolis: University of Minnesota Press, 1987.

Deleuze, Gilles, and Felix Guattari. *Anti-Oedipus*. Trans. Robert Hurley, Mark Seem, and Helen R. Lane. Minneapolis: University of Minnesota Press, 1983.

Derrida, Jacques. *Of Grammatology*. Trans. G. C. Spivak. Baltimore, MD: Johns Hopkins University Press, 1976.

———. *Of Grammatology*. Trans. Gayatri Chakravorty Spivak. Baltimore, MD: Johns Hopkins University Press, 1976.

De Olaso, Ezequiel. *Jugar en serio: Aventuras de Borges*. Mexico City: Paidós, 1999.

De Toro, Alfonso, and Fernando de Toro, eds. *Jorge Luis Borges: Thought and Knowledge in the Xxth Century*. Madrid/Frankfurt: Vervuert/Iberoamericana, 1999.

Del Carril, Sara Luisa, and Mercedes Rubio de Sacchi, eds. *Borges en Sur 1931–1980*. Buenos Aires: Emecé Editores, 1999.

Dicarlo, Chris. "What Is Philosophy? A Causal Explanation." *Eidos* 6 (1987): 129–141.

Dickie, George. *Art and the Aesthetic: An Institutional Analysis*. Ithaca, NY: Cornell University Press, 1974.

Diether, Jack. "Notes to the Program." Carnegie Hall, November 4, 1997, 19.

Di Giovanni, Norman, ed. *The Borges Tradition*. London: Constable, 1955.

Doyle, Arthur Conan. *Through the Magic Door*. London: John Murray, 1920.

Eagleton, Terry. *Literary Theory: An Introduction*, 2nd edition. Minneapolis: University of Minnesota Press, 1996.

Eco, Umberto. *Apocalittici e integrati*. Milan: Bompiani, 1964.

———. *Apocalypse Postponed*. Ed. Robert Lumley. Bloomington: Indiana University Press, 1994.

———. "Casablanca. A Cult Movie." *Substance* 47 (1985): 1–13.

———. *Experiences in Translation*. Toronto: Toronto University Press, 2001.

———. *Foucault's Pendulum*. Trans. William Weaver. New York: Harcourt, Brace, Jovanovich, 1989.

———. *Interpretation and Overinterpretation*. Cambridge: Cambridge University Press, 1992.

———. *The Island of the Day Before*. Trans. William Weaver. New York: Harcourt, Brace, Jovanovich, 1995.

———. *Kant e l'ornitorinco*. Milan: Bompiani, 1998. Trans. as *Kant and the Platypus*. New York: Harcourt, Brace, Jovanovich, 1999.

———. *The Limits of Interpretation*. Bloomington: Indiana University Press, 1990.

———. *The Name of the Rose*. Trans. William Weaver. New York: Harcourt, Brace, Jovanovich, 1983.

———. *The Open Work*. Cambridge, MA: Harvard University Press, 1984. Trans. of *Opera aperta*. Milan: Bompiani, 1962.

———. "The Poetics of the Open Work." In *The Role of the Reader: Explorations in the Semiotics of Texts*. Bloomington: Indiana University Press, 1984.

———. *Postscript to The Name of the Rose*. Trans. William Weaver. New York: Harcourt, Brace, Jovanovich, 1983.

———. *The Role of the Reader*. Bloomington: Indiana University Press, 1979.

———. *In Search of the Perfect Language*. Trans. James Fentress. Oxford: Blackwell, 1993.

———. *Semiotics and the Philosophy of Language*. Bloomington: Indiana University Press, 1984.

———. *Six Walks in the Fictional Woods*. Cambridge, MA: Harvard University Press, 1994.

———. *Sugli specchi e altri saggi*. Milan: Bompiani, 1985.

———. *A Theory of Semiotics*. Bloomington: Indiana University Press, 1976.

———. *Vocali*. Napoli: A. Guida, 1991.

Eco, Umberto, and Thomas Sebeok, eds. *The Sign of Three. Peirce, Holmes, Dupin*. Bloomington: Indiana University Press, 1983.

Edmundson, Mark. *Literature against Philosophy, Plato to Derrida: A Defense of Poetry*. Cambridge: Cambridge University Press, 1995.

Eldridge, Richard. *Beyond Representation: Philosophy and Poetic Imagination*. Cambridge: Cambridge University Press, 1996.

————. *Leading a Human Life. Wittgenstein, Intentionality, and Romanticism.* Chicago, IL: The University of Chicago Press, 1997.

Feagin, Susan L. *Reading with Feeling: An Aesthetics of Appreciation.* Ithaca, NY: Cornell University Press, 1996.

Federman, Raymond. *Critifiction. Postmodern Essays.* Albany: State University of New York Press, 1993.

Fiedler, Leslie A. *The Collected Essays of Leslie Fiedler*, Vol. II. New York: Simon and Shuster, 1971.

Flay, Joseph, "What Is Philosophy?" *Personalist* 47 (1966): 206–217.

Foster, David William. *Buenos Aires: Perspectives on the City and Cultural Production.* Gainesville: University Press of Florida, 1998.

Foucault, Michel. *The Archaeology of Knowledge.* Trans. A. M. Sheridan Smith. New York: Pantheon Books, 1972.

————. *Language, Counter-Memory, Practice.* Ed. Donald F. Bouchard. Ithaca, NY: Cornell University Press, 1977.

————. *The Order of Things: An Archaeology of the Human Sciences.* New York: Pantheon Books, 1970.

————. *The Order of Things: An Archeology of Human Sciences.* London: Tavistock, 1970.

————. *The Order of Things: An Archeology of Human Sciences.* Trans. Richard Howard. New York: Vintage, 1973.

————. "What Is an Author?" Trans. Donald F. Bouchard and Sherry Simon. In *Language, Counter-Memory, Practice: Selected Essays and Interviews.* Ed. Donald F. Bouchard. Ithaca, NY: Cornell University Press, 1977: 113–138.

Frank, Manfred. *Unendliche Annäherung: Die Anfänge der philosophischen Frühromantik.* Frankfurt: Suhrkamp, 1997.

Frege, G. "On Sense and Reference." In *Translations from the Philosophical Writings of Gottlob Frege.* Ed. and trans. P. Geach and M. Black. Oxford: Blackwell, 1952.

Fricaud, S. "Les figures du temps dans *Fictions* ou Comment la fiction d'un Temps idéal ébranle le mythe de la littérature." In *Borges, "Fictions" mythe et récit*, ouvrage colleicf. Paris: Ellipses, 1988.

Fuentes, Carlos. "Jorge Luis Borges: La herida de Babel." In *Geografía de la novela.* Mexico City: Fondo de Cultura Económina, 1993.

————. "The Accidents of Time." In *The Borges Tradition.* Ed. Norman Thomas di Giovanni. London: Constable, 1995.

Gabler, Neal. *Life the Movie. How Entertainment Conquered Reality.* New York: Alfred. A. Knopf, 1998.

Gabriel, G. "Sobre el significado en la literatura y el valor cognitivo de la ficción." In *Figuras del Logos: Entre la filosofía y la literatura.* Trans. and ed. Ma. Teresa López de la Vieja. Mexico City: Fondo de Cultura Económica, 1994: 57–68.

Gadamer, Hans-Georg. "Goethe and Philosophy." In *Literature and Philos-*

ophy in Dialogue: Essays in German Literary Theory. Trans. Robert H. Paslick. Albany: State University of New York Press, 1994.

———. "Plato and the Poets." In *Dialogue and Dialectic: Eight Hermeneutical Studies in Plato*. Trans. P. Christopher Smith. New Haven, CT: Yale University Press, 1980.

———. *Truth and Method*, 2nd revised edition. New York: The Continuum Publishing Company, 1989.

———. *Truth and Method*. Trans. Joel Wiesheimer and Donald G. Marshall. New York: Crossroads, 1991.

Gasché, Rodolphe. "Ideality in Fragmentation." Foreword to Peter Firchow's translation of Friedrich Schlegel's *Philosophical Fragments*. Minneapolis: University of Minnesota Press, 1991.

———. *Inventions of Difference. On J. Derrida*. Cambridge, MA: Harvard University Press, 1994.

Genette, Gérard. *Palympseste. Littérature au second degré*. Paris: Seuil, 1982.

———. *Seuil*. Paris: Seuil, 1987.

Giovannoli, Renato, ed. *Saggi su Il nome della rosa*. Milan: Bompiani, 1985.

Gómez Martínez, José Luis. "Posmodernidad, discurso antrópico y ensayística latinoamericana. Entrevista." *Dissens* 2 (1996).

González, Eduardo. *The Monstered Self: Narrative of Death and Performance in Latin American Fiction*. Durham, NC: Duke University Press, 1992.

González Mateo, Adriana. "Borges y Toledo: zoología fantástica." *Poligrafía: Revista de Literatura Comparada* 1 (1996): 151–162.

Gracia, Jorge J. E. *A Theory of Textuality: The Logic and Epistemology*. Albany: State University of New York Press, 1995.

———. *Texts: Ontological Status, Identity, Author Audience*. Albany: State University of New York Press, 1996.

Gray, Rickwell. *The Imperative of Modernity: An Intellectual Biography of José Ortega y Gasset*. Berkeley: University of California Press, 1989.

Gregorich, Luis. "La literatura: Creación e industria." In *Buenos Aires: Historia de cuatro siglos*. Ed. José Luis Romero y Luis Alberto Romero. Buenos Aires: Editorial Abril, 1983.

Guibert, Rita. *Seven Voices*. New York: Vintage, 1973.

Habermas, Jürgen. "Excurs zur Einebnung des Gattungsunterschiedes zwischen Philosophie und Literatur." In *Der Philosophische Diskurs der Moderne*. Frankfurt: Suhrkamp, 1985: 219–247.

———. "Philosophie und Wissenschaft als Literatur?" In *Nachmetaphysisches Denken*. Frankfurt: Suhrkamp, 1988: 242–266.

Halliwell, S. "Philosophy and Literature: Settling a Quarrel?" *Philosophical Investigations* 16, 1 (1993): 6–16.

Hampshire, Stuart. "Logic and Appreciation." In *Aesthetics and Language*. Ed. William Elton. Oxford: Basil Blackwell, 1959.

Hayn, Rudolf. *Die Romantische Schule*. Hildsheim: Georg Olm Verlagsbuchhandlung, 1961.

Hegel, G. W. F. *The Phenomenology of Spirit*. Trans. A. V. Miller. New York: Oxford University Press, 1977.

Heidegger, Martin. "The Origin of the Work of Art." In *Poetry, Language, Thought*. Trans. Albert Hofstadter. New York: Harper & Row, 1971: 17–81.

Hernadi, Paul, ed. *What Is Literature?* Bloomington: Indiana University Press, 1978.

Hirsch, E. D., Jr. "Objective Interpretation." *PMLA* 75 (1960): 463–479.

———. *Validity in Interpretation*. New Haven, CT: Yale University Press, 1967.

———. "What Isn't Literature?" In *What Is Literature?* Ed. Paul Hernadi. Bloomington: Indiana University Press, 1978: 24–34.

———. "Counterfactuals in Interpretation." In *Interpreting Law and Literature: A Hermeneutic Reader*. Ed. Sanford Levinson and Steven Mailoux. Evanston, IL: Northwestern University Press, 1988: 55–68.

Huch, Richarta. *Die Blützeit der Romantik-Ausbreitung, Bluzeit und Verfall der Romantik*. Tubingen: R. Wunderlich, 1951.

Huerta, David. "La querella hispánica de Borges." *Letras Libres* 1, 8 (1999).

Hutcheon, Linda. *A Poetics of Postmdoernism. History, Theory, Fiction*. London, New York: Routledge, 1992.

Innerarity, Daniel. "La verdad de las mentiras: Reflexiones sobre filosofía y literatura." *Diálogo Filosófico* 24 (1992): 367–380.

Irwin, William. *Intentionalist Interpretation: A Philosophical Explanation and Defense*. Westport, CT: Greenwood Press, 1999.

———. "Philosophy and the History of Philosophy: On the Advantage of Nietzsche." *American Catholic Philosophical Quarterly* 75 (2001): 25–43.

———. "What Is an Allusion?" *The Journal of Aesthetics and Art Criticism* 59 (2001): 287–297.

Jameson, Frederick. *Postmodernism or The Cultural Logic of Late Capitalism*. Durham, NC: Duke University Press, 1991.

Jauß, Hans Robert. "Italo Calvino: *Wenn ein Reisender in einer Winternacht* Pladöyer für eine postmoderne Ästhetik." In *Studien zum Epochenwandel der ästhetischen Moderne*. Frankfurt: Suhrkamp, 1989: 267–302.

Jones, Peter. *Philosophical Aspects of the Novel*. Oxford: Clarendon Press, 1975.

Joyce, James. *Ulysses*. New York: Penguin Books, 1988.

Judovitz, Dalia. "Philosophy and Poetry: The Difference between Them in Plato and Descartes." In *Literature and the Question of Philosophy*. Ed. Anthony J. Cascardi. Baltimore, MD: The Johns Hopkins University Press, 1987: 24–51.

Kafka, Franz. "In the Penal Colony." In *The Complete Stories*. New York: Schocken, 1977: 163–166.

Kahler, Erich. "What Is Art?" In *Problems in Aesthetics*. Ed. Morris Weitz. New York: The Macmillan Company, 1959: 157–171.

Kainz, Howard. "The Definition of Philosophy." *Epistemologia* 17 (1994): 197–203.

Kant, Immanuel. *Critique of Pure Reason*. Trans. W. Pluhar. Indianapolis: Hackett, 1996.

———. *Critique of Pure Reason*. Trans. Norman Kemp Smith. New York: St. Martin's Press, 1965.

Khatchadourian, Haig. "Common Names and Family Resemblances." *Philosophy and Phenomenological Research* 18 (1957–58): 341–358.

Kreyche, Gerald F. "What Is Philosophy?" *Listening* 21 (1986): 56–65.

Lacoue-Labarthe, Phillipe, and Jean-Luc Nancy. *The Literary Absolute: The Theory of Literature in German Romanticism*. Albany: State University of New York Press, 1988.

Lamarque, Peter. *Fictional Points of View*. Ithaca, NY: Cornell University Press, 1996.

———, and Stein H. Olsen. *Truth, Fiction, and Literature: A Philosophical Perspective*. Oxford: Clarendon Press, 1994.

Landow, George. *Hypertext: The Convergence of Contemporary Critical Theory and Technology*. Baltimore: The Johns Hopkins University Press, 1992.

Lange-Churrión, Pedro, and Eduardo Mendieta. "Philosophy and Literature: The Latin American Case." *Dissens* 2 (1996): 37–40.

Laporte, R. *Une voix de fin silence II. Pourquoi?* Paris: Gallimard, 1967.

Lévi-Strauss, Claude. "The Structural Study of Myth." In *Structural Anthropology*. Trans. Claire Jacobson and Brooke Grundfest Schoepf. New York: Basic Books, 1963: 206–231.

Lukács, Georg. *Soul and Form*. Trans. Anna Bostock. Cambridge, MA: MIT Press, 1971.

Lyas, Colin. "The Semantic Definition of Literature." *The Journal of Philosophy* 66 (1969): 81–95.

Mandelbaum, Maurice. "Family Resemblances and Generalizations Concerning the Arts." *American Philosophical Quarterly* 2 (1965): 219–228.

Manser, A. R. "Games and Family Resemblances." *Philosophy* 42 (1967): 210–225.

Marshall, Donald G., ed. *Literature as Philosophy: Philosophy as Literature*. Iowa City: University of Iowa Press, 1987.

McGinn, Colin. *Ethics, Evil, and Fiction*. Oxford: Clarendon Press, 1997.

McHale, Brian. *Constructing Postmodernism*. London and New York: Routledge, 1992.

Merleau-Ponty, Maurice. *The Visible and the Invisible*. Trans. Alphonso Lingis. Evanston, IL: Northwestern University Press, 1968.

Molloy, Sylvia. *Las Letras de Borges*. Buenos Aires: Editorial Sudamericana, 1979.

Monegal, Emir Rodríguez. *Jorge Luis Borges: A Literary Biography*. New York: Dutton, 1978.

Nehamas, Alexander. "What Should We Expect from Reading (There Are Only Aesthetic Values)." *Salmagundi* 111 (Summer 1996): 27–58.

Nicholson, Shierry Weber. *Exact Imagination, Late Work: On Adorno's Aesthetics*. Cambridge, MA: MIT Press, 1977: 139–145.

Nietzsche, Friedrich. *The Will to Power*. Trans. Walter Kaufmann and R. J. Hollingdale. New York: Vintage, 1967.

Nussbaum, Martha. *Love's Knowledge: Essays on Philosophy and Literature*. New York: Oxford University Press, 1990.

———. *Poetic Justice: The Literary Imagination and Public Life*. Boston: Beacon Press, 1995.

———. "Exactly and Responsibly: A Defence of Ethical Criticism." *Philosophy and Literature* 22, 2 (October 1998): 343–365.

Ohmann, Richard. "Speech Acts and the Definition of Literature." *Philosophy and Rhetoric* 4 (1971): 1–19.

Oliva, Achille Bonito. *Luoghi del silenzio imparziale. Labirinto contemporaneo*. Milan: Feltrinelli, 1981: 39–50.

Ortega y Gasset. "Decline of the Novel." In *The Dehumanization of Art and Other Essays on Art, Culture, and Literature*. Princeton, NJ: Princeton University Press, 1968.

———. *Meditations on Quixote*. Trans. Julián Marías. New York: W.W. Norton, 1961.

———. "The Novel as a Sluggish Genre." In *The Dehumanization of Art and Other Essays on Art, Culture, and Literature*. Princeton, NJ: Princeton University Press, 1968.

———. *The Revolt of the Masses*. Trans. Anthony Kerrigan. Notre Dame, IN: University of Notre Dame Press, 1985.

———. "Taboo and Metaphor." In *The Dehumanization of Art and Other Essays on Art, Culture, and Literature*. Princeton, NJ: Princeton University Press, 1968.

Permiola, M. *Il Metaromanzo*. Milan: Silva Editore, 1966.

Plato. *The Collected Dialogues of Plato Including the Letters*. Ed. Edith Hamilton and Huntington Cairns. New York: Pantheon Books, 1961.

———. *Phaedrus*. In *The Collected Dialogues of Plato Including the Letters*. Ed. Edith Hamilton and Huntington Cairns. New York: Pantheon Books, 1961: 475–525.

———. *Republic*. In *The Collected Dialogues of Plato Including the Letters*. Ed. Edith Hamilton and Huntington Cairns. New York: Pantheon Books, 1961: 575–844.

Pompa, L. "Family Resemblance." *Philosophical Quarterly* 17 (1967): 63–69.

Posner, Richard A. "Against Ethical Criticism." *Philosophy and Literature* 21, 1 (April 1997): 1–27.

———. "Against Ethical Criticism: Part Two." *Philosophy and Literature* 22, 2 (October 1998): 394–412.

Prado, C. G. *Making Believe: Philosophical Reflections on Fiction*. Westport, CT: Greenwood Press, 1984.

Quinton, Anthony. *The Divergence of the Twain: Poet's Philosophy and Philosopher's Philosophy*. Warwick: University of Warwick, 1985.

Read, Malcolm K. *Jorge Luis Borges and His Predecessors, or Notes Towards a Materialist History of Linguistic Idealism*. Chapel Hill: North Carolina Studies in the Romance Language and Literatures, 1993.

Rest, Jaime. *El laberinto del universo: Borges y el pensamiento nominalista*. Buenos Aires: Ediciones Librerías Fausto, 1976.

Rodríguez Huéscar, Antonio. *José Ortega y Gasset's Metaphysical Innovation: A Critique and Overcoming of Idealism*. Trans. Jorge García-Gómez. Albany: State University of New York Press, 1995.

Rodríguez Monegal, Emir, and Alasdair Reid, eds. *Borges: A Reader*. New York: E. P. Dutton, 1981.

Romero, José Luis. *El desarrollo de las ideas en la sociedad argentina del siglo XX*. Mexico City: Fondo de Cultura Económica, 1965.

Rorty, Richard. *Consequences of Pragmatism*. Hussocks, Sussex: Harvester 1982.

———. "Philosophy as a Kind of Writing: An Essay on Derrida." In *Consequences of Pragmatism*. Minneapolis: University of Minnesota Press, 1982.

———. "The Necessity of Inspired Reading." *The Chronicle of Higher Education* 42, 22 (February 9, 1996): A48.

Rosa, N. *Los fulgores del simulacro*. Santa Fe: Cuadernos de Extensión Universitaria, 1987.

Rushdie, S. "Umberto Eco." In *Imaginary Homelands: Essays and Criticism 1981–1991*. London: Penguin Books, 1992.

Sacerio-Garí, Enrique, and Emir Rodríguez Monegal, eds. *Textos cautivos: Ensayos y reseñas en El Hogar (1936–1939)*. Barcelona: Tusquets Editores, 1986.

Sarlo, Beatriz. *Jorge Luis Borges: A Writer on the Edge*. London: Verso, 1993.

———. "Un ultraísta en Buenos Aires." *Letras Libres* 1, 8 (1999).

Sartre, Jean Paul. *What Is Literature?* Trans. Bernard Frenchtman. New York: Philosophical Library, 1949.

Schenkel, Elmar. "Circling the Cross, Crossing the Circle: On Borges and Chesterton." In *Jorge Luis Borges: Thought and Knowledge in the Xxth Century*. Ed. Alfonso de Toro and Frenando de Toro. Madrid/Frankfurt: Vervuert/Iberoamericana, 1999.

Schildknecht, Christiane. "Entre la ciencia y la literatura: Formas literarias de la filosofía." In *Figuras del logos: Entre la filosofía y la literatura*. Trans. José M. González García and ed. María Teresa López de la Vieja. Mexico City: Fondo de Cultura Económica, 1994: 21–40.

Schlegel, Friedrich. *Dialogue on Poetry*. Trans. Ernst Behler and Roman Struc. New York: Continuum, 1982.

———. *Philosophical Fragments.* Trans. Peter Firchow. Minneapolis: University of Minnesota Press, 1991.

———. *Friedrich Schlegel Kritische Ausgabe.* 35 vols. Ed. Ernst Behler et al. Paderborn: Ferdinand Schoenigh, 1958.

Searle, John R. "The Logical Status of Fictional Discourse." In *Expression and Meaning.* Cambridge: Cambridge University Press, 1979.

Seyhan, Azade. "Fractal Contours: Chaos and System in the Romantic Fragment." In *Beyond Representation. Philosophy and Poetic Imagination.* Ed. Richard Eldridge. Cambridge: Cambridge University Press, 1996.

Simon, Michael A. "When Is a Resemblance a Family Resemblance?" *Mind* 78 (1969): 408–416.

Sisson, Edward O. "What Is Philosophy: A Proposed Definition." *Philosophical Review* 57 (1948): 167–175.

Sobel, Dava. *Longitude.* New York: Walker and Co., 1995.

Sorrentino, Fernando. *Seven Conversations with J.L. Borges.* Troy, NY: The Whitston Pub. Co., 1982.

Sparshott, F. E. "On Saying What Philosophy Is." *Philosophy in Context* 4 (1975): 17–27.

Spinoza, Baruch. *Ethics Demonstrated in Geometric Order and Divided into Five Parts.* Trans. Edwin Curley. Princeton, NJ: Princeton University Press, 1994.

Stecker, Robert. "Apparent, Implied, and Postulated Authors." *Philosophy and Literature* 11 (1987).

———. "What Is Literature?" *Revue Internationale de Philosophie* 4 (1996): 681–694.

Stephens, Walter E. "Ec(h)o in fabula." *Diacritics* (Summer 1983): 51–64.

Stevens, Wallace. "A Collect of Philosophy." In *Opus Posthumous*, rev. ed. New York: Knopf, 1957.

Stewart, Susan. *On Longing: Narratives of the Miniature, the Gigantic, the Souvenir, the Collection.* Baltimore, MD: Johns Hopkins University Press, 1984.

Strong, Beret E. *The Poetic Avant-Garde: The Group of Borges, Auden and Breton.* Evanston, IL: Northwestern University Press, 1997.

Sussman, Henry. *Afterimages of Modernity: Structure and Indifference in Twentieth-Century Literature.* Baltimore, MD: Johns Hopkins University Press, 1990.

———. "Kafka in the Heart of the Twentieth Century: An Approach to Borges." In *Afterimages of Modernity: Structure and Indifference in Twentieth-Century Literature.* Baltimore, MD: Johns Hopkins University Press, 1990.

———. *The Aesthetic Contract: Statutes of Art and Intellectual Work in Modernity.* Stanford, CA: Stanford University Press, 1997.

Tarski, A. "The Semantic Conception of Truth." In *Semantics and the Philosophy of Language.* Urbana: University of Illinois Press at Urbana, 1952.

Taylor, Julie. *Paper Tangos*. Durham, NC: Duke University Press, 1998.

Vargas Llosa, Mario. "Borges político." *Letras Libres* 1, 11 (1999).

Vattino, Gianni, and Pier Aldo Rovatti, eds. *Il pensiero debole*. Milan: Feltrinelli, 1984.

Walsh, Dorothy. *Literature and Knowledge*. Middletown, CT: Wesleyan University Press, 1969.

Waugh, P. *Metafiction: The Theory and Practice of Self-Conscious Fiction*. London: Methuen, 1984.

Weinberger, Eliot. "Borges: La biblioteca parcial." *Letras Libres* 1, 8 (1999): 36–38.

———, ed. *Jorge Luis Borges: Selected Non-Fictions*. Trans. Esther Allen, Suzanne Jill Levine, and Eliot Weinberger. New York: Viking, 1999.

Weitz, Morris. "The Role of Theory in Aesthetics." *The Journal of Aesthetics and Art Criticism* 15 (1956): 27–35.

Wellek, René. "What Is Literature?" In *What Is Literature?* Ed. Paul Hernadi. Bloomington: Indiana University Press, 1978: 16–23.

White, Hayden. *Metahistory: The Historical Imagination in Nineteenth-Century Europe*. Baltimore: Johns Hopkins University Press, 1973.

———. "The Value of Narrativity in the Representation of Reality." *Critical Inquiry* 7, 1 (1980).

Wimsatt, William, Jr., and Cleanth Brooks. *Literary Criticism: A Short History*. New York: Vintage, 1957.

Wimsatt, W. K., and Monroe C. Beardsley. "The Intentional Fallacy." In *The Verbal Icon: Studies in the Meaning of Poetry*. Lexington: University of Kentucky Press, 1954: 3–18.

Wittgenstein, Ludwig. *Philosophical Investigations*. New York: Macmillan, 1953.

———. *The Blue and Brown Books*. Oxford: Basil Blackwell, 1958.

———. *Tractatus logico-philosophicus, Logisch-philosophische Abhandlung*. Frankfurt: Suhrkamp, 1966; London: 1922.

Wolfson, Martin. "What Is Philosophy?" *The Journal of Philosophy* 55 (1958): 322–336.

Wood, Michael. "Productive Mischief." *London Review of Books* 21, 3 (February 4, 1999): 7–9.

Woodall, James. *The Man in the Mirror of the Book: A Life of Jorge Luis Borges*. London: Hodder and Stoughton, 1996.

Woscoboinik, Julio. *El alma de "El Aleph": Nuevos aportes a la indagación psicoanalítica de la obra de Jorge Luis Borges*. Buenos Aires: Nuevo Hacer, 1996.

———. *The Secret of Borges: A Psychoanalytic Inquiry into His Work*. Trans. Dora C. Pozzi. Lanham, MD: University Press of America, 1998.

Yates, Donald A., and James E. Irby, eds. *Labyrinths*. New York: New Directions, 1962.

Zamora, Lois Parkinson. *Writing the Apocalypse: Historical Vision in Contemporary U.S. and Latin American Fiction*. Cambridge: Cambridge University Press, 1989.

———. "Magical Romance/Magical Realism: Ghosts in U.S. and Latin American Fiction." In *Magical Realism: Theory, History, Community*. Ed. Lois Parkinson Zamora and Wendy B. Faris. Durham, NC: Duke University Press, 1995: 497–550.

———. *The Usable Past: The Imagination of History in Recent Fiction of the Americas*. Cambridge: Cambridge University Press, 1997.

Zangara, Irma, ed. *Borges: Obras, reseñas y traducciones inéditas, colaboraciones de Jorge Luis Borges en la Revista multicolor de los sábados del diario 'Crítica,' 1933–1934*. Buenos Aires/Santiago: Editorial Atlántida, 1955.

Notes on Contributors

Ermanno Bencivenga is Professor of Philosophy at the University of California, Irvine. He is the author of twenty books and more than fifty articles. Among his more recent books are *I delitti della logica* (1998), *A Theory of Language and Mind* (1997), *My Kantian Ways* (1995), *Logic and Other Nonsense: The Case of Anselm and His God* (1993), and *Freedom: A Dialogue* (1997).

Rocco Capozzi is Professor of Contemporary Italian Literature at the University of Toronto. He is the author of *Bernari. Tra fantasia e realtà* (1984), *Scrittori, critici e industria culturale* (1991), and many articles. He has edited *A Homage to Moravia* (1992), *Scrittori e le poetiche letterarie in Italia* (1993), and *Reading Eco* (1997) and co-edited *La relaciones: Borges y Eco* (1999).

Anthony J. Cascardi is Richard and Rhoda Goldman Distinguished Professor in the Humanities and Professor of Spanish, Comparative Literature and Rhetoric at the University of California at Berkeley. He is the author of *Consequences of Enlightenment: Aesthetics as Critique* (1999), *Ideologies of History in the Spanish Golden Age* (1997), *The Subject of Modernity* (1995), *The Bounds of Reason: Cervantes, Dostoevsky, Flaubert* (1986), and *The Limits of Illusion: A Critical Study of Calderón* (1984). He is also the author of more than eighty articles and reviews and the editor of *Literature and the Question of Philosophy* (1986).

Rodolphe Gasché is Eugenio Donato Professor of Comparative Literature at the State University of New York at Buffalo. He is the author of seven books. Among the most recent are *Of Minimal Things: Essays on the Notion of Relation* (1999), *Rajankäyntiä* (1998), *The Wild Card of Reading: On Paul de Man* (1998), *Inventions of Difference: On Jacques Derrida* (1994), and *The Tain of the Mirror: Derrida and the Philosophy of Reflection* (1968, fifth printing 1998). He is also author of nearly ninety articles.

Jorge J. E. Gracia is Samuel P. Capen Chair and SUNY Distinguished Professor of Philosophy at the State University of New York at Buffalo. He is the author of nine books. Among the most recent are *Hispanic/Latino Identity: A Philosophical Perspective* (2000), *Metaphysics and Its Task: The Search for the Categorial Foundation of Knowledge* (1999), *Texts: Ontological Status, Identity,*

Author, Audience (1996), *A Theory of Textuality: The Logic and Epistemology* (1995), and *Philosophy and Its History: Issues in Philosophical Historiography* (1992). He is also the author of more than 150 articles and the editor or co-editor of more than a dozen books.

William Irwin is Associate Professor of Philosophy at King's College (Wilkes-Barre). He is the author of *Intentionalist Interpretation: A Philosophical Explanation and Defense* (1999) and ten articles. He is the editor of *Seinfeld and Philosophy: A Book about Everything and Nothing* (1999), *The Death and Resurrection of the Author* (2002), and *The Simpsons and Philosophy* (2001).

Deborah Knight is Associate Professor of Philosophy at Queen's University. She is the author of over twenty articles, including "Why We Enjoy Condemning Sentimentality: A Meta-aesthetic Perspective," *Journal of Aesthetics and Art Criticism*, "Being Don Juan: Metafiction, Identity and the Conflict of Genres," *Film and Philosophy* (1999), "Aristotelians on Speed: Paradoxes of Genre in the Context of Cinema," in *Film Theory and Philosophy*, edited by Murray Smith and Richard Allen (1997), "Does Tom Think Allworthy Is Real?" *Philosophy and Literature* (1997), and "A Poetics of Psychological Explanation," *Metaphilosophy* (1997).

Carolyn Korsmeyer is Professor of Philosophy at the State University of New York at Buffalo. She is the author of *Making Sense of Taste: Food and Philosophy* (1999), co-author of *Feminist Scholarship: Kindling in the Groves of Academe* (1985), and editor of *Aesthetics: The Big Questions* (1998), *Feminism and Tradition in Aesthetics* (1995), and *Aesthetics in Feminist Perspective* (1993).

Wladimir Krysinski is Professor of Comparative Literature at the University of Montréal. He is the author of *Carrefours de signes. Essais sur le roman moderne* (1981), *Le paradigme inquiet. Pirandello et le champ comparatif de la modernité* (1996), *La novela en sus modernidades. A favor y en contra de Bajtin* (1998), and many articles. Among the most recent articles are "Frye and the Problems of the Modern(ity)," in *The Legacy of Northrop Frye*, edited by A. A. Lee and R. D. Denham (1994), and "Récit de valeurs: les nouveaux actants de la 'Weltliteratur,'" in *Weltliteratur Heute. Konzepte und Perspektiven Beiträge des Symposiums zur Weltliteratur*, edited by M. Schmeling (1995).

Elizabeth Millán-Zaibert is Assistant Professor of Philosophy at De Paul University. She has published translations of two books—from Spanish, Mauricio Beuchot's *Mexican Colonial Philosophy* (1998), and from German, *The Philosophical Foundations of Early-German Romanticism* (in press). She has also published over fifteen articles and reviews. Among these are (with Leonardo Zaibert) "Individualism, Collectivism, and Group Rights," in

Hispanic/Latinos in the US: Ethnicity, Race, and Rights, edited by Jorge J. E. Gracia and Pablo De Greiff (2000), "The Essay as Literary Form and the Problem of Spain's Identity in Ortega's Philosophy," *Dissens* (1996), and (with Jorge J. E. Gracia) "Latin American Philosophy," in *Oxford Companion to Philosophy,* edited by Ted Honderich (1995).

Henry Sussman is Julian Park Professor of Humanities and Chair of Comparative Literature at the State University of New York at Buffalo. He is the author of seven books. Among the most recent are *The Aesthetic Contract: Statutes of Art and Intellectual Work in Modernity* (1997), *Psyche and the Text: The Sublime and the Grandiose in Literature, Psychopathology, and Culture* (1993), *Kafka's Unholy Trinity: The Trial* (1993), *Afterimages of Modernity: Structure and Indifference in Twentieth-Century Literature* (1990), and *High Resolution: Critical Theory and the Problem of Literacy* (1989). He is also the author of more than twenty articles and has edited two books.

Lois Parkinson Zamora is Professor of English at the University of Houston. She is the author (with Wendy Watriss) of *Image and Memory: Photography from Latin America 1866–1994* (1998), *The Usable Past: The Imagination of History in Recent Fiction of the Americas* (1997), and *Writing the Apocalypse: Historical Vision in Contemporary US and Latin American Fiction* (1989). She has edited two collections: *Contemporary American Women Writers: Gender, Class, Ethnicity* (1998) and (with Wendy B. Faris) *Magical Realism: Theory, History, Community* (1995). She has also published translations from the Spanish and authored more than thirty articles.

Index